Prieto

ENVISIONING CUBA

Louis A. Pérez Jr., editor

Envisioning Cuba publishes outstanding, innovative works in Cuban studies, drawn from diverse subjects and disciplines in the humanities and social sciences, from the colonial period through the post–Cold War era. Featuring innovative scholarship engaged with theoretical approaches and interpretive frameworks informed by social, cultural, and intellectual perspectives, the series highlights the exploration of historical and cultural circumstances and conditions related to the development of Cuban self-definition and national identity.

Prieto

Yorùbá Kingship in Colonial Cuba during the Age of Revolutions

Henry B. Lovejoy

The University of North Carolina Press CHAPEL HILL

This book was published with the assistance of the Authors Fund of the University of North Carolina Press.

© 2018 The University of North Carolina Press
All rights reserved
Set in Merope Basic by Westchester Publishing Services
Manufactured in the United States of America

The University of North Carolina Press has been a member of the Green Press Initiative since 2003.

Library of Congress Cataloging-in-Publication Data
Names: Lovejoy, Henry B., author.
Title: Prieto : Yorùbá kingship in colonial Cuba during the age of revolutions / Henry B. Lovejoy.
Other titles: Envisioning Cuba.
Description: Chapel Hill : University of North Carolina Press, [2018] | Series: Envisioning Cuba | Includes bibliographical references and index.
Identifiers: LCCN 2018016246| ISBN 9781469645384 (cloth : alk. paper) | ISBN 9781469645391 (pbk : alk. paper) | ISBN 9781469645407 (ebook)
Subjects: LCSH: Prieto, Juan Nepomuceno, approximately 1773–approximately 1835. | Yoruba (African people)—Cuba—19th century—Biography. | Yoruba (African people)—Cuba—Social conditions—19th century. | Yoruba (African people)—Cuba—History—19th century. | Cuba—Race relations—History—19th century.
Classification: LCC F1789.Y6 L68 2018 | DDC 972.91/05092 [B]—dc23
LC record available at https://lccn.loc.gov/2018016246

Cover illustration: Figure of angel and text from 1820s archival document (Archivo Nacional de Cuba, Comisión Militar, series 11/1). Reproduction of the original document provided courtesy of the Archivo Nacional de Cuba.

To Francis

Contents

Figures, Graphs, Maps, and Tables

TABLES

Acknowledgments

I never could have imagined how my first trip to Havana to learn how to play drums would have led to writing about the history of Lucumí religion and culture. This project began and revolved around the many people I met in Cuba over several trips. I would not have discovered such a profound interest in this topic if it were not for the generosity of so many people. I am indebted to the anthropological research team, Proyecto Orunmila: Ernesto Valdés Jané, Omar García Ruiz, Michael Hernández López, and Julio Valdés Jané. I owe many thanks to Yanet Valdés Hernandez, her mother Lourdes, her sister Laura, and to Yazek Manzano, Alexander Ramirez, Rogelio E. Yamarit Rondón, Ana Clara Tamayo, and their friends and families. They welcomed me into their homes and shared their knowledge about the myths, traditions, beliefs, music, animals, flora, and fauna of African-Cuban culture.

I am certainly privileged to have had such a wonderful education. I want to thank my father, who has given me such a deep interest in learning and travel. I cannot say enough about his influences and support on my research and life. In terms of graduate school, I give special thanks to: Andrew Apter, Lauren Derby, Edward Alpers, Kevin Terraciano, Jacqueline DjeDje, Ghislaine Lydon, Lynn Hunt, Margaret Jacob, José Curto, David Trotman, Michele Johnson, Sydney Kanya-Forstner, Michael Marcuzzi, and Francisco Aguabella. This gratitude extends to my postdoctoral supervisors, Alejandra Bronfman, David Eltis, and Toyin Falola. It has been such an honor studying under such generous and knowledgeable people.

I would like to thank some of my colleagues, most especially Olatunji Ojo, who has been involved in much of my research as an interpreter and guide through Yorùbá culture. Jane Landers has been an academic godmother walking me through the depths of Cuba's archives. Marial Iglesias Utset has helped me navigate Cuban bureaucracies, shared obscure materials, and helped obtain copies of images. Jorge Felipe has shared his digital archives. Robin Law has been instrumental in terms of Yorùbá historiography and the interpretation of colonial ethnonyms. And Manuel Barcia has engaged in countless discussions related to interpreting Yorùbá identity, culture, and resistance in the Atlantic world.

This project was made possible with the support of many, including Roseanne Adderley, Akintunde Akinyemi, Juan Bosco Amores, Richard Anderson, Steve Behrendt, Judith Bettelheim, Nielson Rosa Bezerra, Alex Borucki, Carolyn Brown, Judith Byfield, Rina Cáceres, Mariana Candido, María del Carmen Barcia, Mariza de Cavalho Soares, Matt Childs, Norton Corrêa, Yacine Daddi Addoun, Ademola Omobewaji Dasylva, Natalie Zemon Davis, Érika Delgado, Adrián López Denis, Daniel Domingues da Silva, Suzan Eltis, Elizabeth Fenn, Raul Fernandez, Marcel Fortin, Henry Louis Gates Jr., Jordan Goodman, Oscar Grandío, Gwendolyn Midlo Hall, Walter Hawthorne, Linda Heywood, Umar Hussein, Sherry Johnson, Katrina Keefer, Sean Kelley, Debbie Klein, Martin Klein, Anne Knowles, Carlos Liberato, Kristin Mann, John Mason, Marjorie McIntosh, Ivor Miller, Joseph Miller, Philip Misevich, Byron Moldofsky, Gregory O'Malley, Ugo Nwokeji, Nick Radburn, Dean Rehberger, David Richardson, Inés Roldan de Montaud, Joel Quirk, Abubakar Babajo Sani, David Sartorius, Suzanne Schwarz, Rebecca Scott, Dallas Sealy, Stacey Sommerdyk, Elisée Soumonni, John Thornton, Bruno Véras, Constanze Weis, David Wheat, and Peter Wood. I also want to thank all archivists, librarians, language teachers, musicians, capoeira masters, writing groups, as well as my in-laws, brothers, sisters, friends, and roommates and their families. I am also thankful to my mother, who as a biographer discussed the methods related to reconstructing the lives of people whose stories need to be told.

Funding for research presented in this book came from Fulbright-Hays, the Social Sciences and Humanities Research Council of Canada, the Universities of California-Cuba Academic Initiative, the University of California, Los Angeles (Department of History, Graduate Division, Latin American Institute, and Center for European and Eurasian Studies), and the Eugene M. Kayden research grant via the University of Colorado Boulder.

To whom this book is dedicated, thanks for discussing every possible scenario regarding Prieto's life — no matter how real or imagined. You helped so much with transcriptions and translations, showed me the wonders of Cuba, provided the sincerest criticisms, and were always a sympathetic ear. This book is as much yours as it is mine.

Notes on Language and Orthography

Yorùbá is a tonal language, whereby a given syllable has different meanings whether it has a high, medium, or low pitch. The dots underneath the vowels of "e" and "o" represent a shorter sound, while the dot under the "ṣ" represents an "sh" sound. The decision to use Yorùbá spelling throughout this book helps avoid confusion, although I do maintain the same spelling in direct citations from Spanish primary sources. Documented Yorùbá words involved transliterations, meaning Spanish speakers wrote down the Yorùbá words they once heard using Spanish phonetics. For example, "Ṣàngó" in Yorùbá equates with "Changó" in Spanish sources.

In this book, all spelling of Yorùbá words conforms to the diacritics and spelling from *A Dictionary of the Yorùbá Language*, which Samuel Àjàyí Crowther first compiled in 1843. By 2007, this dictionary had undergone numerous editions, impression, and reprints. I have also consulted more obscure spellings with Akintunde Akinyemi (University of Florida) and Olatunji Ojo (Brock University). The meanings of Yorùbá terms are explained at first instance in the text.

Prieto

Introduction
Slave, Soldier, and Lucumí Leader

On Sunday, 12 July 1835, word spread around Havana that a group of Lucumí slaves, free persons, and enslaved Africans liberated by the Anglo-Spanish antislave trade commission were attempting to seize Havana and overthrow the colonial government. Despite the involvement of only about thirty people in some kind of a disturbance in a city with tens of thousands of residents, military police and concerned citizens mobilized themselves and then descended on the small group violently. In a matter of minutes, the angry mob killed four people of African descent and injured the remaining participants. That evening, officials from the island's military court began searching for the underlying motives of the alleged crime. Within four days, officials identified the participants, imprisoned the suspects, and executed the leaders by firing squad. Then they displayed their decapitated heads in cages around the city to serve as a warning to others. Over the course of the swift trial for what was but a minor disturbance, authorities speculated that a major conspiracy was afoot and that a network of people of African descent were organizing an islandwide revolt in pursuit of Cuban independence and the abolition of slavery.

Two days into the investigation, Manuel de Moya, police captain of the Havana neighborhood of Jesús, María y José, alleged that "the *negro* Juan Nepomuceno Prieto leader of the *nación Lucumi Elló* [Ọ̀yọ́] had participated in the conspiracy."[1] Moya believed Prieto—whose name means "black"—was the architect of this plot, which he had organized along ethnic lines. The majority of the participants that Sunday were "Lucumí," a colonial designation for those who are generally identified as Yorùbá in Cuba today. Prieto was a well-known leader of a *cabildo de nación* Lucumí, which was a legally sanctioned and church-sponsored socioreligious brotherhood for Lucumí in Havana. His *cabildo* was formally known as the Mutual Aid Society of the Lucumí Nation of Santa Bárbara (*Sociedad de Socorros Mutuos Nación Lucumí de Santa Bárbara*). Prieto led this *cabildo* for nearly two decades after he retired as second sergeant of Havana's Loyal Black Battalion (*Batallón de Morenos Leales de la Habana*).

1

In attempts to prove his innocence, Prieto emphasized his loyal military service. This information was relevant to the investigation because the arresting officer accused the Lucumí leader of "being involved at some other time in a conspiracy movement against white people in 1812, which demarcated the *Conspiracy of Aponte*."[2] Over twenty years before Prieto's arrest, authorities uncovered what was considered an islandwide plot to overthrow the colonial regime and obtain independence from Spain. During the suppression and trials, it was revealed that its leader, José Antonio Aponte who was a captain in the black militia, had not only sought independence and abolition but also had been inspired by ideologies linked to the American, French, and Haitian revolutions.[3] While Prieto was not involved in the Aponte Rebellion, except perhaps in its repression, this biography of a slave, soldier, and *cabildo* leader provides uncanny insights into the experiences of people of African descent in the Atlantic world.

Prieto's life occurred during a series of movements that shaped the modern world in a period often referred to as the "Age of Revolutions." The intellectual and philosophical movement of the Enlightenment—which advanced ideologies related to reason, liberalism, liberty, independence, and human rights—directly resulted in the transformation from monarchial rule to constitutional states or republics. Prieto was born at the height of the kingdom of Ọ̀yọ́, which was a major slave trading state in West Africa. He arrived in Cuba after the American Revolutionary War which ended in 1783 and before the start of the French Revolution in 1789. He then served in the Spanish military in Cuba during the Haitian Revolution, Napoleonic wars, and Spanish-American Wars of Independence. Prieto also lived in Havana during the most aggressive phase of the Bourbon reforms when the Spanish colony underwent drastic economic, social, and cultural transformations, including the militarization of the island, the rapid expansion of the plantation economy, the free import of enslaved Africans, and a fundamental shift in the pattern of landholding. This period, which Dale M. Tomich refers to as "second slavery," forms part of the economic and political restructuring of the world economy during the industrial revolution whereby new zones of slavery emerged, most especially around the production of cotton in the southern United States, sugar in Cuba, and coffee in Brazil.[4]

Prieto possessed a remarkable ability to traverse a society that was increasingly fearful of the population of African descent, which grew exponentially once the slave trade to the Spanish colony opened in 1789 and the sugar industry in the French colony of St. Domingue collapsed in the 1790s. Over the course of Prieto's life, nearly 450,000 enslaved Africans landed in Cuba, and over three-quarters of that total arrived after 1810.[5] As a soldier, Prieto supervised the enslaved population arriving in unprecedented numbers, and he contributed to the same oppression he had once himself endured as a slave. Toward the end of his life, he led a Lucumí *cabildo* during the mass arrival of Yorùbá speakers to Cuba following *jihād* emanating from the Sokoto Caliphate, which contributed to the collapse of Ọ̀yọ́ between 1817 and 1836. His success in Havana meant he navigated through new and different social, political, and cultural networks, which continued to change as much as the world around him. Prieto's life was therefore anything but static. It was *experienced*.

THE DECADE-LONG PROCESS of research surrounding this historical subject has brought together primary and secondary sources, both oral and written, from many countries and in multiple languages. Prieto's story begins with records housed in Cuba's national archives under the Military Commission series. This file, entitled "The Lucumí uprising in Jesús, María and Juan Nepomuceno Prieto," contains over four hundred pages, among other loose documents. Two-thirds of this dossier relate to the trial proceedings (including Prieto's testimony) of more than a dozen people accused of being involved in the Lucumí unrest in Havana on 12 July 1835. The remaining third of this file revolves around Prieto's arrest, whereby the police searched his home and confiscated weapons, religious shrines, as well as a stack of papers in what amounts to the Lucumí *cabildo* archives. Prieto's personal documents, which were submitted as evidence to the trial, have survived from a period when people of African descent generally could not read or write. These records, many of which Prieto signed, include a last will and testament, property deeds, receipts, festival licenses, and printed images of Catholic saints (figures 5.1–5.5).

Due to this documentation alone, Prieto is a person of note who warrants further study. Most of this book derives from how the secretary of a colonial military court used Prieto's testimony to record the following biographical sketch in the third person: "Juan Nepomuceno Prieto of the Lucumí nation, *Católico Apostólico Romano*, widowed status, of an age that could not be established apart from saying that he came in the period of Sr. Gálvez Governor of this city [Havana], being a large boy, retired Second Sgt. of the Battalion of Loyal Blacks."[6] This passage, which is cited frequently herein, only touches upon Prieto's affiliations, religious beliefs, and identities. Without deeper research, this description of a significant historical figure does not adequately explain his upbringing in West Africa in the 1770s and 1780s; his involuntary participation in the transatlantic and inter-Caribbean slave trades; his more than twenty years of service in Spain's colonial army in Cuba and Florida; the death of his wife of more than thirty-five years, María Francisca Camejo, during a cholera epidemic in 1833; his ascension as the leader of a Lucumí *cabildo*; and the false accusations leading to his arrest in July 1835.

Filling in the many gaps of Prieto's life with information from the available primary sources has been challenging. This complex individual participated in a multifaceted, multicultural, and oppressive world. Reconstructing his portrait has involved Natalie Zemon Davis's strategy of "sometimes imagining" the past to contend with meaningful and sometimes contradictory "silences in the contemporary record." This method ultimately involves researching "the persons, places, and texts that good evidence affirms or suggests" he knew, or what he "would have been likely to see or hear or read or do."[7] To supplement Prieto's testimony and archives, this biography therefore incorporates government correspondences, military records, ecclesiastical sources, notarial documents, judicial proceedings, other evidence of Havana's *cabildos*, travel accounts, business transactions, and large databases of primary sources. Finding Prieto at various points in his life could not be accomplished without open-access and crowd-sourced digital projects, such as Cuban Genealogy Center, Legacies of British Slave-ownership, Liberated Africans, SHADD: Studies in the History of the African Diaspora – Documents, Slave Societies Digital Archive, Voyages: The Trans-Atlantic Slave Trade Database, among others. Linking together "big data" has meant engaging in processes of elimination to follow Prieto's odyssey as he crossed the Atlantic from the Bight of Benin hinterland to Barbados to Jamaica to Cuba, and then from Cuba to Florida and back to Cuba again.

Due to the lack of written records specific to Prieto, I have incorporated an anthropological and ethnomusicological approach to writing this biography. A key theoretical method has involved piecing back Prieto's life while contemplating complex processes sometimes called "creolization" or "transculturation." According to Sydney Mintz and Richard Price, such concepts refer to historical reconstitutions of diverse cultures in the Americas through "new social bonds."[8] In essence, Prieto was an "Atlantic Creole," which Ira Berlin defined as someone with "linguistic dexterity, cultural plasticity, and social agility."[9] He was just one of millions of enslaved Africans who Paul Lovejoy considers "found creative if also often desperate ways of adjusting to their bondage, of course relying heavily on familiar ideas and practices, but adopting innovation out of necessity."[10] For example, Prieto and many others in his community "syncretized," "re-blended," and/or "fused" Christian theologies with African and indigenous cosmologies in opposition to the institution of slavery.[11] Creolization theory, which tends to revolve around themes of resistance, has been necessary to envision how Prieto operated in a colonial slave society.

The knowledge I received through cultural immersion from different perspectives undoubtedly shaped how I came to conceptualize Prieto's religious beliefs in the past. My initiations into African-derived religions in Cuba began when I first traveled to Havana for several months over the summer of 2001.[12] This fieldwork followed the "special period" when the island was still recovering from an economic crisis related to the dissolution of the Soviet Union. As the island opened its doors to tourism, I chose to avoid hotels and resorts by residing in the home of an anthropological research team known as Proyecto Orunmila in the Havana neighborhood of Regla. Since the 1970s, this group has been consulting a network of local priests to consolidate, on a rolling basis, over sixty volumes of religious texts, ceremonies, manuscripts, treaties, and the deep ritual language of one of the most widely practiced religions of African persuasion in Cuba, commonly known as Santería.[13] During my graduate and postgraduate education, I returned to Havana for months at a time to grow my social network, while continuing to learn about Cuban religions from an Atlantic perspective. Over the past ten years, my religious indoctrinations expanded into the Havana neighborhoods of Guanabacoa, El Cerro, and Santiago de las Vegas. Beyond Cuba, I have also participated in rituals and ceremonies across North America, Europe, Brazil, and Nigeria.

Like Prieto must have once done, I have trudged the streets of Havana during the hot summer months trying to find religious paraphernalia and sacrificial objects, such as animals, plants, and stones. In 2001, I watched my own name being entered into church records at the baptism of my godson, Henry, who was coincidently born on my birthday.[14] I have had bananas spontaneously arrive when none were to be found in the markets, and once when I needed it most, I miraculously caught a pigeon after it landed at my feet. I have learned basic rhythms and theories surrounding *bàtá* talking drums, along with other music and dance.[15] I have brought flowers to almost every Catholic church in Havana, whose priests accept the "double consciousness" that pantheons of African gods hold over the saints, and vice versa.[16] I have even explored Palo Monte, whereby I received my "scratches" (*rayamiento*) and became a priest (*tata nganga*). The value of these personal experiences has brought an added perspective to question the racist bias found in the surviving colonial documentation, especially as it pertains to Lucumí oral traditions, legends, myths, and folklore.

AS A NARRATIVE STRATEGY, biographies of Africans have the capacity to transcend broad generalizations of complex historical processes. Arguably, Philip Curtin pioneered this methodological approach in *Africa Remembered*, published in 1967. This collection contains ten narratives of West Africans during the era of the transatlantic slave trade, of which three were Yorùbá speakers.[17] The introductions, annotations, and maps about authorship provided a deeper background related to the personal dimensions of slavery from an African perspective. Since then, the ongoing research into the personal stories of Africans in diaspora informs just as much about the authors themselves, as well as the world in which they lived. Prieto epitomized what it meant to be Lucumí in the late eighteenth and early nineteenth centuries, as well as what it entailed to be a slave transitioning to freedom. His story forms part of an already large and growing body of biographical literature of enslaved Africans whose lives straddled, crisscrossed, and influenced the history of the Atlantic world in countless, unimaginable ways.[18]

Prieto is especially worthy of a biography because his life illuminates the early development of Santería. As a major branch of a world religion generalized into "òrìṣà worship," Santería refers to the "syncretization" of Catholic saints with a pantheon of Yorùbá gods (òrìṣà).[19] David H. Brown describes how this "Afro-Cuban religion known variously as La Regla de Ocha, La Regla de Ifá, La Religión Lucumí, and La Santería ("The Religion") has been studied since the late nineteenth century in Cuba and the 1940s in the United States from diverse disciplinary perspectives and thematic bases."[20] Scholars have long debated the function of the *cabildo* in the earliest stages of the expansion of African derived religions in Cuba. According to Roger Bastide, "The *cabildo* incontestably forms the starting point for the African *santaria* of Cuba."[21] Most scholars agree that *cabildos* had provenance in the Iberian Peninsula and then transferred to the Americas, where authorities permitted groups of people of African descent to organize around ethnic lines.[22] Amazingly, Prieto's testimony and personal archives reveal the inner workings of a Lucumí *cabildo* and proves beyond doubt how he was a key religious figure within the Cuban branch of a major global religion.

In spite of a paper trail, modern-day practitioners have not remembered Prieto by name within their genealogical lists, but they do, however, recall an early nineteenth-century Lucumí *cabildo* remembered as Ṣàngó tẹ̀ dún.

In some of the earliest recorded Lucumí oral traditions related to the 1830s—that is, in Prieto's time—Fernando Ortiz described this Lucumí *cabildo* as popular and wealthy.[23] Separately, Lydia Cabrera refers to another prestigious Lucumí *cabildo* by the same name from the 1870s, after Prieto died, suggesting the continuation of an institutional legacy.[24] Without attaching specific dates, Brown states how this organization is "the most widely remembered and important Lucumí *cabildo* in Cuba's history."[25] As a documented *cabildo* leader, Prieto followed Catholicism, òrìṣà, and other belief systems simultaneously. During the 1835 trial, Prieto candidly described in an apparent act of self-incrimination how *"Changó, which is the same as saying King, or Santa Bárbara, [was] who we venerate as God."*[26] This documented statement, which is also cited frequently herein, is remarkable because it was one of, if not the earliest references, to a common òrìṣà/saint paradigm still observed in Cuba and elsewhere today. It also affirms to me that Prieto holds a prominent place within the long history of the Lucumí religion in Cuba.

The honorific title of Havana's most famous Lucumí *cabildo* obtained from two sets of oral sources has many variant spellings in the secondary literature: *Changó Tedún, Changó Terddún, Shangó-Tedumn, Sàngó ti edun, Sàngó tè dún, Sàngó tèdó,* among others. As a result, scholars have since provided many interpretations as to its meaning. Brown has argued that it appears to represent a Yorùbá phrase *"Sàngó ti edun,* meaning, 'Changó becomes the thunderstone,' i.e., the celts that this òrìṣà is thought to hurl from the sky when lightning strikes the earth."[27] From interviews with a prominent Havana priest in the 1980s, John Mason determined that it was either *Sàngó tè dún,* meaning "Sàngó imprints with noise," or *Sàngó tèdó,* signifying "Sàngó arrived and planted."[28] Without discrediting these noteworthy interpretations, I would like to add that in Catholic terms, the *cabildo* title might relate to a Christian hymn with the opening Latin line *Te Deum laudamus,* meaning "Thee, O God, we praise"—that is, *"Sàngó te Deum* [thee, O God]." In the spirit of creolization theory, I consider all versions correct, but based on my discussions with Mason, I elect to use the Yorùbá phrase, *Sàngó tè dún.*

Associating Prieto with the legacy of this Lucumí *cabildo* requires further clarification because it has been historically misrepresented in the secondary literature until recently. Since the 1960s, a distinguished Cuban historian, José Luciano Franco, asserted that the alleged mastermind of the 1812 Aponte Rebellion (in which authorities had implicated Prieto in 1835) was the original leader of *Sàngó tè dún.*[29] Over the next decades, other scholars who only cited Franco's work repeated this notion as historical fact.[30] By 2002, Stephen Palmié recognized that this claim was based on "anything *but* documentary evidence."[31] Matt D. Childs, who has conducted extensive research into Aponte and Cuba's *cabildos*, validated Palmié's assertion because it never entered court record that "Aponte was a member of the *cabildo* Chango-Tedum or any other *cabildo* for that matter."[32] Additionally, María del Carmen Barcia's extensive study of dozens of Havana's documented *cabildos* between the sixteenth and nineteenth centuries demonstrates that the earliest Lucumí *cabildo* dedicated to Santa Bárbara never had any links to Aponte at all.[33] Following a trend in Cuban scholarship in the mid-twentieth century, Franco did not cite his sources properly, if ever. But like Ortiz and Cabrera, this respected scholar interacted with many African-Cuban communities, and any number of his undocumented informants might have told him that Aponte led *Ṣàngó tẹ̀ dún*, which cannot be ignored or discredited. In my view, however, Aponte was not the leader of *Ṣàngó tẹ̀ dún*. Rather, the written evidence proves how it is was Juan Nepomuceno Prieto. As a result, Franco's storyline has distorted Prieto's prominence in the history of Lucumí religion and culture, which this book will resolve.

IDENTITY IS A MAJOR THEME in this book. As an analytical concept, identity is full of contradictory meanings of particularistic claims.[34] Prieto held multiple identity markers in which he was able to establish singularity within diverse and racially stratified groups. Raised as a Yorùbá speaker in West Africa, he was captured by Dahomey as a child in warfare. He was then a slave on at least two slave ships. He became a "raw" Spanish slave (*bozal*). He understood his African origins from the Lucumí nation (*negro de nación Lucumí*). He earned the title of free black (*moreno libre*). He was a soldier, who rose through the ranks as a second sergeant (*sargento segundo*). By the time of his arrest as a *cabildo* leader, Prieto could have used a lengthy honorific title along the lines of *negro de nación Lucumí, moreno libre, sargento segundo retirado de la Batallón de Morenos Leales de la Habana*; and *capatáz de la Sociedad de Socorros Mutuos de Nación Lucumí Santa Bárbara*, aka *Ṣàngó tẹ̀ dún*. Within the limitations of a colonial slave society, his status demonstrated a high social standing, perhaps even of royal stature within Havana's Lucumí community.

The most difficult of Prieto's identities to conceptualize is "Lucumí." Colonial procedures meant enslaved Africans were assigned a "nation" after arriving in the Americas. In Cuba, slave traders and owners grouped people according to broad geographic associations with the African continent, as well as vague ethnonyms related to language and/or ethnicity. José Antonio Saco, a liberal Cuban-born intellectual from Prieto's time, criticized and questioned this process:

> How does one figure out the homeland for the various Africans who come to the New World? Many of them [were] driven from the interior regions of Africa down to the Atlantic coast, accumulated there among the coastal peoples, sold by the hundreds, transported to the Americas afterwards, [and] finally distributed into groups, getting passed around from man-to-man without retaining a single trace of the name of the nation from which many of them belong. And in the middle of so much uncertainty, it is not possible, not even in times of prosperity, to figure out the homeland of so many Africans.[35]

Stressing "the middle of so much uncertainty" relates to Paul Lovejoy's view that "the struggle for survival began in Africa . . . [and] the emphasis on Africa is important because it places the 'Middle Passage' in the middle. What happened before the shipboard trauma had ramifications affecting the historical development of the African diaspora, the other side of the 'middle' for the enslaved."[36] Diverse languages, ethnicities, and cultures effectively "creolized" *within* Africa long before anyone traveled to the Americas. Much like Catholicism "fused" with òrìṣà in Cuba, J. D. Y. Peel argued that the religion and culture of Yorùbá-speaking people meshed with many West African religions and cultures, including Islam, because it "was overwhelmingly and conspicuously of the 'mixing' kind."[37]

The study of "Lucumí" has been ongoing since the late nineteenth century when police brutally persecuted the African-Cuban population for practicing witchcraft (*brujería*) and scholars of criminology, phrenology, and evolutionary anthropology considered the legacy of slavery in shaping Cuba as a modern nation.[38] As the *afrocubanismo* movement emerged at the turn of the twentieth century, intellectual pioneers such as Fernando Ortiz began to historicize African derived cultures through religion, music, and dance. Ortiz argued that *"lucumís are equal to the Yorubas."*[39] However, this perspective failed to recognize that the term "Yorùbá" (يوربا), or some variation thereof, was first a designation in Hausa, Kanuri, Songhay, Arabic, and probably other languages in the African interior since the sixteenth century, if not earlier. It referred to people speaking a common language called Yorùbá today.[40] "Lucumí" was equally complex because the term surfaced in documentation in the Spanish Americas in the sixteenth century. It was similar in usage to other ethnonyms, such as "Nagô" and "Terranova," and clearly referred to people who spoke a common language, most likely Yorùbá.[41] As Robin Law has shown, the popularization of Lucumí as an ethnonym in Cuba coincided with the expansion of the kingdom of Ọ̀yọ́ after the middle of the seventeenth century.[42] However, not every Lucumí person documented in colonial Cuba could be considered "Yorùbá" because they could have belonged to any ethnolinguistic group found throughout the Bight of Benin hinterland, such as Nupé, Hausa, Fon, Mossi, Màhi, Borgu, Igala, Bornu, among others.

Late in his life, Prieto chose to identify himself as "Lucumí," but it was really his documented belief in Ṣàngó that truly places his birth place within the geographic context of Yorùbá-speaking regions in the Bight of Benin hinterland. At the time of his enslavement in the second half of the eighteenth century, Ọ̀yọ́ was the dominant kingdom in this area. Its initial development is usually attributed to the strategic location of its capital in the savannah, also known as Ọ̀yọ́ (or "Katunga" in Hausa and Kanuri), almost 250 kilometers inland from the coast along major trade routes near the Niger River in what is modern-day Nigeria. Ọ̀yọ́ participated in the transsavannah trade from Gonja northward to the Hausa states, primarily in kola nuts, salt, textiles, and slaves; and eventually firearms, iron products, and cowrie shells.[43] Ọ̀yọ́'s sizeable military, famous for its cavalry, facilitated commercial expansion and imperial conquest. At the kingdom's height around the time of Prieto's birth, Ọ̀yọ́'s population was close to one million people, and the total area was around 46,000 square kilometers.[44] Prieto was a victim of Ọ̀yọ́ grandeur and an unwilling participant in the kingdom's struggle for control over access to European trade at the coast in the late eighteenth century.

This microhistory within this larger picture therefore situates Prieto's upbringing in Ọ̀yọ́ and his involvement in the transatlantic and inter-Caribbean slave trades. His passage from Ouidah to Bridgetown to Kingston, and then to Havana was part of a macrohistory that has been described as forming the "Yorùbá diaspora." Between 1616 and 1863, nearly two million people boarded slave ships at the Bight of Benin, and the majority were Yorùbá speakers. According to estimates, the hundreds of thousands of victims departing this region at different intervals primarily went to Brazil (about 600,000 people), St. Domingue (200,000), Cuba (111,000), Jamaica (75,000), and due to British pressure to suppress the transatlantic trade after 1807, Sierra Leone (50,000). Following British emancipation in 1833, groups of those "recaptured" relocated from Sierra Leone, and to a lesser extent from Cuba to other British Caribbean colonies, especially Trinidad, the Bahamas, and British Honduras, as well as Europe. Otherwise, groups of people returned from the Americas and Sierra Leone back to the Bight of Benin hinterland too.[45]

As this biography demonstrates, Prieto's involvement within the Yorùbá diaspora occurred via a much smaller, more ethnically diverse migration in the late eighteenth century. His historical significance is even more prominent because he became a Lucumí *cabildo* leader throughout the largest migration of enslaved Yorùbá speakers when over 35,000 arrived to Cuba during Ọ̀yọ́'s disintegration.[46] An analysis of Prieto's life within this context exhibits how the conceptual meaning of "Lucumí" transformed when Ọ̀yọ́-centric repertoires fused with established socioreligious paradigms in Cuba which had already undergone processes of creolization in earlier periods. Prieto's life, therefore, bridges older generations of Lucumí who arrived in the eighteenth century with much larger groups arriving during Ọ̀yọ́'s collapse.

THE SUBTITLE OF THIS BOOK, "Yorùbá Kingship in Colonial Cuba during the Age of Revolutions," requires explanation. First, it is undoubtedly problematic to refer to Prieto as "Yorùbá." The people called "Yorùbá" today never used the term to refer to themselves as a people in the late eighteenth and early nineteenth centuries. However, Prieto grew up in the Bight of Benin hinterland speaking the Yorùbá language, he was part of what scholars have called the "Yorùbá diaspora," and he played a significant role in the development of Santería because he worshipped the òrìṣà. Even if Prieto never referred to himself as "Yorùbá," he still self-identified as "Lucumí," which forms part of the history of a global pan-Yorùbá identity. For the subtitle, I am therefore using "Yorùbá" retroactively to situate Prieto within this broader context. Second, the use of "kingship" is complicated too. Obviously, the Spanish monarchy and the authoritarian colonial regime never recognized a former slave from Africa as a "king" in colonial Cuba. Nonetheless, Prieto was the undisputed leader of a wealthy and prosperous Lucumí *cabildo* in Havana, which authorities officially acknowledged and allowed to operate. This book will argue how Prieto made dynastic claims through òrìṣà worship; hence he promoted, consolidated, and upheld the royal status of a "king" within Havana's Yorùbá-speaking community.

This book's organization follows Prieto's life chronologically. The first chapter examines his childhood and enslavement in West Africa during Ọ̀yọ́'s struggle to control the slave trade at the coast during the destruction of the port of Badagry in September 1784. Chapter 2 places Prieto on board the *Golden Age* and his subsequent arrival in Havana via Jamaica by 1785.

The next chapter looks at Prieto's early years in Havana as a *cabildo* member, his enlistment in the military after the start of the Haitian Revolution, his marriage to María Francisca Camejo, and their manumission. The fourth chapter follows the bulk of Prieto's military service, including his involvement in the suppression of the Aponte Rebellion of 1812 and his service in Florida during the War of 1812 and the Creek War in 1814. Chapter 5 explores the festivals, rituals, and innerworkings of *Ṣàngó tẹ̀ dún* from c. 1818 to 1835. The next chapter examines the growth of the Lucumí community in Havana through an examination of the Bight of Benin migration to Cuba during Ọ̀yọ́'s collapse when Camejo and Prieto were *cabildo* leaders. Chapter 7 examines the ramifications of the Yorùbá diaspora when warfare from Ọ̀yọ́ carried over to plantations to the west of Havana during the cholera epidemic of 1833. The final chapter looks at events leading to Prieto's arrest, imprisonment, and disappearance from historical record in 1835. The conclusion discusses Prieto's legacy within the history of the Lucumí religion in Cuba, and his place within the formation of a broader pan-Yorùbá identity.

CHAPTER ONE

Badagry

Where did Prieto come from in Africa? And what were the events leading up to his embarkation on a slave ship as a child? This challenging line of inquiry requires careful consideration because slave traders and masters actively deleted details about the lives of millions of men, women, and children absorbed into the Atlantic trade. Enslaved people did not have control over their lives, let alone what written evidence appeared in the surviving, fragmentary documentation. To complicate matters, most non-Muslim peoples in the Bight of Benin hinterland were illiterate until former slaves, Liberated Africans, and Christian missionaries, such as Samuel Àjàyí Crowther, returned to their homelands and developed Yorùbá orthography in the mid-nineteenth century.[1] A major problem in reconstructing sociocultural changes in diaspora has been finding specific evidence about individuals who influenced colonial slave societies. Even the names of renowned political and spiritual leaders, such as Juan Nepomuceno Prieto, have almost disappeared from modern memory. Today's practitioners and scholars of the Lucumí religion, for example, have taken a long time to connect Prieto's documented leadership with the famous Lucumí *cabildo* remembered as Ṣàngó tẹ̀ dún. This biography brings Prieto to the forefront because he not only represents a major branch of the Lucumí genealogical tree, but he also deserves recognition within the global study of Yorùbá history, culture, and religion.

Much about what can be known about Prieto's childhood in West Africa relates to how he emerged as a central figure in an eminent branch of a world religion known as òrìṣà worship. As simplified theories explain, enslaved people carried their cultures, religions, and traditions from Africa across the Atlantic, which then transformed in the Americas through complex processes of creolization.[2] The Lucumí religion in Cuba, which continues to be marginalized, undeniably has roots among the West African ethnolinguistic group known today as "Yorùbá." Despite a lack of written evidence, Prieto's childhood requires careful reflection to eliminate stereotypes about his African upbringing as a means in which to enhance his successes in Cuban slave society. Using clues from the records about Prieto found in Cuba in the nineteenth century, it has been possible to piece back together parts of his early life. Tidbits of evidence found in his deposition and last will establish a basic chronology related to his birth. In 1835, Prieto testified that he arrived in Havana as a "large boy" when "Señor Gálvez [was] Governor of this city."[3] This deliberate recollection demonstrated his own intention to date his arrival in Havana during a four-month window when Bernardo de Gálvez was captain general between February and May of 1785. His memory showed an awareness about the global implications following the American Revolutionary War, which included naval campaigns in the Caribbean Sea.[4] By taking into account the time it took to cross the Atlantic Ocean and arrive in Cuba, Prieto must have boarded a slave ship at the Bight of Benin between late 1784 and early 1785. His description of being a "large boy" at the time of his enslavement suggests he was probably not born before 1773.

Without any documented proof, Prieto's African origins and conditions of enslavement will forever be a matter of interpretation. In his last will, Prieto generalized his heritage, first and foremost, as a "native of Africa from the Lucumí nation."[5] The self-identification of "Lucumí," which was a term that slave traders assigned to Prieto involuntarily upon his arrival to Cuba, indicates that late in his life he actively embraced his African roots according to Spanish colonial perceptions of the region of his birth. Prieto's acceptance of "Lucumí" implied that he spoke Yorùbá and climbed on board a ship along a broad African region formerly known as the "Slave Coast." This shoreline in the Bight of Benin included ports between Little Popo and Lagos (Èkó) but that centered at Ouidah, which was the second most voluminous point of embarkation for enslaved people in all of Africa during the era of the slave trade.[6] Among an estimated one million people leaving this region during the Age of Revolutions, Prieto's experiences leading up to his departure from Ouidah culminated with the destruction of Badagry, a rival port to Ouidah, on 24 September 1784.[7]

Before exploring events at Badagry, two additional clues from Cuban records establish more details about Prieto's African origins. At his incarceration in 1835, the arresting officer, Manuel de Moya, knew Prieto as "Lucumí Elló," which was an additional identity marker which referred to the kingdom of Ọyọ.[8] Prieto corroborated his loyalty by identifying shrines devoted to "Changó," or in Yorùbá "Sàngó," the principal god worshipped in this prominent West African kingdom.[9] Such incredibly rare descriptions confirmed how Prieto spoke the Yorùbá language. However, this remarkable evidence of an African god recorded in Spanish colonial sources still cannot specify with any precision Prieto's place of birth or how he ended up on a slave ship. But by juxtaposing such clues with primary and secondary sources about West Africa in the nineteenth century, and alongside modern-day cultural practices, it is conceivable to project backward a society and culture Prieto might have encountered as a child.

The people in the Old World did not use New World identities. Prieto's African family never considered themselves part of a "Lucumí nation" or even "natives of Africa." Yorùbá-speaking peoples generally chose to identify themselves within their own communities by an "ancient place of origin," called *oríkì orílè*.[10] Prieto's story clearly did not start at his birth, but with a long line of ancestors who participated in long-distance trade and foreign relations with other diverse peoples across West Africa and beyond. According to the appellations, attributions, and epithets of *oríkì orílè*, Prieto's predecessors told stories about how they migrated from somewhere inland to found a new village or how they inserted their family into the social fabric of a pre-existing town. Through oral traditions transmitted over great distances and extended periods of time, people from similar lineages shared socio-cultural practices, such as food taboos, funeral customs, music, dance, occupations, and religious beliefs. Prieto's background, therefore, stemmed from a complex genealogical tree stretching back into times of legend, folklore, and mythology—one family heritage of millions of people transported from Africa to the Americas.

In Yorùbá-speaking societies, families or kinship groups were mostly polygamous patrilineages. According to Karin Barber, marriage increased a male's social standing, whereby each succeeding wife would represent "another improvement in status." For women, marriage and motherhood provided influence within the family compound, or house, called *ilé*. Villages, towns, and cities, of which there were many in the region, varied in population, but no matter the size, they all contained many houses which were "the fundamental social and political units of the town."[11] If Prieto's father could support multiple wives, then his mother would have negotiated social standing within the house's hierarchy, which for children generally revolved around their mother's order in marriage, followed by gender, then age. Marjorie McIntosh has argued that "the domains in which Yorùbá women functioned were affected by economic, social, political, and religious factors, including the gender definitions and forms of patriarchy present at particular times and places."[12]

Through oral and archeological sources, scholars know that Yorùbá-speaking communities cultivated a variety of social statuses.[13] Wealthy families owned slaves, meaning Prieto could have been born into slavery. Individual identities linked to a wide range of institutions or corporations within the house, and even slaves accessed basic resources tied to membership within the extended kinship group. In contrast to plantation slavery in the Americas, which was mostly a racialized and economy-driven institution, slavery in the Bight of Benin hinterland generally occurred for political and social reasons, such as to expand lineages and gain prestige. Scholars have often considered African slavery to be more assimilative, whereby the enslaved could increase status over the course of their lives or over generations. According to Sean Stilwell, the slave's role "was not solely centered on production," but slaves often "slept within the same general household and ate out of the same pot."[14] Even if Prieto was born into slavery, he still grew up with a sense of belonging to a community, culture, and people.

The Yorùbá birth name of "Prieto" was never documented (and hence the main reason the Spanish name has had to be used in the African context). Nonetheless, his parents (or owners) undoubtedly gave him a Yorùbá name shortly after his arrival into the world. According to Samuel Johnson, who recorded Ọ̀yọ́-centric traditions in the late nineteenth century, the naming of a baby boy occurred on the ninth day after birth. The ceremony, called "bringing the child out" (kò ọmọ jáde), represented the first time the mother and child left the birthing room together. Depending on wealth, Prieto's community brought presents, held feasts, offered sacrifices, and consulted oracles.[15] Even today, Yorùbá describe naming practices with a proverb: "The house precedes the child, who is born out of it" (ilé ni à n wò kí a tó sọ ọmọ ní orúkọ).[16] Modupe Oduyoye explains that "one could write a complete grammar of the Yorùbá language using nothing but names for illustration."[17] Through observations made at birth, Prieto's Yorùbá name could have referred to religious beliefs, wealth, disease, drought, warfare, fertility, reincarnation, ancestors, or his physical characteristics. His Yorùbá name, which he carried across the Atlantic, probably gave him a sense of belonging within his birth community, especially if he had expectations to live up to its meaning, whatever that was.[18]

Prieto worshipped Ṣàngó in Cuba, which implied that his kin group venerated this god too. Written records describing òrìṣà have not survived from the late eighteenth century, if indeed any existed at all. However, Hugh Clapperton, a British diplomat, was in Badagry in 1825, which at that time had a population of about "five thousand inhabitants." He wrote how people worshipped "different fetishes" yet believed "in a supreme being . . . too far removed from mankind to attend to their prayers and their wants—excepting thro' the medium of the fetish which they worship."[19] Clapperton's use of "fetish" stereotyped these religious beliefs as primitive idolatry, but in essence he referred to fundamental *òrìṣà* theology. In Cuba today, believers do not worship the high god Olódùmarè directly; instead, they revere a pantheon of gods, who act as conduits between humanity and the Almighty.[20]

Prieto practiced, preached, and philosophized *òrìṣà* throughout his life. His polytheistic beliefs, which changed over time, viewed the pantheon as incestuous, androgynous, paradoxical, and full of ever-shifting manifestations.[21] As a child, Prieto learned about the creation of the habitable world. In Cuba, he retold variations of those stories, much like modern-day observers of the Lucumí religion retell them today. According to myths of creation, Olódùmarè gave life to Odùduwà, a god of light and creation, who descended from the heavens on a chain toward a planet covered in water. In one hand, Odùduwà carried a handful of dirt, and in the other, a rooster. He threw down the dirt onto the water world and put the rooster on top, which then scratched about to form the continents. Prieto knew the holy site of Odùduwà's descent as Ilé Ifẹ̀—the cradle of all Yorùbá civilization and a thriving city in modern-day Nigeria.[22]

According to the *Encyclopedia of the Yorùbá*, there are 401 deities in the pantheon, "although that figure should be viewed as a sacred metaphor and not a scientific fact."[23] Taking into account variations of myths, traditions, and beliefs, Prieto's pantheon centered on a group of principal deities. Odùduwà, the *òrìṣà* of light and creation, stood at the head, and he gave birth to Èṣù/Ẹlẹ́gbára, the trickster of the crossroads; Ògún of iron and war; Ṣàngó of thunder, lightning, and war; Ifá of divination; Òṣun of rivers; Yẹmọja of oceans; Olókun of deep water; Ọya of wind and rivers; Ọbàtálá of wisdom; and others. In most circumstances, the pantheon relates to places and elements observed in the environment, such as rocks, stones, hills, mountains, water sources, plants, trees, groves, animals, and diseases. John Pemberton III explains how personal belief tended to center on one *òrìṣà* within a "cluster of sacred symbols."[24] The vast liturgy and iconography for each god includes handcrafted objects, colors, spaces, numbers, and temporal dimensions, which seamlessly pass through spiritual and material planes. Existence depends upon the philosophical concept of a life force called *àṣẹ*, which runs through all living and inanimate objects. Like most world religions, *òrìṣà* worship involves purifications, sacrifices, prayers, stories, music, dances, proverbs, festivals, masquerades, burials, ancestors, divinations, possessions, and initiations.

Once missionaries from Sierra Leone and Europe began arriving in the region of Prieto's birth, evidence of Ṣàngó surfaced in written sources from the mid-nineteenth century onward. In the past and present, Sàngó's colors have been red and white, which symbolize thunder and lightning. In 1852, missionary James White described "a piece of wood, shaped in the form of an axe with two sides, by which the god [Sàngó was] represented."[25] From among the religious items confiscated from Havana in 1835, Prieto described an "Opachangó signifying that it [was Sàngó's] scepter."[26] Devotees and priests also carried làbà, a red and white embroidered ritual bag, which held spiritually charged materials.[27] In 1851, James Huber, another missionary, described how Sàngó priests used this bag "to show [their] authority."[28] In Havana, Prieto possessed a "little bag . . . used to make orations."[29] Modern-day practitioners continue to invoke Sàngó with his thunder axe and carry ritual items in làbà bags.

Prieto observed Sàngó in music and dance. As a mnemonic device, performances memorialized stories about ancient origins, migrations, rituals, ancestors, and òrìsà. In West Africa and Cuba today, òrìsà music includes a vast repertoire of instruments.[30] Among the more essential, bàtá are a trio of double-headed, hourglass-shaped "talking" drums, which belong to Sàngó. When played in unison, polyrhythms imitate the tones of the Yorùbá language.[31] The sérèé rattle, a red-and-white painted calabash on a stick and filled with stones, replicated the sound of thunder when shaken.[32] The choreographies imitated Sàngó's personality, which Johnson described as "a very wild disposition, [and] fiery temper."[33] Andrew Apter explains how the god's movements summoned "legendary associations with lightning, fire, war, demolition, differentiation, death, and even immolation."[34] In his 1835 testimony, the Lucumí leader ambiguously referred to music and dancing on several occasions.[35]

Prieto's schooling in òrìsà began at a young age and continued throughout his life. John Peel recognizes how phases of religious instruction started "at birth, or at the age of the baby's teething, or at adolescence, [while] further stages of initiation might take place later in life, giving deeper degrees of access to the mystery and power."[36] J. Lorland Matory describes how Sàngó priests recruited prepubescent children because of concerns they might adopt the beliefs and practices of competing gods or religious institutions.[37] In 1846, Crowther explained how Sàngó priests seized children without warning and took them to a "sacred grove" a few miles east of Badagry.[38] In the following year, William Marsh, a missionary, watched as Sàngó priests kidnapped upward of five hundred children for initiation and held them over periods spanning between seven and fifteen months.[39] Although it is not known what rituals Prieto underwent as a child in Africa, the missionary, Samuel Pearse, described Ṣàngó initiations extensively in 1869. Priests and parents made "necessary arrangements" whereby the priest knocked an initiate unconscious "by a sudden tap on the head . . . with a fetish rod [likely Ṣàngó's thunder axe], and ere he recovers himself, he is born away in triumph in the fetish house, where he finds others old and young in a similar predicament." During the months of seclusion, initiates memorized ritual languages, songs, music, and dances. They recited oaths of allegiance, received body and facial scarifications, and drank "hallucinogenic elixirs," which were believed to "become deadly at any period of their lives, [if] they [were] unfaithful." They also took new names, which "they must be called ever afterwards."[40] If Prieto acquired a second Yorùbá name or scarifications, they too were not documented in Cuba. His renaming as "Juan Nepomuceno Prieto" epitomized a lengthy process of integration, initiation, positioning, and sense of belonging within different slave societies throughout the Atlantic world.

During his religious education, Prieto learned Ṣàngó's history, whereby the mythology overlapped with dynastic claims to kingship. Among the various Yorùbá-speaking kingdoms, royal families considered themselves to be the direct descendants of the mythical Odùduwà. According to oral traditions, the "king of all kings" fathered several princes who left Ilé Ifẹ̀ to found their own kingdoms. According to legend, Odùduwà's grandson, Ọ̀ranmiyàn "the universal conqueror," subjugated peoples to the southeast of Ifẹ̀, where he had a son, Eweka I, the founder of the Ẹ̀dó-speaking Benin dynasty. After that, Ọ̀ranmiyàn went to the northwest, where he established the Ọ̀yọ́ capital, became "the father of all Ọ̀yọ́s," and crowned himself the "owner of the palace" (aláàfin). Ọ̀ranmiyàn's two sons, Àjàká and Ṣàngó, succeeded the throne and were also deified after their deaths.[41] In Cuba, Prieto understood the mythology associated with dynastic claims. In 1835, he testified, "Changó, which is the same as saying King."[42]

Prieto evaluated his ancestral origins, whatever they were, within ever-evolving state initiatives tied to divine royalty. His heritage ties into the apex of Ọ̀yọ́'s greatest territorial extent, which Matory has called the "Age of Ṣàngó."[43] Since the seventeenth century, Ọ̀yọ́'s military conquered many towns in the savannah to gain control over access to European trade at the "Slave Coast." Ọ̀yọ́ colonists either moved into unoccupied lands or installed new rulers in existing towns. Robin Law rationalizes how spontaneous claims to Ọ̀yọ́ occurred because "there were obvious attractions in claiming a spurious royal ancestry." If Prieto's house was not from Ọ̀yọ́ proper, his kinship group could have asserted such claims, which "might equally be fabricated for purposes of prestige."[44] Claims and counterclaims among warring houses revised the rankings of chiefs and gods in the pantheon, the house, the town, and the region. According to Apter, "deep knowledge" (ìmọ̀ jínlẹ̀) made òrìṣà worship powerful across the Atlantic and "informed syncretic revisions of dominant hierarchies in the New World."[45]

Ọ̀yọ́ imperialism in the eighteenth century coincided with the popularization of "Lucumí" as an identity marker for people in Cuba arriving from the Bight of Benin.[46] Prieto was no exception. According to John Thornton, Yorùbá "had emerged as a lingua franca along the coast" from the Volta River to the kingdom of Benin.[47] "Lucumí" might have been a Yorùbá salutation meaning "my friend," or a pejorative Èdó phrase from the kingdom of Benin meaning "young animal," which traders used to describe slaves who spoke Yorùbá.[48] In the seventeenth century, Jean Barbot, a French merchant, described how this inland nation terrorized "all adjacent countries."[49] By the time of Prieto's birth, Ọ̀yọ́ had colonized the areas of Ìbàràpá, Ẹgbádo, Àwórì, and Ànàgó, and subjugated to tributary status many Ìgbómìnà towns, as well as Ẹ̀gbá, Òwu, Kétu, Ṣabé. Ọ̀yọ́ also held authority over non-Yorùbá-speaking territories, such as Dahomey, as well as parts of Màhi, Borgu, and Nupé.

Throughout the Age of Revolutions, slave traders and owners from Cuba recorded dozens of Lucumí subclassifications, such as "Lucumí Elló" (Ọ̀yọ́). These subgroups generally referred to the diversity of people, languages, kingdoms, confederations, provinces, and towns in the Bight of Benin hinterland and beyond. However, in some circumstances the terms had no correlation with anything in Africa. According to their interpretations, anyone classified as "Lucumí," including Prieto, could have theoretically come from distant, inland places, including Asante, Mossi, Borgu, Hausa, Borno, or Igala, especially if many people from these regions could have spoken Yorùbá, which was a common language throughout the region. Therefore, it is feasible that Prieto came from the deep hinterland. However, David Eltis has argued that the Atlantic slave trade "generated captives and shifted slave provenance southward—closer to the coast."[50] To confirm this argument, the interpretation of dozens of Lucumí subclassifications from colonial Cuba more often than not reflected Yorùbá-speaking kingdoms, confederations, and towns close to the coast, and mostly along the savannah/forest divide. These places extended up from the coast through the Àwórì, Ẹgbádo, Ẹ̀gbá, Òwu areas, most of which were under Ọ̀yọ́ control (map 1.1 and table 1.1).

The geography of the savanna/forest divide is another clue to help explain Prieto's African origins. His affinity toward Ṣàngó and Ọ̀yọ́ suggests that he and his family did not hold strong allegiances to the Yorùbá-speaking kingdoms located deep in the forest, such as Ifẹ̀, Ìjẹ̀bú, and Ìjẹ̀sà. Ọ̀yọ́'s impressive cavalry, a majority of which was composed of Hausa-speaking slaves, never conquered the forest because of the tsetse fly, which thrives naturally in this ecological zone. This insect transmits trypanosomiasis, a microscopic parasite that reproduces in the blood of horses and causes swelling, loss of appetite, dehydration, fever, and eventually paralysis. The disease therefore made it impossible to raise horses in the forest; hence Ọ̀yọ́'s cavalry dominated the savannah, which did not have tsetse flies. Between the Niger River and the Atakora Mountains, Ọ̀yọ́'s strategic position in the grasslands facilitated agricultural production and enabled easy transportation of goods and slaves overland, or along large rivers flowing toward the coast.[51] Based on his belief in Ṣàngó, Prieto was born within Ọ̀yọ́'s sphere of influence and almost certainly closer to the coast, where most enslaved people originated before crossing the Atlantic.

As a rival and tributary to Ọ̀yọ́, Prieto's upbringing revolved around the Fon-speaking kingdom of Dahomey. In the early seventeenth century, Aja princes from the kingdom of Allada migrated inland toward the Abomey plateau to found Dahomey. In order to control the coastal trade at Ouidah, Dahomey became more powerful than Allada, conquered its parent state, and destroyed the coastal kingdoms of Wemẹ, Whydah, and Jakin, whose people scattered along the lagoons.[52] Even though Dahomey grew into a dominant kingdom, Ọ̀yọ́ subjected Dahomey to tributary status in 1723. Colonial authorities recognized to some degree this linguistic and political division through usages of the colonial designation "Arará," which derived from sixteenth-century references to Allada.[53] It is worth noting that Prieto never identified as "Arará" in Cuba, which generally referred to Fon-speakers or victims of Dahomey trade. Nevertheless, some of his relatives could have come from any number of internal migrations.

As a child, Prieto had exposure to many diverse and multicultural communities. The peoples living along the lagoons in the Badagry and Porto Novo areas were collectively known as Egun. During Ọ̀yọ́ and Dahomey expansion, refugees mostly from Wemẹ and Whydah, along with people displaced from the Ègbádo, Ànàgó, and Àwórí areas, settled at Badagry, which was originally a farming hamlet located at the confluence of the Yẹwá River and lagoons. Likewise, refugees from Allada flooded the trading center of Hogbonou (called Àjàṣẹ́ in Yorùbá), which the Portuguese renamed

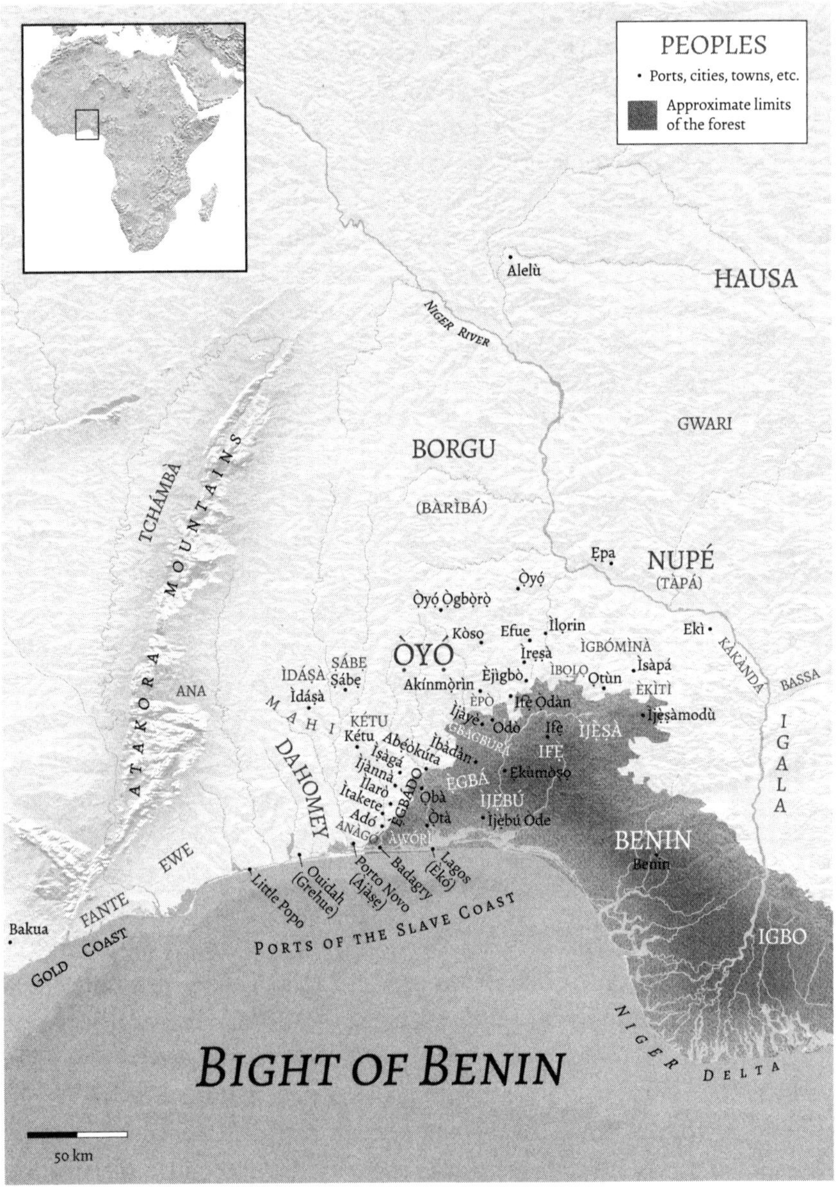

MAP 1.1 Selected interpretations of Lucumí subgroups documented in colonial Cuba and plotted on a map of the Bight of Benin hinterland. Source: Henry B. Lovejoy, *African Diaspora Maps*, 2018.

TABLE 1.1 Interpretation of selected Lucumí subgroups documented in colonial Cuba during the era of the transatlantic slave trade

Lucumí Subgroup	Interpretation	Lucumí Subgroup	Interpretation
Adó	Adó	Ejibo, Ellico, Eyibó,	Èjìgbò
Aguza, Aguzá, Ausá,	Hausa	Eki, Ki	Ekì
Jausá		Ekiti, Ekitin	Èkìtì
Ainá	Ana	Engüei, Engüey	Ewe
Alagua, Bragurá,	Gbágbùrá	Epá	Ẹpa
Egruá		Epó	Èpò
Alelú	Alelù	Fanti	Fante
Allom, Aylló, Ayó, Ayones,	Òyọ́	Fee, Fée, Ife, Nife	Ifẹ̀
Elló, Eyo, Eyó, Oyó		Feodán	Ifẹ̀ Ọ̀dàn
Anagó, Anagonou,	Ànàgó	Guari, Guarí	Gwari
Anagunú, Nanga,		Ibadá, Ibadán	Ìbàdàn
Nangas, Nego		Ibanya, Llainá, Llané,	Ìjànnà
Apapá chiquito, Popo	Little Pópó	Yanés	
Aro, Lara	Ìlarò	Igara	Igala
Ayasé, Ayasí	Àjàsẹ́	Ijaye, Layí, Llallí	Ìjàyè
Babá, Barba, Barbá,	Bàrìbá	Ijesa, Iyesá, Iyesha,	Ìjẹ̀sà
Barbaes, Baríba,	(Borgu)	Iyecha, Yesa, Yesá,	
Barubá, (Bogú)		Yecha	
Banín, Beni, Benin,	Benin	Ilabú, Iyebú, Yavú,	Ìjẹ̀bú
Biní		Yebú	
Basa	Bassa	Ilorin	Ìlọrin
Bolo	Ìbọ́lọ́	Irecha	Ìrẹsà
Bona	Ìgbómìnà	Iyesamoddú	Ìjẹ̀sàmodù
Cacanda	Kàkàndá	Juda, Judá, (Grefé),	Ouidah
Chabas, Chamba,	Tchámbà	(Grife), (Grifé),	(Grehue)
Chambá, Chamvá,		(Griffé)	
Machamba, Tembú		Kangá	Kanga
Chaga, Chagga, Isagá,	Ìsàgá	Kete	Ìtakete
Ishagá, Sagá, Shagá		Ketu	Kétu
Dagñame	Dahomey	Komoré, Komorén	Akínmọ̀rìn
Dasá	Ìdásà	Koso	Kòso
Ebá, Egbá, Egguá,	Ẹ́gbá	Maji, Mají	Mahi
Egwá, Evá		Oba	Ọbà
Ecumachó	Ẹ̀kùmòsọ	Obiokutá	Abẹ́òkúta
Efú	Efue	Odó	Odò
Edwardo, Egguado,	Ẹ́gbádo	Opu	Opu (Igala)
Egwalubo		Ot, ota, otá, oti	Ọ̀tà

(continued)

Lucumí Subgroup	Interpretation	Lucumí Subgroup	Interpretation
Otan	Òtùn	Tapa, Tapá, Tapo,	Takpa (Nupé)
Ouori	Àwórì	Tapós	
Oyóboro	Ọ̀yọ́ Ọ̀gbọ̀rọ̀	Yacuó, Yacó	Bakua
Sabé	Ṣábẹ	Zapa	Ìsàpá

Source: Lucumí subgroups obtained from Bremer, *Homes of the New World*, vol. 3, 181–85; Carmen Barcia, *Los Ilustres apellidos*, 417; Childs, *1812 Aponte Rebellion*, 105, 239; Deschamps Chapeaux, "Marcas tribales," 70–71; Deschamps Chapeaux, *El negro*, 41–44; Dumont, *Antropología y patología*, 4, 21; Guanche, *Africanía y etnicidad*, 217–21; Lachatañeré, "Tipos étnicos," 12; López Valdés, "Notas para el estudio," 72–73; López Valdés, *Africanos de Cuba*, 164, 189, 193–94; H. Lovejoy, "Old Oyo Influences"; H. Lovejoy, "Registers of Liberated Africans: Transcription," 129; Martín, *De dónde vinieron*, 7; Ortiz, *Hampa afro-cubana*, 26–33; and Wetohossou, "Las migraciones," 172. Interpretations of Lucumí subgroups discussed in person, or via email and phone, with Andrew Apter, Robin Law, Paul Lovejoy, and Olatunji Ojo, 2008–2017. Table 1.1 and Map 1.1 do not illustrate a number of Lucumí subgroups. These include (1) ethnic groups, states, towns, subgroups, and ethnonyms: Achanti, Chante, Chanté (Asante); Akokó (Akoko); Aku (Yorùbá speakers in Sierra Leone); Arará (common ethnonym in Cuba, generally refers to Fon-speakers from Dahomey or their victims); Barnó (Borno); Bibi (Ibibio); Ibo Aro (Igbo; *aro* are Igbo traders); Ketza, Keza (Ketsa); Krooman (Kru or Kroo, an ethnic group from eastern Liberia who settled along the West African coast, notably Sierra Leone and Bight of Benin); Mina (common ethnonym found in Cuba; generally refers to people from the western Bight of Benin and eastern Gold Coast, such as Akan or Ewe); Mossi, Mosi, Mosé (Mòssi); Pobe (Pobé); Yoruba, Yobá (Yorùbá). The missing subgroups also include the following (2) debatable interpretations: Amanga, Bambara, Bambaras (Wangara, Bambara?); Aro (Ilaro, Igbo trader?); Efon, Efons, Efún (Fon, Àfọ̀n, Èfọ̀n?); Efuché (possibly refers to the priestess Ña Rosalía Efuche and head of a branch of Ochá in Cuba); Ezza (Ìdáṣà?); Ibanya (Ìjànnà, Ìgbómìnà?); Zezá (Ìjẹ̀ṣà, Ketsa?); and (3) possible phrases: Agaín/Agani Ota (refers to regions in the western Bight of Benin and eastern Gold Coast; Ata is a town north of gold coast); Ará Iyaé, Arafé, Aralorí (*ará* means "people," or "inhabitant of place"; hence *ará* Ìjàyè, *ará* Ifẹ̀, and *ará* Ìlọrin); Aratakua, Atacua, Aratako (*ará takwa*, people from western Bight of Benin or eastern Gold Coast); Takwa, Takua, Takuá, Tacua, Tapkua, Ekuá, Cecuá (*takwa* possible Akan or Kru word); (4) unknown interpretations: Abaya, Abya (?); Aguerefé (Ifẹ̀?); Akuleku; Amaroniki; Aná Ayashé Odina, Oná Ayaché Odina (Ana subgroup and possibly something to do with Àjàṣẹ́); Arailú, Aralú (*ará ìlú*, inhabitants of town); Arufá (?); Aya Die (?); Ayabadó (aja Ẹgbádo?); Camisa (Spanish word for shirt?); Chiquioni (?); Ekubí (?); Ellico (?); Kanga (?); Laguí (?); Mosokue (?); Okó Manigbó (?); Orudó (?); Oyó Ameko, Oyó Ayilodá, Oyonisi (Ọ̀yọ́ towns that might not exist today?); Yogo de Ota (from Òtà?); Yudusi (?).

Porto Novo in 1724. By the 1780s, John Adams, a British slave trader, estimated how Porto Novo had a population of upwards of seven thousand to ten thousand people. He conducted business with Pierre Tammata, who was Hausa and a prominent Muslim slave trader from the deep interior living in Porto Novo. Enslaved as a child, Tammata learned to read, write, and keep accounts in France. His master, who eventually granted him freedom, helped start his business in the port city "by granting him credit for a considerable amount."

TABLE 1.2 Total documented embarkations at the Bight of Benin by European flag, 1777–1785

	Portugal	France	Britain	Total	Percent
1777	2,120	6,225	726	9,071	11.1
1778	6,514	6,559	806	13,879	17.0
1779	2,788	871	609	4,268	5.2
1780	8,023	0	0	8,023	9.8
1781	9,060	0	0	9,060	11.1
1782	8,035	726	1,675	10,436	12.8
1783	5,728	543	450	6,721	8.2
1784	5,052	3,152	1,955	10,159	12.4
1785	4,833	4,598	622	10,053	12.3
Total	52,153	22,674	6,843	81,670	
Percent	63.9	27.8	8.4		

Source: Voyages (database: 1777–85, Bight of Benin).

By the time Prieto boarded a slave ship, Tammata owned many wives, domestic slaves, and a large house containing "upwards of thirty apartments."[54]

At the time of Prieto's enslavement, Portugal, France, and Britain had each built a trading fort in Ouidah. According to Law, this city had an estimated population of eight thousand people and "was a cosmopolitan community, in which European (and American) and African populations and cultures underwent intensive interaction."[55] Estimates of the total departures from the Bight of Benin corroborate Prieto's claim that he arrived during Bernardo de Gálvez's governorship in Cuba. Between 1777 and 1785, Portugal, France, and Great Britain combined to load over 81,000 people onto over 240 documented slave ships. Nearly 65 percent of those people went to Brazil on Portuguese ships, signifying that Prieto was not among that majority. He therefore had to reach the Caribbean through either the French or British trade, which accounted for over 25 percent and less than 10 percent of the total, respectively. Based on known departures, there were no documented voyages leaving the Bight of Benin for the Caribbean at the peak of the American Revolutionary War in 1780 and 1781. Consequently, Prieto boarded a ship once the French and British slave trade resumed in 1782 and when Gálvez held office in 1785 (tables 1.2 and 1.3).[56]

Prieto's embarkation on a slave ship overlapped with Ọ̀yọ́ policies seeking to destabilize Dahomey's control of the slave trade at Ouidah. Prieto grew up during the reigns of Abíọ́dun of Ọ̀yọ́ and Kpengla of Dahomey. In

TABLE 1.3 Documented departures of slaves at the Bight of Benin by destination, 1780–1785

	1777	1778	1779	1780	1781	1782	1783	1784	1785	Total
Brazil	2,120	6,514	2,788	8,023	9,060	8,035	5,728	5,052	4,833	52,153
Amazonia	0	0	0	0	0	0	0	300	0	300
Bahia	1,485	6,223	2,478	7,760	8,802	7,817	5,728	4,752	4,833	49,878
Pernambuco	635	291	310	263	258	218	0	0	0	1,975
British Caribbean	726	806	609	0	0	1,675	450	1,955	622	6,843
Antigua	0	0	0	0	0	0	0	0	408	408
Dominica	0	0	0	0	0	0	0	273	0	273
St. Lucia	0	0	0	0	0	424	0	0	0	424
Grenada	0	359	0	0	0	0	0	162	214	735
Jamaica	726	447	446	0	0	1,251	450	1,520	0	4,840
Tobago	0	0	163	0	0	0	0	0	0	163
French Caribbean	6,225	6,559	871	0	0	726	543	3,152	4,598	22,674
French Guiana	0	570	475	0	0	0	0	0	0	1,045
Guadaloupe	0	0	0	0	0	359	0	0	0	359
Martinique	359	0	0	0	0	0	0	0	0	359
St. Domingue	5,866	5,989	396	0	0	367	543	3,152	4,598	20,911
Totals	9,071	13,879	4,268	8,023	9,060	10,436	6,721	10,159	10,053	81,670

Source: Voyages (database: 1777–85, Bight of Benin).

the early 1770s, Ọ̀yọ́ traders generally brought slaves to Abomey-Calavi, a Dahomey town on the western side of Lake Nakoué. Middlemen then sold slaves at the European forts in Ouidah and helped transport people in large canoes across the lagoons and heavy surf to slave ships. To eliminate Dahomey from the supply chain, Abíọ́dun diverted trade to the east of Lake Nakoué toward Porto Novo and a lesser extent Badagry. By 1777, Olliver de Montaguère, director of the French fort at Ouidah, stated that Badagry and Porto Novo "were full of ships."[57] By 1780, Montaguère maintained how the trade thrived at Porto Novo above all other places because "the King of the Ailleaux [Ọ̀yọ́, i.e., Abíọ́dun] . . . does hardly anything in the other places [which] has made Juda [Ouidah] decline greatly."[58] European merchants, who had no control over Ọ̀yọ́'s embargo on Ouidah, reacted by sending their ships eastward toward Porto Novo and Badagry.

The competition for access to Ọ̀yọ́'s supply of people at the coast contributed to Prieto's enslavement. As Abíọ́dun declared Porto Novo the principal outlet of the slave trade, an alliance of coastal towns, which included Badagry, Epe, Agonsa, Ketonou, among others, united to oppose Ọ̀yọ́ sanctions. When Prieto was about eight years old and no slave ships departed for the Caribbean, this coalition openly defied Ọ̀yọ́ by successfully raiding Porto Novo in 1781. Montaguère, who keenly watched these events unfold, explained that "through jealousy of their trade [this alliance] seized the sea-side, [which] has restored the trade of Juda [Ouidah] to its ancient splendor."[59] Shortly after, Abíọ́dun ordered Porto Novo, with Dahomey support, to mount a counterattack, whereby Ọ̀yọ́ destroyed Epe, Agonsa, and Ketonou, but not Badagry.[60] Once again, trade declined at Ouidah, which coincided with the end of the American Revolutionary War and the return of the slave trade to the British and French Caribbean.

To support the argument that Prieto did not come from the deep interior, Abíọ́dun overextended his military resources at the coast and neglected Ọ̀yọ́'s northern frontiers. In July 1783, Lionel Abson, who spoke Fon and served as director of the British fort in Ouidah for thirty-six years, reported that Ọ̀yọ́ had received a "total overthrow from a country by the name Barrabbas [Bàrìbá], having lost in battle 11 umbrellas and the generals under them."[61] This conflict to the north of Ọ̀yọ́ resulted in the Borgu kingdom of Kaiama revolting against its tributary status, which ultimately severed a major supply line for slaves from the deep interior to the coast.[62] In September 1783, Abson observed how eight slave ships waited off the coast of Badagry, and "from there nobody had purchased a single slave for better than 2 months, [while] Porto Novo [had] 6 ships and none of them [had] purchased a slave in 3 months."[63] Overall estimates of the trade at the Bight of Benin echoed this decline in trade from the interior, whereby less than seven thousand people went to the Americas in 1783, compared to averages hovering around ten thousand individuals in previous and subsequent years.[64]

Due to conflicts for control of the lagoons, Prieto probably did not board a ship for the Caribbean in late 1783 or early 1784. The Dahomey and Porto Novo alliance under Ọ̀yọ́ command unsuccessfully attempted to sack Badagry on two separate occasions during these two years.[65] According to Isaac Adeagbo Akinjogbin, Badagry proved too powerful, and Abíọ́dun retreated during the rainy season between April and July 1784 to assemble a more "powerful army consisting of Dahomey, Kétu, Mahi, and Porto Novo."[66] The *aláàfin* of Ọ̀yọ́ convinced the kingdom and port of Lagos (Èkó), which had previously allied with Badagry, to switch sides by cutting off food supplies leading up to the campaign.[67] Joseph Fayrer, the British captain who arguably took Prieto to the Caribbean, complained how he waited for months in late 1783 and most of 1784 because there was "no trade during the war at all. The war was between that king [Kpengla] and one Port Agray [Badagry]."[68] During these months, the slave trade at the Bight of Benin came to a standstill, indicating that Prieto had an even greater chance of boarding a slave ship after the rainy season in 1784.

On 24 September, Abíọ́dun's strategy paid off, and his powerful coalition destroyed Badagry.[69] Prieto, who was about eleven or twelve years old, was almost certainly among the victims. Archibald Dalzel, who was Fayrer's friend and foremost authority on Dahomey at the time, explained how the army from Porto Novo attacked Badagry from the lagoon with a fleet of war canoes, while the Dahomey, Kétu, and Mahi alliance "marched overland north of the lagoon, through [Ọ̀yọ́] territory."[70] William Devaynes, a British slave ship captain who traded at Ouidah in the 1780s, observed how "the old, the lame, and the wounded [were] often put to Death on the Spot, to save the Trouble of bringing them away; the young and the healthy, if not immediately sold, [were] kept for another Market," that is, the transatlantic slave trade.[71] Fayrer confirmed how prisoners "were mostly killed and their heads ordered to be carried up to the king of Dahomy."[72]

Having survived the Badagry massacre, Prieto witnessed death, destruction, and greed, which was surely traumatizing for a young boy. Fayrer described how "the drums of the [Dahomey] soldiers were decorated with human skulls and jaw-bones."[73] Prieto likely contemplated *xwetanù*, which was the Fon term for a ceremony the British knew as the "Yearly Head Business" or "Annual Customs." This well-known celebration held at Abomey, Dahomey's capital, involved mass human sacrifices by decapitation.[74] The victims were usually war captives or criminals, and the event took place over several weeks toward the end of the dry season in January or February.[75] Europeans believed the tradition was a religious ritual held in honor of ancestors and gods, but *xwetanù* primarily served a political function "for the annual resolution and reformulation of competing national goals."[76] Beside the human sacrifices, the event involved the distribution of gifts, tributes, military parades, and speeches. Fortunately for Prieto, he did not travel to Abomey.

For most people involved in the transatlantic slave trade, it is impossible to know precisely when and where they came from inland before boarding ships. But by reviewing key events surrounding Prieto's chronology and the historical context of the "Slave Coast," it is possible to begin to imagine several plausible scenarios. The first of which, takes into account how Prieto was born and raised in Badagry. This port consisted of diverse people with multicultural backgrounds. The town, which never developed a central administration, had key divisions consisting of several prominent houses grouped into wards. Descendants of refugees from the destroyed kingdom of Whydah formed the wards of Ahoviko, Asago, Ahwanjigo, and Boeko; and families from the kingdom of Wemẹ occupied the Ijegba, Posuku, and Ganho wards. Badagry also became home for migrants from Ọ̀yọ́'s colonization into the Ẹ̀gbádo, Ànàgó, and Àwórí areas.[77] If Prieto was born in Badagry, his more "ancient origins" could have therefore belonged to any combination of people displaced during Ọ̀yọ́ and Dahomey expansion. In this period, his kin group could have claimed origins from Ọ̀yọ́ to increase status in Badagry, and therefore he grew up revering Ṣàngó to prove their loyalty to the *aláàfin*.

Another interpretation considers how Prieto grew up in the vicinity of Badagry among the predominately Yorùbá-speaking Ànàgó and Àwórí areas. Even for purposes of initiations, kidnapping was prevalent in the region. Children were easy targets; thus, it is easy to imagine a young Prieto being snatched from his home, wherever that might have been, and forced into slavery or even for purposes of religious education. Slave merchants, who felt the squeeze of Ọ̀yọ́ blockades in the 1780s, almost certainly hunted for victims in nearby Àwórí or Ànàgó towns and villages. According to oral traditions, many diverse Àwórí and Ànàgó peoples claimed dynastic traditions linked to Ifẹ̀ but at this time owed direct allegiance to Ọ̀yọ́. Again, this context suggests that Prieto's ancestors came from elsewhere but could have made ancestral claims to Ọ̀yọ́ for purposes of prestige (map 1.2).[78]

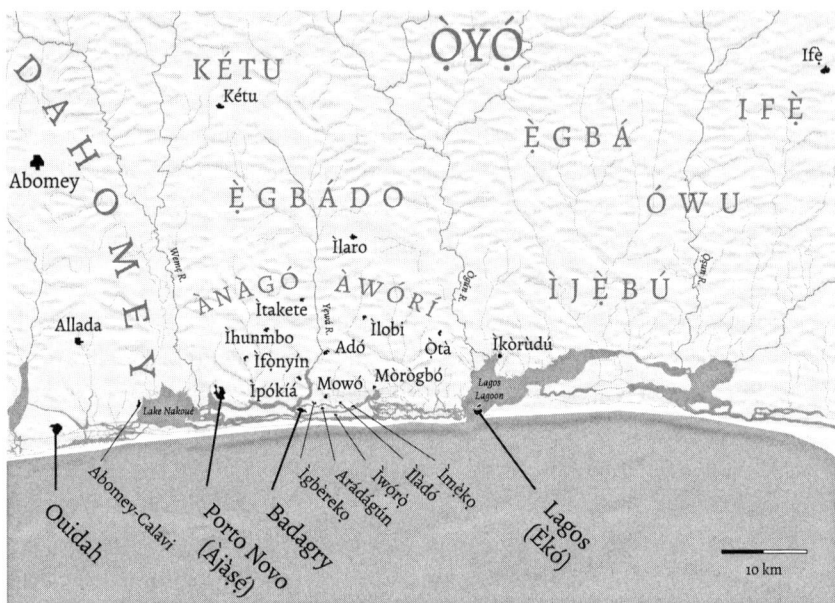

MAP 1.2 Ànàgó and Àwórí towns, c. 1783.
Source: Henry B. Lovejoy, *African Diaspora Maps*, 2018.

Without any available written evidence, the details about Prieto's upbringing can never be known with any precision. After all, any slave route from the deep interior was possible. Prieto could have been born a slave in some far inland location beyond the Niger River or Atakora Mountains. If this were the case, Prieto would have probably been sold and resold many times in the West African interior before reaching the coast. If this alternative, albeit less likely, scenario holds true, then as a child he entered Ọ̀yọ́ trade networks during the Age of Ṣàngó, where he had ample time to begin to speak Yorùbá and learn òrìṣà mythology. Ọ̀yọ́ merchants funneled people toward Porto Novo, which Badagry had been raiding since 1781. Robert Norris, who was a ship captain and friends with Dalzel and Fayrer, described how slaves awaiting shipment at the coast were kept in "Slave Holes," which referred to "a strong Room in every Slave-merchant's House."[79] Prieto might well have had such an experience, that is, until the Dahomey army "rescued" him from enslavement at Badagry, but only to reenslave him to be sold to European traders.

No matter what Prieto experienced as a child in West Africa, he boarded a slave ship and ended up in Cuba by 1785. Due to his achievements and belief in Ṣàngó in Cuba, Prieto arguably grew up in a relatively wealthy house in or around Badagry, where he was educated from a young age in Ṣàngó belief, practice, and mythology. After the attack upon the region of his hometown in September 1784, Prieto was captured by Dahomey soldiers (perhaps even during initiatory seclusion) and grouped among hundreds of victims for sale to European merchants. Several weeks before Gálvez became captain general of Cuba, Dalzel described how the Dahomey army marched their prisoners along the beach through Porto Novo and then into Ouidah.[80] Paul Erdmann Isert, chief surgeon to some Danish properties at the coast, described how merchants restrained all males, even "a child of five years old."[81] In the days immediately following Badagry's destruction, Prieto discussed the human sacrifices taking place in Abomey. While walking down the beach, he also gazed heavily upon the Atlantic Ocean, where there was a flotilla of more than a dozen slave ships moored off the coast, including one captained by Joseph Fayrer.[82]

CHAPTER TWO

Golden Age

How did Juan Nepomuceno Prieto travel from Ouidah to Havana? And what were his experiences during the Middle Passage involving the inter-Caribbean slave trade? To answer these questions requires scrutinizing large amounts of primary sources in multiple languages stemming from the transatlantic slave trade. State officials and merchants in Europe, along with their agents in Africa and the Americas, produced inventories, bills of sales, and correspondences to itemize and monitor slave voyages. As human commodities, however, the people they trafficked rarely had their names recorded or registered, that is, until after British abolition efforts in 1807.[1] At the time Prieto crossed the Atlantic between 1782 and 1785, nearly nine hundred documented transatlantic slaving voyages left from all of Africa, meaning an estimated 300,000 individuals mostly had their identities omitted from the historical record.[2] Since no written evidence exists that specifically places Prieto on board a ship, or at any point of sale, there will always be uncertainty in terms of how this boy reached Cuba. But by eliminating the vessels he logically could not have boarded due to fluctuations in trade surrounding the American Revolutionary War, his odyssey can be reconstructed within a certain degree of accuracy. What can be learned from Prieto's middle passage embodies the experiences of thousands of others leaving Africa during the Age of Revolutions; more importantly, however, his journey represents wealth passing through a global mercantile community.

As established in the previous chapter, Prieto embarked upon a slave ship when British and French trade from the Bight of Benin to the Caribbean resumed after 1782, and he arrived in Havana around Bernardo de Gálvez's four-month tenure as Cuba's captain general in early 1785. This basic timeline greatly reduces the number of documented slave vessels Prieto could have boarded. Between 1782 and 1785, the transatlantic trade from all of Africa to the circum-Caribbean involved over five hundred voyages and 175,000 people. The British and French combined for over 90 percent of this trade, with minimal involvement from the Netherlands, Denmark, and the United States. The majority departed the Bight of Biafra, where the British concentrated most of their efforts; then West Central Africa, which was the center of French activity; followed by the Gold Coast, Upper Guinea Coast,

Bight of Benin, and finally Southeast Africa. During this three-year period, just over 7 percent of the total trade to the Caribbean originated at the Bight of Benin, which involved just over 12,500 enslaved Africans, including Prieto (table 2.1).[3]

Throughout most of the eighteenth century, Spain did not participate in the transatlantic slave trade directly but contracted other European nations to deliver slaves to its New World colonies under a contractual trade agreement called the *asiento*. This situation further complicates Prieto's biography because it means he had to have reached Cuba on a least two different slave ships, whereby one crossed the Atlantic and at least one other was trading between Caribbean islands. From 1700 until the start of the uprising in St. Domingue in 1791, roughly 33,000 people arrived in Cuba directly from all of Africa and almost entirely through British and French networks. However, over one-quarter of Cuba's direct slave trade from Africa occurred between 1762 and 1765, which was during and immediately after the British capture of Havana for eight months during the Seven Years' War.[4] Thereafter, the Spanish government heavily regulated foreign trade until a royal decree fully opened the slave trade in 1789, which was approximately when the period of "second slavery" began and the sugar revolution in Cuba entered its golden age.[5]

When Prieto arrived in Cuba, the British and French were the only two European powers moving people from the Bight of Benin to the Caribbean—and no known ship traveled directly from this West African region to Cuba. Among all the French and British possessions in the Caribbean, Prieto had the greatest likelihood of reaching Havana via Jamaica, which had an extensive history of supplying slaves to the Spanish colony. From 1765 until 1789, the inter-island slave trade into Cuba operated through a licensing system, whereby Spanish authorities awarded select members of the colonial elite exclusive permission to acquire slaves from neighboring islands.[6] Between 1775 and 1789, an estimated total of 38,000 enslaved people reached Cuba with more than 70 percent arriving from Africa indirectly—that is, through the inter-Caribbean slave trade. Through these licenses, British traders, especially in Jamaica, supplied just over 31,000 people of that total. When Britain was at war with Spain and France, British trade declined considerably, and in 1777 and 1778, the French introduced over 6,800 individuals to Cuba from St. Domingue. Prieto did not board a slave ship in 1780 and 1781 because British and French ceased their trade both at the Bight of Benin and in the Caribbean to Cuba. With the signing of the Peace of Paris in September 1783, trade resumed as if war had never happened.[7]

Although not every transatlantic voyage was documented, Prieto almost certainly boarded one of thirty-four known slave ships leaving the Bight of Benin for the Caribbean between 1782 and 1785.[8] Of this total, twenty French ships carried over seven thousand people to St. Domingue, and fourteen British vessels transported over four thousand people to the West Indies—half of whom went to Jamaica, with the remainder going to Grenada, Antigua, Dominica, and the French colonies of St. Lucia and Guadeloupe. Despite a remote possibility that Prieto traveled via French networks, this route appears highly unrealistic. The price of slaves in St. Domingue was not only disproportionately higher than in Jamaica, but also the estimated inter-island trade from French colonies was not only nominal in 1782 and 1783, but also nonexistent in 1784 and 1785 (tables 2.1, 2.2, and 2.3; graphs 2.1 and 2.2).

Eliminating the ships Prieto likely did not take suggests further that he crossed the Atlantic on a British vessel to Jamaica.[9] Out of the seven remaining slavers, the ship named the *Golden Age*, which contains a wealth of documentation, emerges as the most viable option for Prieto. It arrived in Kingston via Barbados on 25 November 1784.[10] Factoring the average nine to ten weeks it took to cross the Atlantic, the unknown date of departure from Ouidah nonetheless coincides with Badagry's destruction in late September 1784.[11] This time frame subsequently would have afforded two months to travel from Jamaica to Cuba before Bernardo de Gálvez became captain general. The *Golden Age* exemplifies what Prieto would have experienced during the Middle Passage even if he boarded another ship, which will always remain a possibility.

During the American Revolutionary War, naval engagements in the Caribbean ultimately led to many prisoners from Badagry crossing the Atlantic on board the *Golden Age*. This merchant vessel was originally built in Havana in 1779, which was the same year Spain declared war on Britain. Even toward the end of the revolution, merchants risked trading between the Canary Islands and Cuba. With peace on the horizon in December 1782, two Spanish ships were returning to Havana "from St. Sebastian's, with very valuable cargos of silks, velvets & etc." As the ships approached the Caribbean, Thomas Windsor, commander of the HMS *Fox*, engaged for "an hour and a half . . . before they struck." After surrender, the *Fox* escorted the prizes to Jamaica. By March, the Vice Admiralty Court in Kingston condemned the two vessels.[12] With the support of some of Britain's most elite traders, captains Joseph Fayrer and Thomas Jolly bought one of these ships at auction for an unknown price, renamed it "the good Ship NANCY," and sailed it to

TABLE 2.1 Arrival of enslaved Africans to the Caribbean by African region of embarkation and flag, 1782–1785

	Britain	France	Denmark	Netherlands	USA	Spain	Portugal	Total	Percent
Upper Guinea Coast	11,677	6,767	1,022	726	290	0	0	20,482	11.6
Gold Coast	21,476	6,757	7,389	4,004	600	0	0	40,226	22.8
Bight of Benin	4,893	7,614	0	0	0	0	0	12,507	7.1
Bight of Biafra	47,359	2,725	0	0	0	0	0	50,084	28.5
West Central Africa	9,893	38,439	0	1,160	0	0	0	49,492	28.1
Southeast Africa	0	3,045	0	0	0	0	0	3,045	1.7
Total	95,298	65,347	8,411	5,890	890	0	0	175,836	

Source: Table compiled from Voyages (estimates: 1782–85, according to each flag, and all African embarkation regions, and British Caribbean, Danish West Indies, Dutch Americas, French Caribbean, Cuba, Puerto Rico, Spanish circum-Caribbean, and other Spanish Americas).

TABLE 2.2 Estimated African and inter-Caribbean slave trade to Cuba by year,
1775–1789

Year	African	Inter-Caribbean	Total
1775	0	2,344	2,344
1776	0	2,273	2,273
1777	0	2,212	2,212
1778	0	4,153	4,153
1779	0	647	647
1780	0	119	119
1781	0	138	138
1782	0	1,191	1,191
1783	998	4,768	5,766
1784	656	1,965	2,621
1785	1,479	2,197	3,676
1786	2,445	1,772	4,217
1787	1,760	1,016	2,776
1788	2,750	616	3,366
1789	1,552	1,032	2,584
Total	11,640	26,443	38,083
Percent	30.5	69.5	

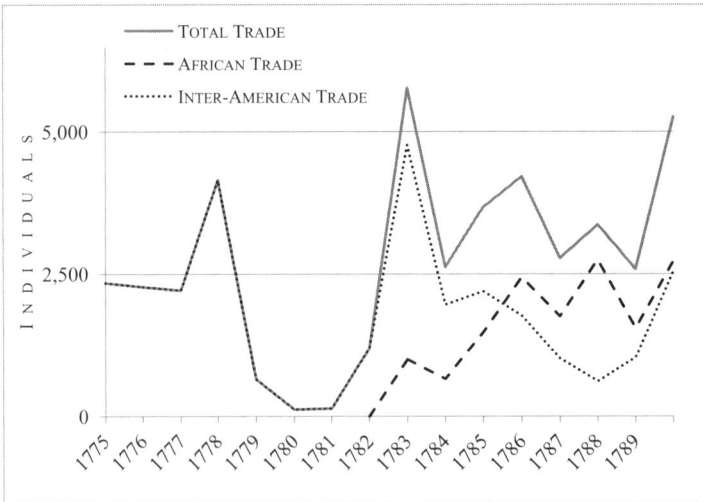

GRAPH 2.1 Estimated African and inter-Caribbean slave trade to Cuba by year,
1775–1789

Source: Compiled by David Eltis and Henry Lovejoy. See also Borucki et al., "Atlantic
History"; Eltis, "interAmertoSpanAmer database"; García Rodríguez, "El mercado";
Lambert, Sessional Papers, vol. 72, "An Account of the Number of Negroes imported into,
and exported from, the Island of Jamaica [1773–87]," 12 May, 1789, 239–40; Lambert,
Sessional Papers, vol. 72, "Import and Export of Negroes, and Negroes retained in the
Island, for 49 Years, viz. 1739–1787, both inclusive; distinguishing the Years of War from
those of Peace," 1790, 207–9; O'Malley, Final Passages; O'Malley, "inter-Caribbean database";
and Torres Ramirez, La Compañía Gaditana. These figures are subject to change with the
release of the "Inter-American Slave Trade Database." See also Voyages.

TABLE 2.3 Estimated African and inter-Caribbean slave trade to Cuba by flag and year, 1775–1789

Year	British	French	U.S.	Total
1775	2,344	0	0	2,344
1776	2,273	0	0	2,273
1777	263	1,949	0	2,212
1778	363	3,790	0	4,153
1779	228	419	0	647
1780	119	0	0	119
1781	138	0	0	138
1782	879	312	0	1,191
1783	5,499	267	0	5,766
1784	2,621	0	0	2,621
1785	3,676	0	0	3,676
1786	3,882	200	135	4,217
1787	2,776	0	0	2,776
1788	3,366	0	0	3,366
1789	2,584	0	0	2,584
Total	31,011	6,872	200	38,083
Percent	81.4	18.1	0.5	

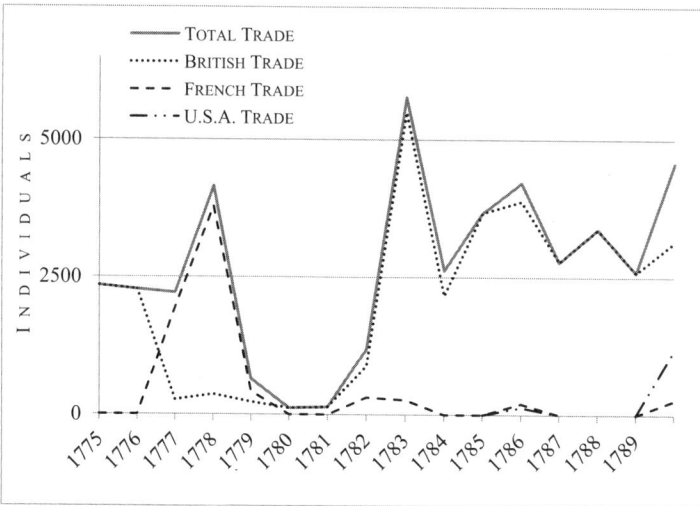

GRAPH 2.2 Estimated African and inter-Caribbean slave trade to Cuba by flag and year, 1775–1789

Source: Compiled by David Eltis and Henry Lovejoy. See also Borucki et al., "Atlantic History"; Eltis, "interAmertoSpanAmer database"; García Rodríguez, "El mercado"; Lambert, Sessional Papers, vol. 72, "AN ACCOUNT OF THE NUMBER of Negroes imported into, and exported from, the Island of Jamaica [1773–87]," 12 May, 1789, 239–40; Lambert, Sessional Papers, vol. 72, "IMPORT and EXPORT of Negroes, and Negroes retained in the Island, for 49 Years, viz. 1739–1787, both inclusive; distinguishing the Years of War from those of Peace," 1790, 207–9; O'Malley, Final Passages; O'Malley, "inter-Caribbean database"; and Torres Ramirez, La Compañía Gaditana. These figures are subject to change with the release of the "Inter-American Slave Trade Database." See also Voyages.

England full of common goods from the Caribbean, such as sugar, indigo, tobacco, wood, and rum.[13]

Wealthy investors from Liverpool funded Prieto's Atlantic crossing. By July 1783, Fayrer solicited investors for a slaving expedition on the *Nancy*, which included five prominent Liverpudlian firms.[14] The board of directors, who renamed this ship the *Golden Age*, involved the mayor, Thomas Earle, and several members of the city's chamber of commerce, including Thomas's brother, William Earle, and their colleague, Daniel Backhouse.[15] They raised over £6,000 from another fifty shareholders in order to convert and outfit the ship into a slaver.[16] The vessel had a carrying capacity of 377 tons and measured 108 feet in length and 28.5 feet in width; it had a square stern, three masts, three decks, copper sheathing covering the hull, and a lion figurehead on the bow.[17] John Matthew, a lieutenant in the British Navy, measured the slave quarters as having an area of 4,898 square feet, which was large enough to transport upwards of eight hundred people.[18]

Prieto's enslavement in Africa was tied into an intricate network of global trade. As Fayrer prepared for the journey from Liverpool to West Africa, dockworkers loaded over £12,500 worth of goods manufactured from around the world. The inventory accounted for every pound, shilling, and pence, and it included a meticulous list for quantities. On board the *Golden Age* were textiles of Irish linens, Persian and Chinese taffetas, Dutch corded dimities, Angola cloth, as well as British-made jackets, gowns, trousers, stockings, tablecloths, and shoes. Quality ranged from superfine satins to bolts of generic cotton. There were plates, salad bowls, sauceboats, tureens, oak dining tables, shaving pouches, scissors, shovels, bellows, irons, umbrellas, pipes, ink pots, jewelry, wrapping paper, and tortoiseshell pen knives. West African demand sought "Guinea stuffs," such as French flints, gunpowder, Caribbean rum, British brandy, port, and beer, as well as bundles of beads, ostrich and peacock feathers, calabashes, cheap tobacco, refined sugar, and cowry shells.[19]

Fayrer sailed the *Golden Age* from Liverpool to Ouidah on 15 October 1783. Depending on weather, this leg of the journey generally took at least a month and a half.[20] Robert Norris, an experienced slave ship captain in the 1780s and expert on the history of Dahomey, explained that the disposition of captains was wide-ranging because "in the African Trade they [were] various."[21] According to Marcus Rediker, captains had to be "tough, hard-driving men, known for their concentrated power, ready to resort to the lash, and ability to control large numbers of people."[22] Fayrer oversaw a crew of fifty, including mates, a surgeon, carpenters, coopers, stewards, cooks, tailors, apprentices, and a couple dozen deckhands. There were also two passengers taken on-board at Liverpool, one of whom was an unnamed "negroe of Governor Abson," who was stationed at the British fort in Ouidah.[23] According to historians of British maritime trade, Fayrer applied his "knowledge and profits as a captain to become an investor."[24] He not only completed twelve voyages involving over six thousand enslaved people, but he also represented a gunpowder manufacturer in Liverpool.[25]

The *Golden Age* arrived in Ouidah sometime in late 1783, after which the captain and crew waited off the coast for nearly a year. Fayrer preferred a quick turnaround but realized how the positioning of Ọ̀yọ́ armies and alliances before Badagry disrupted trade. Before and during the rainy season, he complained how he had "only bought seven Slaves . . . by reason that the trading men and all the great men were obliged to attend the war, instead of going to market."[26] To stimulate trade, Fayrer accompanied Abson to the Dahomey capital on two occasions. In early 1784, they first witnessed the annual human sacrifices, which were "done in abundance and the most horrid manner . . . [with] private parts being cut away."[27] Months later, Fayrer went back to Abomey "in consequence of the badness of the trade," hoping to have "influence with the king," that is, Kpengla.[28]

Once the Badagry campaign ended in September 1784, the Dahomey army marched their prisoners down the beach, which was probably when Prieto went to Ouidah's slave market. There, royal traders took possession of these people, who stood naked, had their heads shaved, and might have been branded. Among the other goods used as barter, cowry shells were a form of local currency, and a boy, such as Prieto, was worth around five thousand pounds of cowries, or upwards of 200,000 shells. In 1783, the British imported to London over 785,000 pounds of cowries from the Maldives in the Indian Ocean, which were generally taken to London, then Liverpool and re-exported to West Africa.[29] The *Golden Age* carried "67 Puncheons of Neat Cowries," or large casks able to hold over three hundred liters each. According to the ship's invoice, this quantity cost nearly £3,000, or a quarter of the total value of goods traded at Ouidah for human beings.[30]

This busy market accommodated and supplied the transatlantic slave trade. For Africans, symbols of the gods resided in the European goods. Ṣàngó came to life in the scarlet cloths and white ginghams, the red and white beads, and rubies and cowries.[31] In the Bight of Benin hinterland, much like in Cuba today, tureens, sauceboats, salad bowls, ink pots, and calabashes housed the *òrìṣà*, while alcohol, tobacco, umbrellas, and feathers were ritual paraphernalia.[32] Dahomey slaves customarily remained with the king's negotiators until they went directly to the ship. Overhead expenses for trading through Dahomey were high but expected. Law explains that the customs tax in 1784 equaled "the value of 12 slaves for a ship of three masts."[33] According to contemporary observers, inland transportation involved porters, servants, and brokers, who earned a weekly salary plus "£3 a Head." Other expenses included provisions for the yearlong delay and provisioning the ship for the crossing. Food was dried meats and fish, live animals, and "Indian Corn, Rice, or Yams." For the crossing, the *Golden Age* carried upwards of 35,000 gallons of water, which amounted to about "50 Gallons per Head, which was an Allowance of Two Quarts per Day." The hazards of moving goods, provisions, and people back and forth between the lagoons and heavy surf required large canoes "manned with 17 Men," which cost "£20 per Trip" plus a commission for each rower.[34]

At the Bight of Benin in the 1780s, European traders bought people with a "measuring stick in hand" and defined a child "at and under Four Feet Four Inches."[35] Prieto probably stood at about that height when he met Fayrer, who procured 650 people at the outset of his Atlantic crossing. Over half were female, which was a particularly high ratio because on average two-thirds of those leaving the African littoral were male.[36] It is unknown how many children Fayrer acquired, but those averages suggest boys and girls represented somewhere between a quarter and a third of the total.[37] In valuing the cost, British merchants made calculations using the "trade ounce," which was a monetary unit assigned to barter exchanges based on the prime cost of goods purchased in Europe. In the 1780s, British traders paid seven to eleven trade ounces for boys at Ouidah, with each unit equaling about £2.27.[38] In such terms, Prieto cost between £15 and £25 sterling. In the 1780s, economic historians of West Africa have calculated the real value of slaves, which was somewhere between £14.8 and £15.6 sterling.[39] As a price comparison, the annual rent for a two bedroom flat in central London in the 1780s was "£10 at the lower end of the scale."[40]

To board the *Golden Age*, Prieto went by canoe over lagoon, heavy surf, and shark-infested waters. He must have marveled at the immense size of the ship. Once hoisted up, the British trader, Norris, described how the crew shackled people together at the ankles, but generally "Boys and Women [were] never in Irons."[41] Sailors forced Prieto below deck. Personal space was not a luxury, and most could not stand upright. The three decks measured five feet in height, and according to Norris, the length allocated was "about Five Feet Ten Inches."[42] People shared communal tubs or buckets, but seasickness was common. The smell was intolerable, even if fresh air was directed through the grated bulkheads, or the rooms cleaned "with Vinegar, or Tar Acid."[43] James Field Stanfield, a sailor turned abolitionist who traveled from the Bight of Benin to Jamaica, complained, "One MINUTE, absolutely spent in the slave rooms on the middle passage, would do more for the cause of humanity, than . . . the whole collective eloquence of the British senate."[44]

As a child, Prieto could have had the opportunity to move around the ship freely. In calm weather, ship captains often permitted children to remain on the main deck and sleep among the sailors.[45] On some voyages, crews hung a platform above the main deck between the mainmast and foremast called the "Booms." This suspended platform could accommodate thirty to forty children. From this vantage, children observed the workings of the ship from a perch. In all likelihood, though, Prieto wallowed in the "Boys Room," which was just a dark, damp crawl space located between decks that measured only a couple of feet in height.[46] Like everyone else, he came up twice a day for mandatory feeding, washing, and exercise.

On the open sea, Prieto witnessed what Stanfield described as "every horrid species of wanton barbarity and oppression."[47] Predicated on violence, Fayrer presided over beatings, torture, rape, and death. His crew separated males from females, administered discipline, and forced people to eat and exercise, among other things. Emma Christopher emphasizes how the crew worked hard at stripping the African of his or her identity to reduce the person into "commodity potential."[48] Stephanie Smallwood adds that these "practices of commodification" muted African agency and consequently produced a stereotype of "an African body fully alienated and available for exploitation in the American marketplace."[49] No matter how brutal the physical and psychological violence, enslaved people acted and reacted. Resistance took many forms, and certainly on the *Golden Age* there could have been hunger strikes, cases of suicide, or attempts at insurrection.[50]

Nonviolent resistance during the Middle Passage was constant, creative, and involved complex processes of creolization. Survival required determination to live as a human, rather than an objectified being.[51] Rediker argues that the millions of victims responded to this horrid environment by creating "new languages, new cultural practices, new bonds, and a nascent community among themselves."[52] Jerome Handler maintains that slave ship crews oftentimes encouraged material culture to circulate on board.[53] Some captains allowed the passengers to arrange "fanciful Ornaments for their Persons with Beads."[54] With access to such items, Prieto would have recognized colors symbolic of the òrìṣà. During daily "dancing" routines, the enslaved had access to instruments, and they sang, danced, and played music in "the Manner of their Country."[55] According to Geneviève Fabre, exercise with music on slave ships instigated "a complex blending of legacies, [which] transformed into new configurations."[56] During Prieto's voyage, Ṣàngó's rhythms and choreographies already began to take on divergent forms.

Captains and crew often allowed the enslaved "Implements of playing at their sundry Games."[57] As a common trade item, cowries littered slave ships. All it took was sixteen shells to have the materials to practice a system of divination popular among òrìṣà devotees.[58] To unsuspecting sailors, casting cowries looked like a game, but it was a powerful method used to invoke gods, foretell the future, and oppose authority. Cowry divination, which could be manipulated by men and women, involved throwing shells on the ground and counting those that landed mouth up. There were seventeen positions in total, whereby combinations from zero to sixteen had a name, and a prophecy, which priests and priestesses memorized. Sandra Greene explains how cowry divination existed between the Volta River and Niger Delta since the eighteenth century if not earlier.[59] It is easy to imagine cowry divination taking place during Prieto's Atlantic crossing and a priest predicting his future as a prominent Ṣàngó devotee.

By the 1780s, shipping technology had advanced to the point that the average ten-week voyage from Ouidah to Jamaica was the shortest it had ever been.[60] Despite careful planning, supplies usually depleted closer to the Caribbean. Slave ships carried upwards of three months' worth of water, but some captains explained that during the approach caution was "necessary in the Distribution."[61] Stanfield complained about "the inexpressible misery of wanting water" and how victims would strain "their weak voices with the most lamentable cries for a little water."[62] In mid-November 1784, the *Golden Age* stopped in Barbados briefly, likely to restock supplies, before heading to Jamaica.[63]

The economics of slave ships were simple: Every slave death counted against the bottom line; hence, the more survivors, the greater the profit. Salaries of captains and ranking crew included hefty incentives. Fayrer received £5 per month, plus a commission of "nearly Six per Cent on the Amount of the Sales."[64] As Stanfield noted, slave ships were full of "mortality and disease."[65] The ship's surgeon attended to the sick and injured, but the overall filthy conditions guaranteed that pathogens lingered longer than average. Suicide, starvation, dehydration, dysentery, diarrhea, scurvy, small pox, and other diseases took many lives. Whippings and beatings resulted in wounds, and long-term restraint in iron chains infected limbs, sometimes requiring amputations.[66] Middle Passage mortality rates averaged about 12 to 13 percent, but the *Golden Age* befell catastrophe with 150 fatalities, as over 20 percent of the people on board this ship passed away for unknown reasons.[67] According to Vincent Brown, many enslaved "believed they would return home to their ancestral lands after death . . . as spirits and ancestors."[68]

Once the *Golden Age* reached Jamaica on 25 November 1784, Fayrer docked at a section of Kingston's wharf owned by the import/export company of Rainford, Blundell & Rainford. For a week after arrival, the crew prepared the enslaved for auction. According to the bill of sales, the captives ate oranges and limes to combat scurvy, as well as potatoes, yams, bread, fish, and meat. The strongest, most valuable people received new shirts, jackets, and trousers.[69] Right before the auction, Prieto stood in a row on the main deck, probably naked, as merchants examined his freshly shaved body, which glistened from an oil used to hide his injuries. He was "sold by scramble," meaning prospective buyers rushed toward the enslaved "in a mad disorderly way, throwing cords . . . around the slaves they wished to purchase."[70] Following a massive hurricane that hit Jamaica in July 1784, demand was especially high. It took less than forty-eight hours to sell all 513 survivors from the *Golden Age*.[71] Indicative of gender, age, and health, Rainford, Blundell & Rainford grouped people into ten categories: "privileged" versus "cargo" men and women; "men boys" and "women girls;" "boys" and "girls;" and the "meagre & sick." The survivors included 264 females and 249 males. If Prieto boarded this ship, then he would have been among the twenty-three "men boys" or twenty-two "boys."[72]

Without Prieto's name explicitly documented at a point of sale, it is impossible to know who bought him and for what price. However, his estimated value of £15 to £25 in West Africa could have doubled or tripled in Jamaica. According to the invoice, the average cost per individual was just over fifty-seven Jamaican pounds, which converted into "£41 Sterling." But the "men boys" and "boys" went at a premium and mostly sold for as high as £65 and £63, respectively. Only thirteen merchants purchased boys from the *Golden Age*, although Alexandre Lindo bought the majority.[73] This famous businessman and prize agent owned large houses, storehouses, warehouses, wharfs, plantations, and ships in Jamaica.[74] In 1784, he purchased nearly 45 percent of the *Golden Age* and paid over £11,000 in local currency for 131 females and ninety-one males. His purchasing power likely drove prices down for the thirteen boys (probably including Prieto), which he bought at the bargain price of £45 Jamaican each.[75]

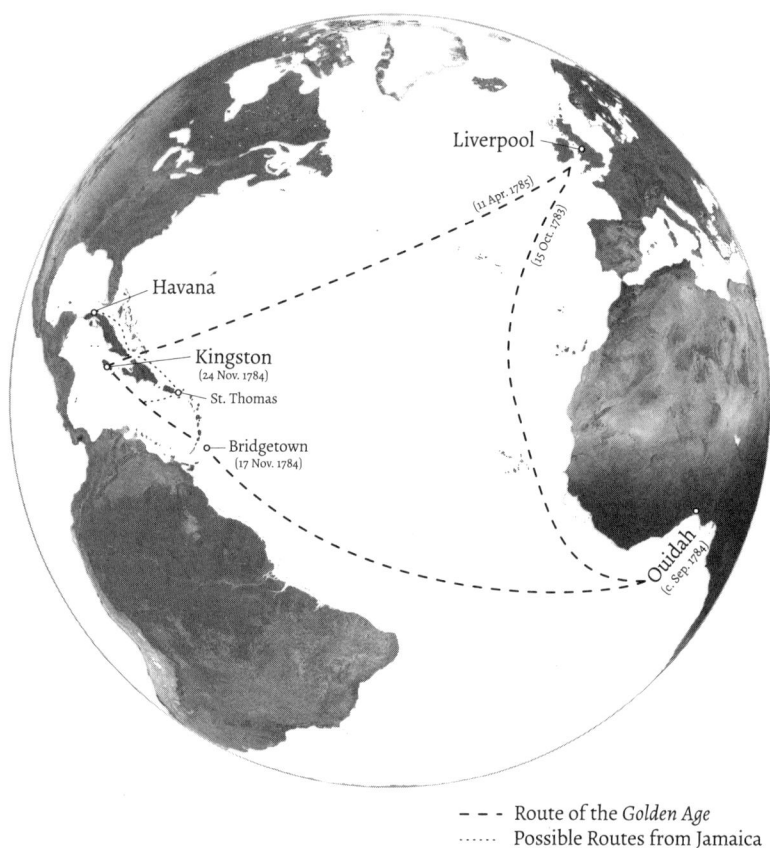

- – - Route of the *Golden Age*
...... Possible Routes from Jamaica

MAP 2.1 Voyage of the *Golden Age* and trade routes from Jamaica to Cuba.
Source: Henry B. Lovejoy, *African Diaspora Maps*, 2018.

If Prieto went to Kingston, how did he end up in Havana? Prieto's outbound voyage from Jamaica almost certainly happened in late 1784 or early 1785. When British and French trade stood still during the American Revolutionary War, Spanish authorities encouraged trade with a royal order in 1780 that effectively opened human trafficking. This legislation permitted Cuban merchants to procure enslaved Africans from any "friendly" or "neutral" colony, which meant anyone except the British. Moreover, it allowed non-British foreign ships to enter Cuba without restriction.[76] However, the overall disruption of trade in 1780 and 1781 meant that few slaves arrived in the Spanish colony until after the war had ended. According to estimates, over 5,500 people entered Cuba, most of whom arrived from Jamaica around the signing of the Peace of Paris in September 1783. In response to this surge of people, the Spanish royal court quickly passed an order in January 1784 prohibiting any foreign vessels from trading in Cuba "under whatever pretext."[77] A month later, another royal order imposed a steep import tax of 9 percent on all goods entering the island, including enslaved people. José Luciano Franco argues that most slave merchants generally avoided paying taxes through smuggling, meaning the final leg of Prieto's journey to Cuba will forever remain murky at best.[78]

In 1784 and 1785, Prieto had the greatest chance of arriving in Cuba with over four thousand enslaved people via British inter-island networks—most of whom did not come from the Bight of Benin hinterland, but rather elsewhere in Africa.[79] Juan B. Amores, who has disentangled the web of slave trading licenses during the 1780s, has effectively confirmed that upwards of three thousand enslaved Africans arrived in Cuba between September 1784 and February 1785. As Cuba's colonial elite petitioned to buy slaves in foreign colonies, most Cuban merchants sold their licenses to foreign companies, who avoided paying taxes by introducing enslaved Africans to Havana in foreign vessels sailing under a Spanish flag. Based on an analysis of licenses as it relates to the Bight of Benin migration to the Caribbean, Prieto likely reached Havana either through the business dealings of Miguel Antonio de Herrera y Chacón or Edward Berry.[80]

The transfer of people from the *Golden Age* to Havana overlapped with the operations of Lieutenant Colonel Herrera, who had served under Bernardo de Gálvez in Spain's Caribbean campaigns during the American Revolutionary War. Issued on 12 September 1784, Herrera's license permitted 560 slaves to enter Havana via the Danish colony of St. Thomas. Herrera then sold his license to the Irish Presbyterian brothers James and Lambert Blair, who negotiated a 12 percent commission on all profits. The Blair brothers, who were based out of St. Kitts, were known associates of Copland & Hodgson and Backhouse & Co., which operated on the British island of Tortola near St. Thomas.[81] These Caribbean agencies had connections with the investors of the *Golden Age*, including Daniel Backhouse, as well as Thomas Hodgson, who was the son of Thomas Earle, the mayor of Liverpool.[82] They likely procured slaves from Jamaica. Herrera exceeded the terms of his license through this network, because by February 1785 he had "introduced 1,013 slaves into Havana," which almost certainly involved Prieto.[83]

In another plausible, albeit less likely, scenario, Prieto could have traveled to Havana via Edward Berry's scheme. In early 1784, the Council of the Indies in Spain, headed by Bernardo de Gálvez's uncle, José de Gálvez, discussed the seemingly endless requests for slave-trading licenses. By 13 February, Berry obtained a one-year contract from the Spanish government to introduce four thousand slaves to Trinidad, which at the time was a Spanish colony.[84] Rather than develop that island, he chased larger profits by redistributing slaves at higher prices in New Granada and Cuba. After Bernardo de Gálvez left Cuba in 1785, Berry had brought 1,800 people to Cuba "in three shipments."[85] Berry purchased most of his slaves through the Liverpool firm of Baker & Dawson, who funded fourteen voyages, mostly leaving Bonny, in 1784 and 1785. These financiers, also from Liverpool, had transported over five thousand people to Trinidad, Jamaica, Cuba, Dominica, and St. Thomas.[86] Besides Trinidad, Berry was also a known associate of Eliphalet Fitch, a partner in the firm of Ludlow & Allwood. Through the 1770s, Fitch traveled to Havana several times and conducted business not only with Herrera but also with Jerónimo Enrilé y Guerci, who oversaw Cuba's *asiento* operations. Enrilé's wife, María de la Concepción Alcedo y Herrera, was likely related to Miguel Antonio de Herrera.[87] In either case, Herrera was at the center of Cuba's most profitable slave trading schemes in 1784 and 1785, suggesting again that Prieto reached Cuba under his business operations.

Without direct evidence, it is still next to impossible to trace Prieto's inter-Caribbean passage to Havana with any precision. However, anyone boarding slave ships at the Bight of Benin mostly went to Cuba via Jamaica and the colonial elite in Cuba controlled trade going in and out of the Spanish colony. Trading firms in Kingston, such as the ones operated by Alexandre Lindo and Eliphalet Fitch, could have sold Prieto to any number of slave traders, who took the boy to another island, where he was resold again to the Blair brothers, Edward Berry, or undocumented smugglers. Prieto could have been sold and resold any number of times before being taken and unloaded anywhere along the coast of the largest island in the Caribbean (after which he could have reached Havana by land). If the Blair brothers actually were the ones to transport Prieto to Cuba, then they went through Matanzas because the evidence shows how they used a Spanish captain to sail the ship into the capital under a Spanish flag to avoid paying taxes.[88] If Berry brought Prieto, then he had the authority with a royal contract from Spain to enter Havana without escort.[89] In other myriad imaginable scenarios, smugglers could have sailed to Jamaica and purchased Prieto by scramble. After which, they would have trafficked the boy into Cuba without any written evidence.

No matter which way Prieto ended up in Havana, this Middle Passage experience to Cuba via the British Caribbean symbolizes the wealth passing through Liverpool investments in the Atlantic trade. The proceeds of the enslaved people on the *Golden Age* turned into "58 Hogsheads of Muscavado Sugar, Ten Barrels Indigo, 2,050 Pieces Nicaragua Wood, 120 pockets of Cotton, [and] 36 Elephants Teeth."[90] Once Prieto was in Havana, the ship had returned to Liverpool on 11 April 1785. The raw goods on board sold for over £7,000 sterling in England.[91] Despite outfitting costs, and a heavy loss of life in crossing, profit totaled just over £2,000 sterling, which was then divided proportionately among the ship's many shareholders.[92] Overall, this three-year venture lost money because such calculations still ignore the cost of the Spanish ship at auction and overhead for the extended waiting off the coast of Africa. Regardless, Liverpool financiers, who invested and financed dozens of other voyages, made huge profits over the long haul.[93] Before its decommissioning in 1793, the *Golden Age* completed five voyages and transported over three thousand enslaved Africans to the Caribbean.[94]

Prieto's legacy further demonstrates affluence within a diverse mercantile community in the Caribbean. The brothers Samuel and Robert Rainford moved from Liverpool to Kingston in 1774, where they met Jonathan Blundell Jr., the son of yet another prominent investor. Between 1779 and 1793, this firm received 8 to 10 percent of all enslaved Africans, or over thirteen thousand people, traded into Jamaica. By 1804, however, their company collapsed due to debt, corruption, and mismanagement.[95] Likewise, Eliphalet Fitch, a native of Boston, became deputy of the office of receiver-general of Jamaica, which empowered him to collect and disburse all pubic revenue. His annual salary of three thousand Jamaican pounds, and his longstanding ties to Cuba implied he made huge profits on the side.[96] Alexandre Lindo was born in Bordeaux, France, and was of Spanish-Sephardic heritage. In his career, Lindo redistributed over twenty-five thousand enslaved Africans around the Caribbean. He made so much money that he loaned Napoleon Bonaparte £500,000 sterling so that the French army could suppress the uprising in St. Domingue.[97] In the end, his investment flopped because Napoleon refused to repay the debt once France abandoned its imperial ambitions in the Americas.

Prieto unknowingly contributed to the success of so many influential people in an emerging free-market system. This boy-commodity was sold and resold by freeloading interlopers, such as the Blair brothers, who held no political affiliation. In the late 1770s, the brothers migrated from Ireland to St. Eustatius, which the economist Adam Smith singled out as a port "open to the ships of all nations."[98] During the American Revolutionary War, the British Navy seized this Dutch colony, whereby Admiral George Rodney intercepted a letter proving the Blairs had been trading "with the Rebellious part of the Continent," that is, the United States. As was his duty, Rodney confiscated all their possessions and banished the two brothers from the island.[99] They relocated to St. Kitts, where they rebuilt their enterprise through inter-Caribbean trade.[100] Being at arm's length to Herrera, the Blairs made huge profits in that deal, possibly involving Prieto, which totaled over £13,500 sterling. By 1799, Lambert Blair & Co. moved from the islands and built seven plantations in British Guiana, Demerara, and Suriname. After emancipation in 1833, the British government paid out £20 million sterling in compensation, and James Blair, the nephew of Lambert, received the largest payout in the British Empire, which totaled over £83,500 sterling in exchange for the freedom of 1,598 men, women, and children.[101]

Prieto's remarkably high value in Cuba typified the view in slave societies that successful development of plantation economies depended on free labor. With high demand and a low supply in Cuba, the crisis of how and when to open the slave trade resulted in unbalanced profiteering among opposing groups of the colonial elite. The mayor of Havana, Ignacio de Urriza, uncovered Herrera's fraud, suspended his license, and sought restitution. According to Amores, Herrera was set to make "19,560 *pesos* in profit," but after being caught he had to pay a fine, and his "profit reduced to 12,000 *pesos*."[102] Urriza challenged Herrera because the mayor had a stake in Pablo Antonio Boloix & Co., which in 1784 was about to secure an exclusive five-year license. The deal fell through when Gálvez arrived in Havana and issued at least ten licenses for two thousand slaves each. Once Gálvez left for Vera Cruz in March 1785, Urriza quickly annulled those licenses, meaning those quotas went unfulfilled.[103] Thereafter, Baker & Dawson, the colleagues of Edward Berry, secured two *asientos* with the Spanish government spanning from 1786 until 1789, when the trade opened unconditionally thereafter.[104] From 1785 until 1795, this Liverpool firm amassed great wealth through thirty-one voyages and transportation of over twelve thousand individuals directly between Africa and Cuba.[105]

Without an itemized paper trail pinpointing Prieto along his slave route, it is necessary to reraise the issue that this boy could have reached Cuba in countless ways. If he did not board the *Golden Age*, he could have arrived on the *Elliott*, which Baker & Dawson owned and operated. It arrived in Kingston from Ouidah with 730 individuals on board in August 1784.[106] Scrutinizing ships, investors, captains, merchants, and licenses has led to the presentation of this circumstantial paper trail, which ultimately points back to how Ọ̀yọ́ sought to control trade at the "Slave Coast" and raised an army to destroy Badagry. After looking extensively into the other possible slave ships, I prefer to imagine Prieto arriving to Havana on board the *Golden Age* via the Herrera license and Blair brothers. His odyssey nevertheless presents an exceptional story following a single, undocumented person through the Atlantic world in an emerging capitalist system during the golden age of revolutions.

CHAPTER THREE
La Habana

Prieto arrived in Cuba as a slave, but as his fortune would have it, he did not end up on a plantation where life expectancy was generally much shorter than urban life.[1] Over the next fifty years, Prieto involuntarily found his home in one of the most influential maritime centers in the Atlantic world: *La Habana*. This port city played a significant role in shaping his life, just as he would come to influence the island's colonial capital as a slave, soldier, and Lucumí leader. As in the previous two chapters, the major problem of reconstructing the biography of an enslaved African relates to the overall lack of documentation relative to the details about his arrival in the New World. Despite concerted efforts to locate written evidence of Prieto in church, military, and state archives in Cuba and Spain in the late eighteenth century, no documented traces of his first twenty-five years in Havana have surfaced. Again, it cannot be known with any precision who initially owned the boy, the circumstances of his military conscription, or details leading up to his emancipation. However, it is possible to explore how the city's militarized setting afforded him opportunities to join a Lucumí *cabildo*, enlist in the military, marry María Francisca Camejo, obtain freedom, and become literate.

Urban life offered enslaved Africans more chances to achieve high-ranking positions in a racially stratified slave society. The city, whose development began in the sixteenth century, was strategically built alongside a narrow inlet opening up into a deep, natural harbor. Historians have emphasized the rise of this commercial hub as a frontier garrison and transient point for Spanish fleets returning to Europe from the American mainland.[2] By the final decades of the sixteenth century, the port's active service economy coincided with demographic growth and diversity. Since the port was constantly under the threat of foreign invasion, the most intense phase of fortification construction occurred following the British occupation of Havana for eight months in 1762 and 1763. Military historians have shown that the Spanish crown deliberately incorporated enslaved labor into defense preparations and soldiers of African descent were present at the earliest stages of the city's development (map 3.1).[3]

Prieto was born in Africa when Cuba entered the most ambitious phase of the Bourbon reforms. As King Charles III of the House of Bourbon and his loyal advisers increased defense spending across the Spanish empire, the cost of a larger military in Cuba meant the crown had to tighten the island's administrative controls, raise taxes, and reduce contraband trade. Reforming Spain's web of political, fiscal, economic, social, and religious institutions mostly involved replacing Cuban-born officeholders with Spanish-born bureaucrats, who were theoretically more loyal to the crown. The colony's militarization involved waves of reinforcements from Spain, as well as enlisting local subjects into the militias, including people born in Cuba and Africa. To finance these strategies, royal officials increased taxes, collected levies, and created monopolies for the production and distribution of the colony's most coveted commodities: sugar, coffee, and tobacco.[4]

Prieto's arrival in Havana in 1785 occurred during a détente after the end of the American Revolution but before the start of the French and Haitian revolutions in 1789 and 1791, respectively. Meanwhile, abolitionism took root in the Atlantic world with the foundation of the Quaker-inspired Society for Effecting the Abolition of the Slave Trade in Britain in 1787, and the French Society of the Friends of the Blacks in 1788. After France granted political rights to free blacks in 1792 and emancipated its slaves in 1794, Great Britain and the United States passed acts to abolish the Atlantic slave trade in 1807. According to Lynn Hunt, "The bulldozer force of the revolutionary logic . . . made its way ineluctably down the social scale in the colonies."[5] While these ideologies existed within Cuba, people on the island engaged in the slave trade until 1866, which was longer than any other place in the Americas. They also abolished slavery in 1886, which made Cuba second-to-last in doing so, behind Brazil in 1888. And Cuba did not achieve independence from Spain until the turn of twentieth century.[6]

On the island, Prieto lived through "second slavery," which Dale Tomich and Michael Zeuske explain as "the systemic redeployment and expansion of Atlantic slavery."[7] Once the Cuban free slave trade law passed in 1789, Spanish-financed voyages sailed directly between Africa and Havana.[8] Meanwhile, Cuban-born planters founded an economic society in 1793, which broke up the hereditary pattern of owning land by Spanish-born elites. As trade opened, Cuban- and foreign-born investors could subdivide, purchase, sublet, and use land without crown intervention.[9] After the revolt in St. Domingue destroyed the most productive sugar economy in the world, sugar prices skyrocketed, and Cuba entered its agricultural boom to take over as the world's largest sugar producer. Franklin Knight argues that the island depended on "imported skill, imported capital, and an imported labor force."[10] From the 1790s through the 1830s, over a half million enslaved Africans landed on the island, which was twenty times more arrivals than the previous three hundred years.[11] Francisco Arango y Parreño, the most influential spokesman of Cuba's planter class in the 1790s, stated "with all frankness . . . the free introduction [of slaves] has allowed the island to prosper."[12]

During and after the Haitian Revolution, which established the first black republic in the Americas, Havana's population grew steadily to over 100,000 people and was among the largest cities in the Atlantic world.[13] Alexander von Humbolt, a Prussian explorer and critic of the slave trade, described Havana when he visited the city on two separate occasions in the first decade of the nineteenth century:

> Havana's appearance from the entrance of the port is one of the most pleasant and picturesque on the coastline of tropical America north of the equator . . . [The city has] diverse elements of a vast landscape: the fortified castles that crown the rocks to the left of the port [with] the city half-hidden behind a forest of masts and sails. . . . When entering the port of Havana, one passes between the Morro (*Castillo de los Santos Reyes*) and the small fort, *San Salvador de la Punta*. Having exited the bottleneck and [passing] the beautiful castle of *San Carlos de la Cabaña* and the *Casa Blanca* to the north, one arrives at . . . three coves — Regla, Guanabacoa, and Atarés. . . . Surrounded by walls, the city of Havana forms a promontory bounded by the Arsenal to the south and by the Punta fort to the north. . . . *Atarés* and *Carlos del Príncipe* guard the city to the west. . . . The suburbs (*arrabales* or *barrios extramuros*) of Horcón, Jesús María [y José], Guadalupe, and Señor de la Salud occupy the middle terrain which, each year, narrows the *Campo de Marte* [parade square]. Havana's great buildings — the cathedral, the *Casa del Gobierno*, the admiralty, the arsenal, the post office or *Correo*, and the Tobacco Factory — are remarkable more for their solid construction than for their beauty. Most roads are narrow and unpaved . . . [and] one marched knee-deep in mud. The multitude of *volantes*, Havana's typical carriages, the dray carts loaded with cases of sugar, and the porters elbowing passersby made the pedestrians' lives positively stressful and humiliating. The smell of *tasajo* (poorly cured meat) infested the houses and the tortuous roads. . . . Near the *Campo de Marte* is the botanical garden, an object worthy of the government's

attention, and something else altogether, whose appearance at once aggrieves and appalls: the barracks [*barracones*] in front of which the pitiable slaves are exposed for sale.[14]

Just about everyone found it difficult to live in this hot, stinky, dirty, and heavily defended military outpost. The city's hospitals cultivated disease, especially yellow fever. The stench must have been intolerable, especially in the summers, as "2,000 beasts of burden" carried merchandise to Havana's markets on a daily basis.[15] As more and more sugar was being produced, people probably had trouble knowing where to store the commodity in the capital city before exporting it off the island.

Despite the city's most obvious inconveniences, economic opportunity drove tens of thousands of people from around the world to pass through the city temporarily, or to settle there permanently. Alan Kuethe describes how the city "served as Spain's primary American military base both for naval and land forces."[16] According to Alejandro de la Fuente, the characterization of the city as a fortified service station "contains elements of truth, but it conflates lived experience . . . [and] reduces the history of the port city and its inhabitants to the functions prescribed for them by the centers of imperial power."[17] By design, Havana's economy centered around the royal docks, markets, fortifications, shipyards, hospitals, factories, taverns, and lodging houses. The social fabric, mostly fueled by local ambition, involved complex interactions among royal officials, bureaucrats, merchants, entrepreneurs, soldiers, seamen, adventurers, privateers, pirates, and slaves. This vibrant, multicultural microcosm became Prieto's home for most of his life. He shared an uneasy coexistence with many diverse people from all over Europe, Africa, the Americas, and Asia.

Since the sixteenth century, people living in Spanish colonies belonged to a corporate society of order (*sociedad de castas*). At the top of the hierarchy were white males born in Spain (*peninsular*). At the other end were African-born slaves, or *bozal*, which was a racist term meaning "new, wild, untamed, raw, and stupid." In between, people born in the Americas were called Creoles (*criollos*), and within that group, race became a major determiner of status. White (*blanco*) was superior to mixed race (*pardo* or *mulato*), which was above black (*negro* or *moreno*). Being an enslaved African meant Prieto started at the bottom of the social order. Over time, he became a *ladino*, which referred to Africans or indigenous peoples from the Americas who learned Spanish. Scholars continue to debate how these stratifications

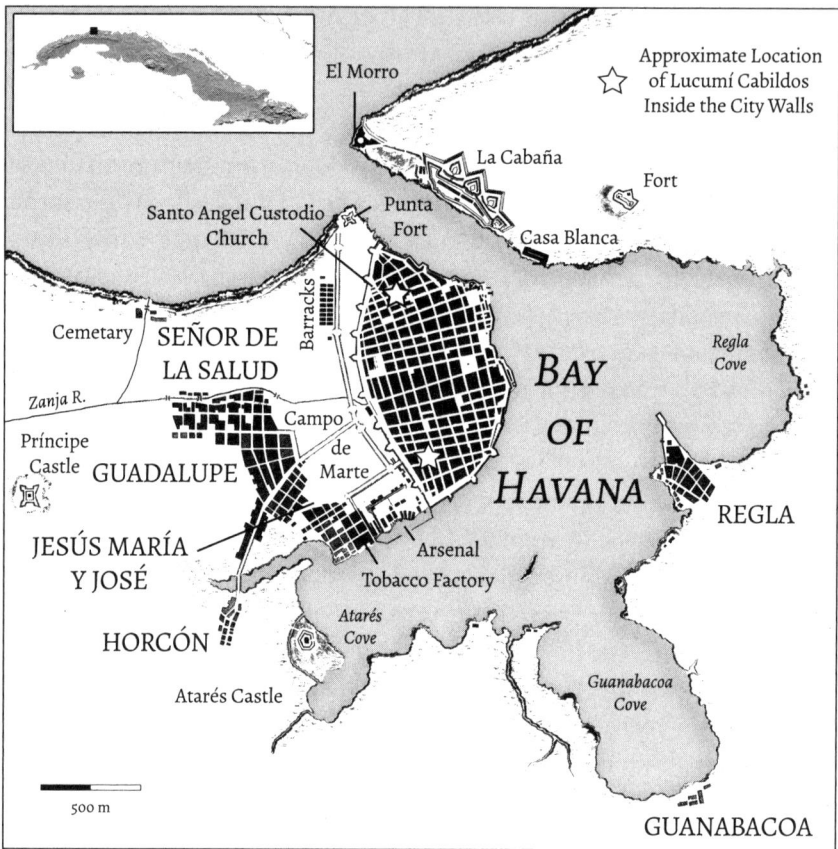

MAP 3.1 Havana, c. 1790.
Source: Henry B. Lovejoy, *African Diaspora Maps*, 2018. Map adapted from
Boto Villa, *Puerto de la Habana*; Del Rio, *Ciudad de la Havana*.

shaped identity, limited political and legal rights, and restricted economic opportunity.[18] William Taylor observes that the Spanish elite "were fond of vertical classifications and graded inequalities, but their standardizing policies . . . strengthened lateral connections and hastened the decline of vertical ones."[19] De la Fuente describes how the tensions of imperial design and local ambition meant the inhabitants of Havana "interacted in complex and sometimes unexpected ways . . . [because] there was much in the Spanish Atlantic that was not Spanish."[20] In this environment, Prieto "creolized" within Havana's social, political, and economic framework and was able to generate his own success.

People born in Africa were disparagingly called *negro de nación*, and Prieto became a part of the Lucumí "nation" because he spoke Yorùbá and came from the Bight of Benin hinterland. Cuban authorities and church officials assigned people African identities often with the help of African interpreters.[21] Most ethnonyms dated back to the sixteenth century, meaning there apparently was a general consensus of the associations between the African "nations" and broad West African geographic regions or languages. Lucumí was one of eight major designations found in Cuba: Mandinga and Gangá (Senegambia and Upper Guinea Coast); Mina, Arará, Lucumí, and Carabalí (Gold Coast, Bight of Benin and Bight of Biafra); Congo (West Central Africa); and Macuá (Southeast Africa). In other cases, some enslaved people were classified as "British," suggesting they came from a British colony via the inter-Caribbean trade and spoke English.[22] All colonial designations, including "Spanish" and "British," were not clearly defined in the late eighteenth century and national identities were as complex then as they are now.

Unless new evidence surfaces, the person who gave Juan Nepomuceno Prieto his new name may forever remain unknown. Throughout the Iberian Atlantic world, "Prieto" was a common surname meaning "black" or "dark-skinned."[23] Any number of wealthy and/or military families from Spain or Cuba could have initially bought the boy. For example, José Prieto was a lieutenant of the Fixed Regiment of Havana.[24] A second José Prieto was an artisan, tradesman, and soldier who eventually owned two houses and a store to the west of Havana.[25] Josef Prieto was a minister in Havana's cathedral in 1772.[26] Juan, the son of a Pedro Prieto, was an officer who went to Louisiana with General O'Reilly in 1769. By the 1780s, he had purchased a shop in New Orleans to trade regularly with Havana.[27] Another Pedro Prieto was a master caulker in Havana's shipyards.[28] Antolín Prieto held stock in Havana's royal commercial company, which monopolized the export of tobacco and sugar before trade opened in 1789.[29]

Prieto obtained his prenames in a Catholic context, closely linked to the glory of Bernardo de Gálvez and the Spanish navy. In hagiography, King Wenceslaus of Bohemia and Romania drowned Ioannes Nepomucenus in the Vitava River because the priest refused to divulge the queen's confessionals. In 1729, Pope Benedict XIII proclaimed Juan Nepomuceno a saint, martyr, and due to the way he died the protector of floods, and drowning.[30] Soon after, San Juan Nepomuceno became patron of Spain's marine infantries.[31] By 1766, the armada launched a 74-gun warship in honor of the saint, and during the Caribbean campaigns in the American Revolutionary War, the vessel fell under Gálvez's command.[32] When Prieto reached Cuba, Gálvez's installation as captain general likely prompted lavish processions as he toured the city inspecting crown enterprises, militias, and fortifications. His departure for Vera Cruz four months later coincided with the saint's feast day on 16 May, which likely involved more military celebrations in the capital city. The fanfare and hoopla surrounding Gálvez's arrival and departure perhaps explains why in 1835 Prieto recalled his own arrival to Havana with the short tenure of one of Spain's most celebrated naval heroes.[33]

Unfortunately, it has not been possible to locate Prieto's baptism record from Havana's church archives, which would undoubtedly shine more light on who named the boy and possibly on when and how he arrived on the island. During the period of Prieto's life in Cuba, a network of priests from several of the city's churches baptized tens of thousands of Africans and their descendants, whom they documented in separate books from white people.[34] Baptisms increased social standing, especially among people from Africa, and Prieto's involvement with the church later on strongly suggests that someone, likely his first owner, had him initiated into Christianity at a young age. If not, then Prieto could have paid for the ceremony himself with money he earned as a soldier. Prieto swore membership to the church, and his commitment to Catholicism should not be undervalued, especially in the context of his belief in òrìṣà worship.

Baptism records from the church of Jesús, María y José in 1784 and 1785 show another cohort of people classified as either Lucumí or Arará, most of whom had likely been involved in the destruction of Badagry and arrived via the inter-Caribbean slave trade. These people were slaves belonging to the Spanish king (esclavos del rey).[35] They worked in the royal tobacco factory and shipyards (table 3.1). It remains unclear whether or not Prieto was a royal slave, but he likely arrived in Cuba with most of these people. Colonial authorities did not always employ crown slaves in state-run corporations, and the state could have easily assigned Prieto to local officials, bureaucrats, or administrators initially as a coachman, stable boy, carpenter, tailor, gardener, musician, stevedore, or domestic slave.

Along with some of the others from Badagry, Prieto joined one of Havana's Lucumí cabildos shortly after his arrival in the 1780s. Derived from the Latin capitulum, meaning municipal council, ecclesiastical order, or corporate guild of mutual aid, Fernando Ortiz demonstrated how these organizations had a strict set of regulations stipulating their operation.[36] Matt D. Childs has since elaborated that the cabildo acted as a residence, school, bank, restaurant, theater, funeral parlor, and conference center.[37] Colonial authorities also permitted people of African descent to form black brotherhoods (cofradías de morenos). Both the cabildo and cofradía shared many defining characteristics, while membership frequently overlapped. In Prieto's

TABLE 3.1 Lucumí and Arará crown slaves baptized in Jesús, María y José, 1785–1786

Date	Name	Nation	King's Slave
1785/03/27	Pedro Alonzo	Arará	Real Factoría de Tabaco
1785/04/03	Narciso José	Arará	Real Factoría de Tabaco
1785/04/03	Gaspar	Arará	Real Factoría de Tabaco
1785/04/03	Esteban Antonio	Arará	Real Factoría de Tabaco
1785/04/03	Baltazar	Arará	Real Factoría de Tabaco
1785/04/03	Francisco Antonio	Lucumí	Real Factoría de Tabaco
1785/04/10	Salvador	Arará	Real Factoría de Tabaco
1785/04/10	Jaun José	Lucumí	Real Factoría de Tabaco
1785/04/10	Florentino	Lucumí	Real Factoría de Tabaco
1785/05/01	Matias	Arará	Real Factoría de Tabaco
1785/05/01	Bartolome	Arará	Real Factoría de Tabaco
1785/05/01	Ramon	Arará	Real Factoría de Tabaco
1785/05/15	Feliciano	Lucumí	Real Factoría de Tabaco
1785/05/15	Domingo Antonio	Lucumí	Real Factoría de Tabaco
1785/05/15	Esteban	Lucumí	Real Factoría de Tabaco
1785/06/05	Juan de Dios	Arará	Real Factoría de Tabaco
1785/06/05	Juan Ignacio	Arará	Real Factoría de Tabaco
1785/06/05	Ceserino	Lucumí	Real Factoría de Tabaco
1785/08/28	Fernando Agustin	Arará	Real Factoría de Tabaco
1785/08/28	Alejo Agustin	Arará	Real Arsenal
1785/12/26	Lazaro	Arará	Real Factoría de Tabaco
1786/01/29	Prudencio	Lucumí	Real Factoría de Tabaco
1786/03/12	José Maria	Lucumí	N/A
1786/04/18	Gabriel	Arará	Real Factoría de Tabaco
1786/04/18	Enrique	Arará	Real Factoría de Tabaco
1786/06/25	Anastacio	Lucumí	Real Factoría de Tabaco
1786/07/25	Bernardo	Lucumí	Real Factoría de Tabaco
1786/08/13	Antonio	Lucumí	Real Factoría de Tabaco
1786/08/13	Bonifacio	Lucumí	Real Factoría de Tabaco
1786/09/03	Ambrocio	Lucumí	Real Factoría de Tabaco
1786/09/03	Rafael	Lucumí	Real Factoría de Tabaco
1786/09/03	José Trinidad	Lucumí	Real Factoría de Tabaco
1786/10/15	Anselmo	Lucumí	Real Factoría de Tabaco

Source: SSDA, JMJ, BPM, vol. 1, 84–110, entry 399–404, 408–10, 421–23, 430–32, 438–40, 450, 451, 480, 484, 490, 504, 505, 516, 522, 524, 525, 530–32, and 547. There does not appear to be other surviving documentation for crown slaves in other church records in Havana in 1784 and 1785.

time, these societies differed slightly, whereby *cabildos* generally organized around ethnic lines, although *cofradías* revolved around professions, such as carpentry, masonry, or leather tanning.[38]

These institutions could be found within the island's largest urban centers. Maria del Carmen Barcia and Israel Moliner Castañeda's extensive analyses of *cabildos* in Havana and Matanzas have demonstrated that the earliest documented *cabildos* emerged in the sixteenth century and continued to thrive into the twentieth century.[39] By the mid-eighteenth century there was an extensive network of twenty-one *cabildos* operating in Havana, several of which were next door to one another.[40] According to Jane Landers, black residents followed church-approved models of organization, "thus guaranteeing a certain conformity."[41] While *cabildos* required sponsorship from the Catholic Church and members openly embraced the Christian faith, Pedro Deschamps Chapeaux describes how these "socio-religious organizations were the African's representative institutions in Cuba."[42] Rafael L. López adds how *cabildos* evoked "the African origin of their members."[43] Even under church supervision, the *cabildo* fostered an environment whereby Catholic saints merged with African deities, who "remained their more covert patrons."[44]

Oral and written sources demonstrate how Yorùbá speakers began to consolidate their culture within Lucumí *cabildos* in Havana before Prieto arrived to the island. According to the interviews of John Mason, it was apparently "in the first decades of the eighteenth century that it [the Lucumí *cabildo*] really became organized."[45] Archival records show how there were at least two Lucumí *cabildos* operating in Havana by 1755—neither of which were affiliated with Santa Bárbara.[46] The Lucumí *cabildo* Camejo and Prieto eventually belonged to had an institutional legacy dating to this time. By the 1780s, two distinct Lucumí *cabildos* operated inside the city walls: one was located on the street of Jesús María and the other on Villegas. Unfortunately, the documentation does not identify the patron saint for either institution.[47] Camejo and Prieto likely met each other as members of one (or possibly both) of these Lucumí *cabildos*. Fannie Theresa Rushing argues that "in a single *cabildo* there might have been between three hundred and fifteen hundred members."[48] Through membership dues, loans, and rent, Lucumí *cabildos* amassed wealth and property, which was redistributed in elaborate celebrations, education, funerals, weddings, baptisms, health care, and support for manumission.

Havana's *cabildo* structure meshed well with West African urban political organization, which generally fell under the authority of a chief in a city ward. In the Bight of Benin hinterland, effective power in Yorùbá-speaking towns depended on wealth and on the number of supporters a leader could organize. According to Robin Law, the leaders of West African city wards frequently transferred authority "from one chief to another . . . for the allegiance of the smaller lineages, which could be secured in the long run only by the distribution of gifts and political favors."[49] In Havana, a Lucumí *cabildo* leader received membership dues and paid taxes—much like local rulers in West Africa collected tributes from local subjects but recognized the authority of larger kingdoms, such as Ọ̀yọ́. As Havana expanded under the Bourbon reforms, it is likely that people of African descent involved in Lucumí *cabildos* reformulated Yorùbá-speaking wards in the Catholic context of a Spanish colonial city.

The reorganization of African communities from the Bight of Benin hinterland into Lucumí *cabildos* led to competition over authority and leadership. Right before Prieto's arrival, a property dispute occurred among members in a Lucumí *cabildo*. In 1780, Manuel Blanco, who was the leader, attempted to prevent the sale of a *cabildo* house that his African-born parents had purchased from a group of new arrivals from Africa.[50] According to court records, the *cabildo* had been founded "many years ago," by "the Lucumí nations, specifically the Nangas and Barbaes," but had recently allowed membership to Lucumí "Chabas and Bambaras."[51] According to Childs, political and ethnic division might have carried over from West Africa and may have been at the root of this dispute.[52] Perhaps the separation into two houses occurred based on support or opposition to Ọ̀yọ́. On the one hand, "Nangas" (Ànàgó) and "Barbaes" (Bàrìbá) fell within Ọ̀yọ́'s sphere of influence, while "Chabas" (Tchámbà) and "Bambaras" (Wangara) reflected groups in opposition to Ọ̀yọ́ hegemony.[53] According to Blanco, "all of them take the name Lucumí, but some are from one homeland and the others from another."[54] Within this politically charged environment, Prieto was slotted into Havana's diverse Lucumí community.

Colonial authorities often regarded militiamen of African descent as loyal subjects who required less scrutiny and were therefore to be trusted to supervise *cabildo* activities.[55] However, after the start of the St. Domingue uprising, a wave of fear struck the white inhabitants living inside Havana's city walls, and in 1792, a royal edict required all *cabildos* and people of African descent, many of whom were free and in the military, to relocate to neighborhoods outside the city walls.[56] The forced evacuation reflected the perceived threat to public security. This sudden relocation, in which Prieto participated, involved an abrupt separation of the *cabildos* from the church. Consequently, people of African descent consolidated their communities with less supervision and they "Africanized" Catholic culture more freely.[57] By the first decade of the nineteenth century, Camejo and Prieto interacted with at least two other Lucumí *cabildos* located outside the walls but they were likely continuations of the earlier ones banished from inside the fortified city.[58]

Exactly how and when Prieto joined the military is a matter of perspective, but it likely revolved around his *cabildo* membership. Lucumí mutual aid societies had leaders and members who were ranking soldiers in Havana's black militia, and some had served during the British occupation of Havana in the 1760s.[59] The titles of leaders utilized in *cabildos* also derived from military ranks and/or hierarchal positions from plantations. Elected leaders, known in colonial terms as "foreman," "overseer," or "captain" (*capatáz*), were in charge of an executive board consisting of lieutenants, sublieutenants, deputies, treasurers, flag bearers, and administrators.[60] According to *cabildo* historians, the leader was often referred to as a "king" among his people.[61] Carmen Barcia argues that the "king" assumed the role of "an ambassador of his African *nación* in front of [Cuba's] captain general."[62] In Lucumí *cabildos*, members probably used other honorific titles in the Yorùbá language, such as "king," "monarch," or "sovereign" (*ọba*), as well as "chief" and "headman" (*olóri, olú*). Lucumí leaders and their "royal" entourage also maintained order and adjudicated disputes. Regardless of this seemingly male-dominated and militaristic *cabildo* culture, Childs emphasizes how women outnumbered men, and although they could not become the *capatáz*, they "influenced, shaped, and ran the organization . . . through voting for leaders and deciding the financial affairs."[63]

Prieto officially enlisted in the military a couple of years after the slave trade opened and Havana's *cabildos* relocated outside the walls. In his testimony from 1835, Prieto stated that he retired from Spain's military after "twenty-four years of having served His Majesty."[64] His retirement occurred no later than 1818, which suggests he joined the military in c. 1794. Once enslaved Africans began arriving en masse and the situation in neighboring St. Domingue escalated beyond control, Cuban authorities conscripted more people of African descent to ensure safety and protect the island from the enslaved population.[65] By the mid 1790s, over three thousand militiamen were of African descent, which amounted to more than a quarter of the island's total armed forces. Evelyn Powell Jennings argues that colonial authorities often enlisted enslaved Africans to the Artillery Brigade, whose patron was Santa Bárbara.[66] Sherry Johnson has estimated that "two-thirds of all adult free colored males in the Havana area *chose* to serve in the militia."[67] Perhaps Prieto's owner, whoever that was, drafted his human property for colonial interests, or Prieto himself took advantage of a crucial historical juncture and made the decision to enlist on his own.

The irony that Cuban officials continuously armed slaves during the Haitian Revolution signified how Spanish military perks far outweighed dissension. Black soldiers received a set of privileges and rights, called *fuero militar*, which granted use of military and civil courts; exemption from taxes, tributes, and labor levies; and the right to bear arms, apply for loans, and own property, such as houses and slaves. Initially awarded only to white soldiers, these rights and privileges were gradually extended by the colonial government to soldiers of African descent during the Bourbon reforms. A jump in social standing also meant Prieto entered the cash economy, collected a small salary, and was promised a pension. With access to military hospitals, he also received the best health care available at this time.[68]

The new social standing signifies that Prieto became what Deschamps Chapeaux describes as Havana's "bourgeoisie of color" or "black elite."[69] Militiamen with benefits had greater social and sexual mobility. The military encouraged marriage to maintain "a certain socio-economic cohesion in the group, but it also assured . . . the possibility to ascend socially, although as always, within the limits imposed by the slave society."[70] Since no marriage certificate has been located in church archives, Prieto probably married María Francisca Camejo in a military wedding, which could occur "without a license if conducted by a superior officer, who was only obliged to give notice that the [ceremony] was executed."[71] According to their will, Camejo and Prieto stated that they had wed as a "Christian husband and wife" at the church of Santo Angel Custodio. By 1832, they claimed that they had been together for "about thirty-five or forty years," suggesting they married shortly after Prieto's enlistment in the mid-1790s.[72]

Little documentation exists for María Francisca Camejo. Her surname, common throughout Spain's empire, remains popular in the tobacco-growing region of Piñar del Rio in western Cuba to this day. Since the eighteenth century, if not earlier, this family engaged in tobacco production for the royal monopoly based at the factory in Havana.[73] By the 1790s, a branch of the Camejos residing in Havana likely owned María Francisca. In Prieto's will, she identified as Lucumí, but baptism records from the early nineteenth century state that she was a "black creole" (*morena criolla*).[74] Like so many people of African descent in the Americas, her heritage remains unknown. Her complex identity suggests she was born in Cuba but had ancestry from Yorùbá speakers originating from the Bight of Benin hinterland.[75] As a Cuban-born child, she could have had to learn how to speak Yorùbá from her parents, Prieto, or members of the Lucumí community in Havana.

In describing the city's highly misogynistic social structure, gender historians of Latin America have argued that "a woman's greatest contributions were to support her husband, to manage her home, and to raise children."[76] In urban areas, the female population was generally higher, as the vast majority of males arriving after 1789 went to the plantations. Even though Camejo and Prieto did not have any known heirs, she could have given birth to children who died at early ages. Urban female slaves typically worked as laundresses, cooks, seamstresses, nurses, day laborers, market sellers, domestics, or prostitutes. Johnson argues that due to the militarization of the island, "family responsibilities were subordinate to their obligations to the Spanish state."[77] After her marriage to Prieto, Camejo could have worked for the military in some capacity. Deschamps Chapeaux describes how military wives made uniforms, caulked ships, washed hospital linens, brought food to the garrisons, or served white officials.[78]

The circumstances surrounding Prieto's liberation are debatable. According to Landers, "Castilian slave law, codified in the thirteenth-century *Siete partidas* and later transplanted to the Americas . . . established mechanisms by which slaves might transform themselves from bondsmen into free vassals."[79] Enslaved people in Havana had access to many opportunities to achieve freedom, and Prieto could have become "free" from numerous situations. As Alexander von Humbolt observed after the turn of the nineteenth century:

> Nowhere in the world where slavery reigns are manumissions as frequent as on the island of Cuba. Far from hindering them or making them onerous, as do the French and British laws, Spanish law favors freedom. The right that every slave has either to *buscar amo* (change masters) or to emancipate himself if he can pay the purchase price; the religious sentiment that inspires many a lenient master to grant freedom to a certain number of slaves in his will; the practice of engaging a multitude of blacks in domestic service and the affections that are born from this proximity to whites; the ease with which slaves can work for themselves and pay only a certain portion of their earnings to their masters—all these are the principal causes that allow so many slaves in the cities to attain their freedom. I would include the lottery and games of chance among the ways in which a slave can obtain the funds to free himself.[80]

Prieto's route to liberation was not likely among those examples Humboldt listed, but rather through meritorious service to the Spanish crown. Without doubt, Prieto understood how the military provided freedom while offering degrees of reciprocal loyalty and privileges from the colonial government. Sherry Johnson describes how Iberian law established conditions that "if a slave performed with exceptional valor in times of war, then he could be freed upon the recommendation of his commanding officers."[81] When exactly Prieto became "free" remains unknown but likely after he had proved his loyalty.

While Prieto earned his liberty through the military, Camejo, who was in all likelihood born into slavery, and probably escaped bondage through a legal system of self-purchase called *coartación*. Accordingly, slaves could make down payments on themselves, and then pay off the debt of slavery in installments. Her Lucumí *cabildo* could have helped with some of these expenses. Historians of Cuba's slave market explain that such persons, although still slaves, had their value "fixed" and that "it could not be altered, in theory at least, even if actual market prices increased later."[82] In 1794, an adult female cost upwards of two hundred *pesos*, meaning if Camejo's initial down payment was ten *pesos*, then she owned one-twentieth of herself. Moreover, if her owners rented her out for work, she "had the right to a percentage of the rental fee or salary paid commensurate with the share [of themselves they] owned."[83] If Camejo owned half of herself, she then had the right to half of any income she earned for her master. The more of herself she owned, the greater her income would be; thus, she could pay off the debt on herself faster. Camejo still required her husband's consent "to loan her services," which Prieto likely approved.[84] He could have also contributed to buying her freedom with his salary.

Despite sexist and racist oppression, Camejo acquired status and autonomy on her own. Margaret and Henry Drewal have argued that women in West Africa "were economically independent, and through trade, they often acquired greater wealth and higher status than their husbands."[85] Yorùbá-speaking women frequently established associations among themselves, such as egbé, which provided social, economic, and religious support to members. N. A. Fadipe writes that by the early twentieth century, even though such organizations were not mandatory, "it was the rule and not the exception to belong to one."[86] Women formed these associations around a particular type of commerce, craft, or service. According to Marjorie McIntosh, members contributed "to unexpected costs of their fellows, such as a family wedding or burial, thereby offering a financial cushion."[87] Possibly through the Lucumí *cabildo*, Camejo participated or helped organize *egbé*, which were instrumental in raising substantial capital that in some circumstances contributed to the purchasing of freedom through the *coartación* system. Over time, she could have also helped finance Prieto's rise as a successful leader of one of Cuba's most famous Lucumí *cabildos*.

Camejo and Prieto clearly benefited from the opportunities afforded to them by the urban setting of *La Habana*. Mutual aid societies played a big role in helping Prieto enlist in the military, arrange his marriage to Camejo, and obtain his freedom. In less than a decade after his arrival, Prieto rose through Cuba's social castes in an auspicious period coinciding with the start of the French and Haitian revolutions and a massive influx of enslaved Africans during Cuba's great expansion of agricultural production. As loyal subjects to Spain and the colony, Prieto (and possibly Camejo) learned to read and write. His signature and writing on his personal papers prove literacy, which he almost certainly acquired due to his involvement in the *cabildo*, church, and military. By the nineteenth century, Landers has shown that militiamen of African descent "established schools in Havana."[88] According to Janet Cornelius, literate people of African descent taught each other and "served as conduits for information with a slave communication network . . . [whereby some people] were able to capitalize on their skills in literacy as a starting point for leadership."[89]

CHAPTER FOUR

Batallón de Morenos

Juan Nepomuceno Prieto performed as a model soldier in Spain's colonial army from the early 1790s until the mid-1810s. He earned promotions from private, to second corporal, to first corporal, and then to second sergeant, after which he retired around 1818. His service coincided with the formation of the Republic of Haiti, the British and United States acts to abolish the Atlantic slave trade, the Peninsular War when Napoleon occupied Spain and Portugal, the start of the Spanish American Wars of Independence, the release of Spain's first constitution, the Aponte Rebellion, and the War of 1812. He spent most of his military career in Havana, although in June 1812, he and his unit, the first company of the *Batallón de Morenos Leales de la Habana*, were deployed to Spanish Florida, whereby he garrisoned Pensacola on the borderlands of a conflict between Britain, the United States, Creeks, and Seminoles. Prieto's time in West Florida overlapped with the surrender of the Spanish fort in Mobile to the Americans on 13 April 1813, and the Creek War from 1813 to 1814. Prieto returned to Havana in September 1814, weeks before the American general, Andrew Jackson, pushed the British out of Pensacola (who had been stationed there on invitation of the Spanish). In Havana, Prieto continued to serve until his retirement, training and recruiting soldiers to control the growing slave population of the island.

Military service in the Iberian Atlantic world included a lifestyle that, as Sherry Johnson explains, had an "ideological impetus [which] came from a long tradition of military glorification."[1] According to regulation, soldiers took an oath "to serve the King, and to defend the Homeland." This commitment emphasized "the utility of whatever Troop depends on his quality, good discipline, subordination, and honor."[2] According to Deschamps Chapeaux, low-ranking soldiers were supposed to follow their superiors with "blind obedience."[3] Prieto clearly adopted this behavior and acted accordingly. All new recruits underwent intensive training after enlistment to acquire rudimentary military skills.[4] Each unit underwent regular reviews to inspect uniforms and equipment. Johnson and Kuethe describe how military exercises occurred at the parade square, called Campo de Marte, as many as four times per day, or as infrequently as once every two months.[5]

Although militia units could be deployed anywhere at any time, Prieto served in Havana for most of his career. According to Johnson, the military also acted as a police force to protect the island's commercial interests.[6] Typical duties for a soldier in the city included patrolling streets or being stationed at one of Havana's many garrisons, fortifications, or along the city wall. As more and more slave ships arrived in Havana, Prieto likely supervised newly arriving Africans at the docks or at a shipping warehouse called *Casa Blanca*. Most of the new slaves disembarked at Regla, located across the bay from the neighborhood of Jesús, María y José. This duty meant Prieto learned about Africa through word of mouth, especially from Yorùbá speakers arriving from the Bight of Benin. There was no specific information on how Prieto treated enslaved Africans, but as a free black soldier, the expectation was to inflict punishment as necessity dictated. Prieto could have also been tasked with controlling Cuba's enslaved population in other ways. Militiamen hunted fugitives (*cimarrones*), conquered maroon communities (*palenques*), and suppressed insurrections. Matt D. Childs has argued that the deliberate decision to have "black soldiers guarding slaves served to reinforce colonial authorities' belief in the loyalty of the militia troops to the Spanish Crown regardless of race."[7]

Soldiers of African descent constantly experienced racial discrimination. Prieto understood that during war he would be ordered into the most dangerous situations first. Kuethe explains how white soldiers frequently viewed their black counterparts as "vicious, morally depraved, stupid, and untrustworthy."[8] As a corollary to racial stratification, a white command group supervised and functioned alongside black and mixed-race units. Captain was the highest rank a black soldier could obtain, which was ten positions above the highest rank Prieto achieved as second sergeant. Standard training involved combat formations, weaponry, and "sufficient instruction" to substitute as a regular artilleryman "for motives of war."[9] Discipline for insubordination could result in imprisonment, docked pay, demotion, forced labor, and in cases of desertion, death.[10] Nevertheless, the military benefits and privileges far outweighed the alternatives, such as working on a plantation, and it is unlikely Prieto ever got into any serious trouble.

Despite the prejudice, black soldiers still received social recognition. Johnson explains that uniforms "set the military member apart from the ragtag ordinary urban dweller."[11] Moreover, military life revolved around the phrase "I must follow my flag."[12] During drills, parades, and ceremonies, battalions of people of African descent marched in formation, carrying flags of patron saints, and playing music with fife and drum. Prieto's uniform was "a blue indigo coat, crimson red collar and border trim, golden brown tailpiece, white pants, and on the collar, a distinctive border made up by a blade, shovel, pick, and bomb."[13] Colonial authorities endorsed loyal service, and soldiers of African descent earned medals that they received in public ceremonies at the parade square.[14]

The iconography of military patron saints often overlapped with those representing the *cabildos*. The infantry revered Nuestra Señora de los Remedios. De la Fuente explains how people from Africa began following this saint in the sixteenth century.[15] Camejo and Prieto knew her as "the Black Virgin" and had images of her in the Lucumí *cabildo* archives confiscated in 1835.[16] On the one hand, this saint does not have a clear equivalent in modern-day òrìṣà worship, which is a reminder of how processes of creolization were not always obvious and consistent over time. On the other hand, Camejo and Prieto owned images of Santa Bárbara, the patron saint of the artillery, who was equated with Ṣàngó.[17] As many modern-day practitioners generalize, the Ṣàngó/Santa Bárbara paradigm emerged at the moment enslaved Africans saw muskets and cannons explode, much like thunder and lightning. Perhaps Nuestra Señora de los Remedios became a symbol of colonial rule suggesting the saint's prominence in the military declined during Cuba's path toward independence after Prieto passed away (figures 5.1 and 5.2).[18]

At a time when independence and abolition became a major topic around the Atlantic world, the elite, slave-owning class in Cuba was naturally apprehensive about training black militiamen. The success of the St. Domingue uprising proved what might happen. Fear and paranoia, characteristic of Cuban society during the Age of Revolutions, intensified as attitudes shifted toward independence. In the first decade of the nineteenth century, the colonies began to look upon Spain as a politically unstable place, especially after Napoleon failed to reclaim St. Domingue yet conquered Spain and Portugal.[19] With King Ferdinand VII in exile, the debate on how Spain would defeat France evolved into questions of who belonged to Spain. In Cuba, some officials and slaveholders openly expressed reservations about arming free people of color. Francisco Arango y Parreño, a person responsible for expanding Cuba's plantation economy, petitioned the crown to disband the militia in the 1790s. According to Childs, arming free blacks "provided contrasting images of stability and destruction in the eyes of different sectors of Cuban society." Despite pleas for disarmament, such attempts failed as the opposition "pointed to the three centuries of loyal service that defined the militia as a distinct social class with special privileges."[20]

Military ideologies of honor, loyalty, and service had implications for citizenship. Prieto paid attention to the debate over definitions of "Spanish" as it affected him as a Lucumí soldier. In 1811, the crown and many colonial representatives met in Cádiz. Arango y Parreño, who was in attendance, defended his vision of slavery and the position to disarm. Landers has shown how liberal members of the royal court "had more enlightened views . . . [and] were anxious to modernize Spain and its empire. Much to the dismay of Cuban planters like Arango [y Parreño], the delegate from Mexico proposed abolition throughout the Spanish colonies."[21] During this meeting, the court drafted Spain's first constitution, which stipulated that

> for those Spaniards who on either side derive their origin from Africa, the door of virtue and merit is open. In consequence, the Cortes may grant letters of citizenship to those who have rendered eminent services to the fatherland, or to those who distinguish themselves by their talent, application, and conduct, provided . . . that they be the offspring of legitimate marriages, the children of free parents, themselves married to free women, and resident in Spanish dominions, and they exercise some useful profession, office, or industry and have capital of their own sufficient to maintain their homes.[22]

In Cuba, authorities mostly censored these constitutional discussions. According to David Sartorius, the 1811 constitution was "a radical document that placed Spain far ahead of other European polities in its embrace of liberalism and its extension of citizenship rights."[23] Despite suppression of such political rhetoric in Cuba, rumors spread as free people of African descent envisioned citizenship and the enslaved contemplated freedom.[24] Prieto probably believed that through merit and service he might one day become a Spanish citizen and that abolition was on the horizon.

The tension between Spanish nationals and people born in the Americas, which precipitated independence movements elsewhere, was much less apparent in Cuba.[25] Spanish-born *peninsulares* and Cuban-born *criollos*, hostile to each other in many ways, often united in their mutual economic interests in promoting the development of the plantation economy and in maintaining slavery. Black militia units felt a backlash from the fear and paranoia, and underwent more stringent supervision. Childs has argued that the failed efforts to disband black militias "undoubtedly contributed to the decline in prestige and appreciation."[26] The strong military presence meant the island remained under effective control, but only as long as its soldiers remained loyal.[27] Even after Prieto's arrest in 1835, the court appeared disinterested in his attempts to prove his innocence after he testified to "twenty-four years of having served His Majesty."[28]

As people took sides on whether Cuba should remain a colony or become independent, Arango y Parreño's opposition to arming people of African descent crystalized in the infamous Aponte Rebellion.[29] It began in mid-January 1812, when a series of revolts erupted across the island. Groups of enslaved people destroyed several plantations a few miles from Puerto Príncipe. This city was the location of a supreme court which held jurisdiction over all Spanish Caribbean colonies as well as Florida. After the uprisings began, the army and armed citizens suppressed the insurrection with a show of force meant to restore public confidence and deter such resistance in the future. In a matter of days, the governor in Puerto Príncipe executed the leaders publically and whipped many alleged participants.

Nearly four hundred miles away, news of these investigations and trials quickly went to Havana where paranoia about an islandwide insurrection reached a fever pitch. The fear was that a much larger action for Cuban independence in the eastern provinces of Bayamo and Holguín was spiraling out of control. The rumors appeared true, because during the nights of 15–16 March 1812, several conspirators under the leadership of Captain José Antonio Aponte traveled to the outskirts of Havana, recruited slaves, and destroyed several plantations. As the rebellion swept throughout the countryside, militiamen of African descent from Havana who had defected apparently organized to prepare an attack on the capital. Childs writes that the goal of the rebellion, directed at one of the most heavily fortified cities in the Americas at this time, "called for the destruction of slavery, just as had been reported in Puerto Príncipe and Bayamo."[30]

As the rebellion spread, Prieto's loyalty was called into question, and his company, which had to have been on high alert since January, was deployed to suppress the insurrection in rural areas around Havana. Prieto must have been on the frontline, especially since black militiamen were the first to be exposed to battle. Once the situation was brought under control, Prieto's unit patrolled the countryside searching for suspects and fugitive slaves. Childs reports that the army, armed citizens, and the militia, including Prieto's unit, "arrested more than 200 slaves and free people of color over the next two months, rapidly filling the island's prisons."[31] During the suppression of this 1812 insurrection, Prieto likely earned the rank of first corporal. According to regulation, promotion occurred through "years of service, acts of heroism, or monetary donations."[32] The timing suggests that loyalty and bravery accounted for Prieto's advancement in status.

Prieto clearly knew José Antonio Aponte before 1812, at least by reputation if not personally. They were both in Havana's black militia, although

Prieto was in the first company and Aponte in the second. Aponte, who served under Bernardo de Gálvez during the Florida campaigns of the American Revolutionary War, was accused of being the mastermind for the conspiracies and various acts of rebellion.[33] On 19 March 1812, authorities arrested this captain and searched his house in the Havana neighborhood of Guadalupe. They found evidence that they attributed to Aponte's leadership, including handwritten copies of the decrees explaining the privileges given to militiamen, as well as reports written by Haitian revolutionary leaders such as Henri Christophe, Toussaint L'Overture, Jean François, and Jean-Jacques Dessalines. Authorities also confiscated a book of drawings with maps depicting streets and garrisons in Cuba, images of black soldiers defeating whites, portraits of black kings from Abyssinia, and accounts of other revolutionary models, such as George Washington. Officials interpreted this documentation as an act of treason. Childs explains how the investigations into the conspiracy determined that Aponte routinely showed the drawings "to members of the free black militia and numerous others during meetings at his house," suggesting that Prieto might have participated in these secret meetings at one time or another.[34]

Prieto was never implicated in the Aponte conspiracy, and his name was not mentioned in the more than six thousand pages of testimony.[35] Over two decades later, however, he would be accused of complicity. According to Childs, the *cabildos* "played a crucial role" in organizing the rebellion, particularly in Havana.[36] Aponte's associate, Salvador Ternero, led the Mina Guagüí *cabildo*, which likely involved members from Gbe-speaking regions of Africa to the west of Dahomey.[37] Aponte was also a member of a *cofradía* established by a guild of carpenters in 1800, which called itself the "Slaves of our Glorious Patron the Patriarch St. Joseph, and of Jesus, and of his Sainted Mother."[38] There has also been much speculation that Aponte was the leader of the legendary Ṣàngó tẹ̀ dún, which is almost certainly untrue.[39]

Throughout the Aponte Rebellion, it became apparent to Prieto that African-born militiamen would never become citizens, despite their loyalty and the fact that they received promotions. Even before the Aponte trial concluded, court officials decided the punishment of the alleged leaders and participants. The Marqués de Someruelos, Cuba's captain general at the time, promised that he would make "a horrifying example [at] the gallows."[40] On 9 April 1812, Aponte and his associates were hung at La Punta, a military fortification guarding the western entrance to the Bay of Havana. The crowd who had gathered applauded the hanging. Afterward, the executioner decapitated the heads of the accused, put each in a steel cage on top of a pole, and displayed the cages at conspicuous places to serve as a warning. Prieto certainly saw these heads exhibited around Havana and around the plantations during his patrols. In addition, everyone in the military knew that dozens of convicted participants were sent to labor camps in St. Augustine, Florida.[41]

As the Aponte investigation ended, the United States openly declared war on Britain on 18 June, marking the start of the War of 1812. Prieto knew that he was going to leave Cuba at any moment to help Spain secure Spanish territory in Florida. As Napoleon expanded France's territory across Europe, American policy shifted to expand their control over much larger regions of continental North America. After the Louisiana Purchase in 1804, the United States confronted British interests in Canada, as well as Spanish Florida.[42] Kathleen DuVal has argued how in the lead up to conflicts over the southern borderlands, "self-styled patriots, organized and backed by the United States, crossed the St. Mary's River into Spanish Florida to foment a 'revolution.'"[43] When the Americans occupied Amelia Island in eastern Florida in March 1812, Juan Ruíz de Apodaca, the captain general of Cuba, made preparations to send reinforcements and supplies from Havana to Spanish Florida in early April. On the same day the war officially started, a royal order explained how "the inhabitants of the Plazas of Florida in Pensacola, [were] threatened by an invasion from the American continent," that is, the United States.[44]

Ten days after the start of the War of 1812, Prieto and his unit traveled to West Florida. On 28 June, the port master in Havana, Antonio Ramón Romanillos, noted that "the Brig of War the Borjas, led by Colonel D. Mauricio de Zúñiga . . . left this Port yesterday to go to Panzacola in order to take charge of the Command of that Plaza provisionally: various officials that are on that ship are members of the auxiliary units and squads; and a company of *Moreno* Militias to increase the garrison."[45] In 1835, Prieto clearly remembered how he "was sent aboard the Brig of his King Juan Francisco de Borjas along with his Company, in order to serve as reinforcements."[46] Prieto could recall his departure because he sailed with Zúñiga, the Spanish governor of Florida. By September, Apodaca had sent "two more companies of *morenos*" from Cuba; one went to Pensacola and the other to St. Augustine in eastern Florida.[47] According to muster rolls from Pensacola in January 1814, the first and second artillery companies of *morenos* from Havana totaled 227 men. Prieto ranked third in command, under First Sergeant José Agüero and Second Sergeants Felipe Carballo and León Monzón.[48] Prieto was listed first among six first corporals, who oversaw five second corporals and seventy-two infantrymen (table 4.1).[49]

Reinforcements from Cuba protected Spanish interests in Pensacola, which was a conduit in the flour trade to Havana through Florida from

TABLE 4.1 Muster roll of the first company of *Batallón de Morenos*, 1814

Rank	Name		
First sergeant	Felipe Carballo	Leon Monzón	
Drummer	Espiritu Santo Aquiro		
First corporal	Juan Prieto	Leocadio Diaz	Pablo Pacheco
	Antonio Villaseca	Nicolas Olaris	Blas Arango
Second corporal	Matias Santa Cruz	Manuel Martinez	Facundo Ramirez
	Bartolo Galvez	Manuel Cabrera	
Soldier	Justo Alvares	Jose Infante	Jose Gonzalez
	Florentino de Flores	Jose Allovin	Antonino Caballero
	Justo Rodriguez	Benito Medirra	Juan Facenda
	Joaquin Pallardo	Pablo Fernandez	Andres Chavarria
	Jose Perez	Tomas Hernandez	Pedro Fagle
	Pedro Menocal	Jose Fernandez	Balentin Penalver
	Patricio del Pilar	Angel Santa Cruz	Dionisio Godoy
	Jose Roque	Pedro Hernandez	Andres Basan
	Jose Almentero	Marcelo Castillo	Belen Bovadilla
	Jose Lisundia	Jose Moya	Miguel Luz
	Alexo de Soto	Facundo Banyas	Claudio Miralles
	Jose de los Rios	Bartasal Aguiar	Francisco Pimienta
	Eucebio Infanzon	Jose Fiallo	Felipe Gonzales
	Francisco Alcalde	Jose Mandeo	Isidoro Franco
	Jose Ramos	Mariano Quinonez	Jose de la Paz
	Manuel Duante	Balentin Belozo	Pablo Blanquisal
	Manuel Moreno	Carlos Gamarra	Jose Castellon
	Juan Quiroga	Juan Martinez	Luis Penalvea
	Francisco Minan	Francisco Noriega	Jose del Pezo
	Jose Arostegui	Manuel Aguilar	Ramon Miranda
	Jose Heredia	Simon Zequeira	Isidoro Castillo
	Marcos Mirando	Pablo de la Cruz	Juan Martinez
	Eduardo Caydo	Isidoro Hernandez	Jose Uguarte
	Julian Barreto	Brifido Ricardo	Juan Castro

Philadelphia or New York. Cuba did not produce much of this vital commodity required to feed the island's growing population. Prieto and his unit moved between the garrisons in and around Pensacola Bay, including Fort San Carlos de Barrancas, Fort San Miguel, and Santa Rosa Punta de Sigüenza. His unit patrolled the city and docks to defend supply lines from the incursions of American settlers, maroons, and native indigenous groups who frequently raided Spanish territory. During the first year of the war, not much action took place, and the initial soldiers ensured the safe delivery of flour. For example, a little more than a month after Prieto arrived, dozens of barrels arrived in Havana through Pensacola.[50]

The area around Pensacola was sparsely populated, but the settlement was politically significant. During the Bourbon reforms, the Spanish government had invested heavily in expanding and repairing the forts.[51] The city formed part of the Deep South, which was primarily occupied by peoples that Prieto knew as "Uchizes" and "Talapusa" in Spanish, or Upper and Lower Creeks among the British and Americans.[52] In Pensacola, Prieto encountered diverse peoples, some of whom were peaceful traders and smugglers, among others who were violent and prone to raiding. According to Nathaniel Millett, Pensacola was "a garrison town that maintained close ties to Cuba and was populated by various Creole whites, diverse Europeans, and a slave and free black population that was African as well as Spanish, French, and Anglo Creole."[53] As described by Claudio Saunt, the Spanish population in the Deep South "fluctuated between 2,500 and 3,500, while Native Americans numbered as many as 16,000."[54] Creek territory, which Prieto never traveled, "stretched from the ridge dividing the Alabama and Tonbigbee rivers east of the Savannah River."[55] These indigenous groups lived in dozens of towns, which had as few as ten families to as many as two hundred or more.[56] Since the early eighteenth century, "wayward Creeks began to form separate settlements in the Alachua prairie" to the west of St. Augustine. The people in these communities, which were also multicultural, came to be known as "Seminoles," which derived from the Spanish word for "runaway" (*cimarron*) or "the Muskogee term *ishti semoli*, meaning 'wild men.'"[57]

By the early nineteenth century, the more powerful Creeks, whose trade had previously relied on deerskin, were engaging in large-scale cattle farming. Many supported the "plan for civilization" implemented by Benjamin Hawkins, whom George Washington had appointed in 1796 as the general superintendent for Indian affairs.[58] After the Louisiana Purchase, Hawkins signed treaties with factions of the Creeks and Seminoles, which ultimately resulted in the United States acquiring a large swath of land that became part of Georgia as well as the perceived right to build a federal road across Creek territory. The year before Prieto arrived to Pensacola, this road opened through Creek lands from Fort Stoddert above Mobile to the Flint River (map 4.1).

Indigenous groups responded differently to European and American occupation of native lands. By September 1811, Creek leaders and warriors held a meeting with different factions, including Shawnees, Choctaws, and

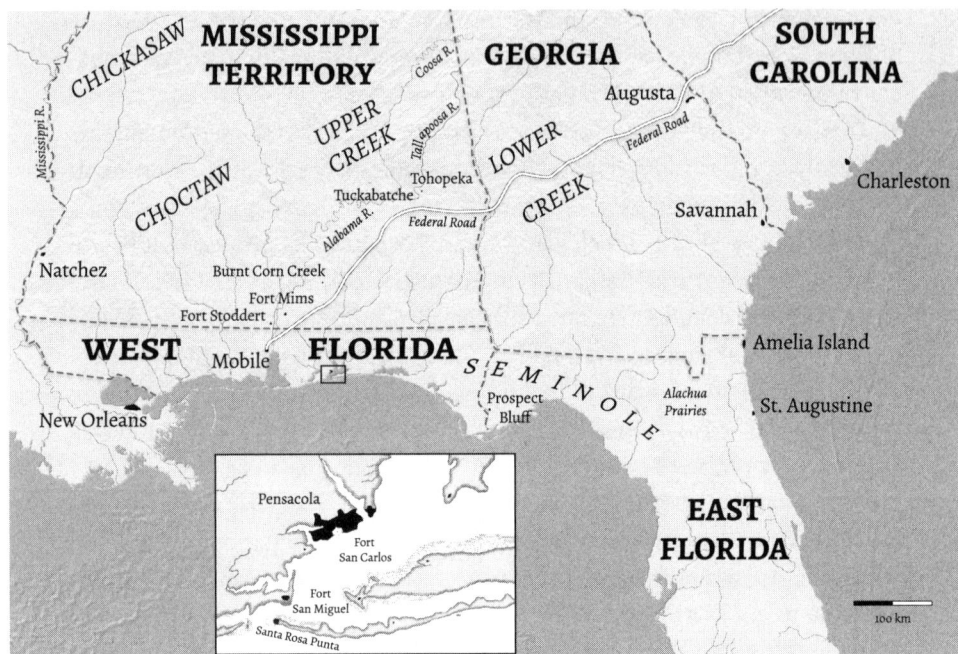

MAP 4.1 Spanish borderlands in continental North America, c. 1812. Source: Henry B. Lovejoy, *African Diaspora Maps*, 2018. Inset map adapted from Romans and Sayer, *Plan of the Harbour of Pensacola*.

Cherokees. Tecumseh, a Shawnee warrior who led this delegation, hoped, as Hawkins described, "to unite all the red people in a war against the white people."[59] Seminoles, allied with runaway slaves, went to war fighting against the Americans especially after the occupation of Amelia Island in Spanish East Florida. During Payne's War from 1812 to 1814, Seminoles attempted to defend the Alachua prairie lands but were ultimately pushed west toward Pensacola. While the Seminoles fought in the Florida peninsula, Creek leaders in support of Hawkins' missions began to crush any dissent inspired by Tecumseh. In April 1813, Creek dissidents led by Little Warrior killed members of the Creek council's police force, who in turn executed Little Warrior and his men. According to Creek historians, these attacks and retaliations marked the start of a "civil war" between the "Redstick Creeks, named for the red clubs that they wielded," and the "Creek leaders and their U.S. allies."[60] As Saunt explains, once the "Redsticks had converted nearly every Upper Creek town to their cause," their army of about 2,500 warriors turned their attention to "slaughtering swine, fowl, and especially cattle . . . [which] symbolized the innovations of the new order."[61] Their leaders, who included

Peter McQueen and Cusseta Tustunnuggee (also known as High-head Jim), mostly came from upper towns on the Tallpoosa, Coosa, and Alabama Rivers.

As the situation north of Pensacola deteriorated, relations between Spain and the United States became tense when a substantial number of American troops arrived at the federal road to Mobile and the Spanish surrendered the fort there without a fight, realizing that resistance was futile.[62] Although the Spanish never officially declared war against the United States, Britain and Spain were allied against Napoleon in Europe. In Florida, the Spanish military therefore leaned toward helping the British and Creek factions who had allied against the United States. By July, McQueen and Cusseta Tustunnuggee, along with "280 warriors," arrived in Pensacola to obtain supplies and ammunition from the Spanish, which included "a small bag of powder each, for ten towns, and five bullets to each man."[63] Prieto's unit stood on guard as McQueen and his men rode into town. They met with Mateo González Manrique, Zúñiga's replacement. The governor of Florida allowed them to search "through houses, looking for one or two Americans who had taken refuge in the Spanish settlement."[64] Henry Adams notes how Manrique's soldiers, which included Prieto, treated McQueen and his men "civilly, and in fear of violence."[65] Following the meeting, the governor reported to Cuba that the "Redsticks intended to attack the Americans as well as their Creek opponents" and that Spain had the choice "to support either the Indians or the United States."[66]

Relations between the United States and Spain declined further, placing Pensacola in a precarious position. News that the rebellious Creeks were obtaining ammunition in Spanish territory quickly spread throughout American settlements. As described by Adams, on 27 July, "white settlers from Tensaw and mixed-blood Creek planters from the Little River area" ambushed Cusseta Tustunnuggee and McQueen's party, whereby they took their ammunition and supplies. This incident, which Prieto likely heard about as the Battle of Burnt Corn Creek, occurred "about eighty miles north of Pensacola." The result was that one "party of twenty-three . . . killed three, and wounded one of the hostile Indians, and brought the scalps to the public square; one other party [took] four negroes from Peter McQueen, and a third party [took] a lad of his family, twelve years old, as prisoner."[67] Prieto likely lived in fear of the volatile situation over which Pensacola was poorly defended.

The ambush escalated into the Creek War. Some of McQueen's men returned to Pensacola to secure ammunition from the Spanish, while others went inland to recruit more warriors. Michael Green explains how McQueen and his men then mobilized and tracked the people who had attacked them to "a makeshift fort hastily constructed around the house of Samuel Mims, an old Georgia trader." On 30 August, they massacred all of them "at the infamous slaughter of Fort Mims."[68] This counterattack was all the Americans needed to justify a full invasion of Creek territory, which they achieved under the leadership of Andrew Jackson, who commanded heavily armed units from Georgia, Tennessee, and the Mississippi Territory, along with help from factions of Choctaws, Cherokees, and Creeks.[69] On 27 March, the Americans and their allies destroyed most of the Creek towns at the Battle of Horseshoe Bend, also known as *Tohopeka*, which was located on the Tallapoosa River nearly 150 miles to the northeast of Pensacola.[70]

Spanish troops at Pensacola were directly involved in the Creek War, as they protected their territory from what Robbie Ethridge describes as "thousands of men, women, children, and warriors who fled into the Coastal Plain."[71] Sometime during this refugee crisis, Prieto was admitted to the military hospital in Pensacola for undisclosed injuries. As he made his recovery, Prieto learned of the heavy losses the Creeks had sustained. Although he was not directly involved in that war, he knew that the Americans had engaged the "Red Sticks in numerous bloody battles . . . [as they] danced and pranced in front of cannons, believing them shielded from the cannonballs by the magic of their prophets."[72] As a soldier, Prieto knew all about the power of Sàngó and the artillery. On 12 May, Prieto was released from the hospital and resumed duty, as monthly muster rolls demonstrate.[73]

Peace negotiations between the United States and Britain began in Ghent in August 1814. By this time, a British blockade of the North American coast had crippled the American economy, and following the end of the Peninsular War, the British occupied and burned Washington to the ground. The Americans almost instantaneously retook the city, inflicting a major defeat on the British. In Havana, Edward Nicolls, lieutenant colonel of the British Royal Marines, was negotiating with Captain General Apodaca to send a detachment of British soldiers and slaves up the Apalachicola River to the east of Pensacola. He was put in charge of building a fort and munitions depot at Prospect Bluff on the river and to train runaway slaves, Seminoles, and Creek refugees for an attack on the Americans.[74] As the fort was being built, manned, and supplied with ammunition, William Henry Percy, captain of the British warship *Hermes*, arrived on the Apalachicola River with instructions for Nicolls to abandon the fort and "bring the arms, ammunition, and everything from the depôt on the Bluff to Pensacola . . . to assist the Spanish nation." With the mass arrival of Creeks, Spanish authorities feared an attack from the Americans and cleared Fort San Miguel, which "was put into the hands of Lieutenant-

Colonel Nicholls; and the British flag was hoisted in conjunction with the Spanish, which . . . was done with the [Spanish] governor's approbation."[75]

Prieto was part of the preliminary Spanish evacuation of Florida. Shortly after Nicholls occupied the fort, Prieto received instructions for his return to Havana along with nine others from his unit on 8 September.[76] Prieto was truly fortunate to have been relinquished from his duty at this time. On 15 September, a considerable force consisting of Creeks and British marines, with the support of four warships, attacked Fort Bowyer on Mobile Point. The Spanish were not involved, and genuinely seemed unaware of these developments. The Americans successfully defended the assault and also sunk the *Hermes*, which was under Percy's command. Once the British returned to Pensacola, the Americans believed the British, Spanish, and Creeks had formed a deeper alliance. Thereafter, Jackson determined "to advance against, and reduce Pensacola . . . until the principles of right and neutrality were better respected."[77]

In early November, after Prieto was reunited with his wife in Havana, Jackson marched upwards of three thousand troops on Pensacola and captured the city, whereby the British blew up Fort San Miguel and abandoned Pensacola, leaving their Creek and Spanish allies to fend for themselves. Jackson wrote to Manrique, the Spanish governor, "It is out of my power to protect and defend your neutrality, as otherwise I should have done. The enemy has retreated; the hostile Creeks had fled for safety to the forest; and I now retire from your town, leaving you to re-occupy your forts, and protect the rights of your citizens."[78] Through military networks, Prieto definitely heard that the Americans briefly occupied Pensacola in 1814, and then how refugee Creeks, Seminoles, and maroons occupied the British fort on Prospect Bluff.[79] He also heard about the "miracle shot," which destroyed the fort in 1816. By 1821 Spain had conceded all of Florida to the United States following two Seminole wars.[80]

Upon his return to Havana, Prieto was likely promoted to second sergeant, but whether that related to the injuries he sustained in Cuba remains a mystery. With higher rank, Kuethe writes, soldiers were "expected to contribute more extensively to managing the details of unit maintenance and discipline."[81] Prieto therefore began training new recruits and free people of African descent to defend Cuba from the threat of independence and abolition. Leading by example, he instructed his subordinates how to manage and control new shipments of enslaved Africans who were continuously arriving to the island. Little is known about his transition to retirement, but by around 1818, he stepped down and began receiving a small pension. At this time, he assumed leadership of a Lucumí *cabildo* dedicated to Santa Bárbara.

CHAPTER FIVE
Ṣàngó Tẹ̀ Dún

Prieto's ascension as leader of a Lucumí *cabildo* happened after his return from Florida. In the midst of the Spanish American wars of independence and increasing pressure from British abolitionism, Cuban authorities were not going to permit just anyone from leading a mutual aid society. Clergy and government officials must have therefore vetted and endorsed this literate second sergeant, whom they determined had loyally policed the enslaved, helped suppress the Aponte Rebellion, and served in Florida. Prieto's crowning as *cabildo* "king" was not documented, but it is clear that he had to obtain support from members of the Lucumí community, who cast their votes through a democratic process. María Francisca Camejo influenced the outcome of this election because, as Matt D. Childs has effectively shown, women often decided new leadership due to their numerical superiority in *cabildos*.[1] With Camejo almost certainly acting as his political adviser, Prieto's platform appealed to the elite Lucumí population in Havana. He was the ideal candidate because he was born in Africa, had served in the military, understood the legal framework of the church and state, revered the *òrìṣà*, and had been a *cabildo* member since the 1790s. Around 1818, Camejo and Prieto garnered a substantial following, and in the end, they consolidated a remarkable socioreligious organization until Camejo's death around 1833 and Prieto's arrest in 1835.

The period in which Camejo and Prieto became the *cabildo* "queen" and "king" marked a period when Cuba prospered during its agricultural revolution. The vast amounts of money made from the production of sugar no doubt trickled down into communities of people of African descent, especially in Havana. Modest improvements in social life affected the prestige of Camejo and Prieto's *cabildo*, which achieved a level of wealth that had not existed previously. Through literacy and rigid record keeping, Camejo and Prieto oversaw one of the wealthiest and most well documented *cabildos* in Cuban history. The reputation of this organization grew during a period that coincided with the mass arrival of enslaved people involved in the collapse of the kingdom of Ọ̀yọ́. Therefore, Camejo and Prieto's story elucidates an enduring legacy about the inner workings of a mutual aid society, which modern-day practitioners of the Lucumí religion have memorialized as

Ṣàngó tẹ̀ dún. As discussed in the introduction, this *cabildo* title has multiple meanings, such as "Ṣàngó imprints with noise," "Ṣàngó arrived and planted," "Ṣàngó becomes the thunderstone," and "Ṣàngó thee, O God, we praise."

In order to assume control of a *cabildo* in Havana, Camejo and Prieto not only required endorsement from the Lucumí community but also church sponsorship, meaning they must have had strong and proven Christian beliefs. The archbishop of Havana, Juan José Díaz de Espada y Fernández de Landa, likely sanctioned Prieto's institution, which ultimately fell under the supervision of José Pedro Infante, the priest of the parish in Jesús, María y José. Every *cabildo* in Havana had a patron saint, and the years of military service influenced the selection of Santa Bárbara. Among Prieto's personal documents, there were over a dozen pamphlets dedicated to this saint with prayers in Latin and Spanish. Soldiers followed this saint as a "glorious virgin and martyr, patron of the royal artillery corps, and special intermediary against lightening, sparks, and sudden death."[2] According to hagiography, Santa Bárbara was "the patron of armories, artillerymen, gunsmiths, carpenters, masons, miners" and "was invoked against storms, thunderbolts, sudden death, and final impenitence."[3] Among Lucumí in Havana, she clearly epitomized Ṣàngó, the revered Ọ̀yọ́ god of thunder, lightning, and war (figure 5.1).

Undoubtedly, Prieto and Camejo simultaneously believed in a creolized pantheon of gods at the root of a modern-day African-derived religion commonly known as Santería. In 1835, authorities confiscated religious paraphernalia from their home, including "a countless number of dolls and trinkets symbolic of his witchcraft."[4] Such colonial perspectives of African-derived religious beliefs devalued Lucumí culture as "primitive," which Prieto openly challenged before a military court. According to his own explanations about the shrines, he stated as a matter of fact, "The biggest doll, which has a sediment of blood on its chest from a Pigeon and other animals, is called *Changó*, which is the same as saying King, or Santa Bárbara, who [we] venerate as God. . . . A stick, with a silk cat-o-nine-tails, is called *Opachangó* signifying that it is the scepter of the King."[5] This quotation is one of the earliest documented statements from a Yorùbá speaker in the Atlantic world to explain the duality of òrìṣà and Catholic worship. Typically, scholars have had to attribute characteristics of Ṣàngó to references of Santa Bárbara based on modern-day observations.[6] Prieto was clearly at ease explaining to his oppressors his culture as a child of Odùduwà within his Christian beliefs. Without revealing too many secrets, however, Prieto exposed a powerful, deep ritual knowledge (ìmọ̀ jinlẹ̀), which according to Apter had

Cristus Rex ve- | Christus cruci-
nit in pace. | fixus est.
Et Deus Homo | Cts. mortuus est.
factus est. | Cts. sepultuus est.
Verbum Caro | Ctus resurrexit.
factum est. | Ctus. ascendit.
Christus de Vir- | Ctus. imperat.
gine natus est. | Christus regnat.
Christus per me- | Cts. ab omni ful-
dium illorum | gure nos defendat
ibat in pace. | Deus nobiscum est.

S. BARBARA

GLORIOSA VÍRGEN Y MARTIR,
PATRONA DEL REAL CUERPO DE ARTILLERÍA,
Y ESPECIAL ABOGADA CONTRA RAYOS, CENTELLAS Y MUERTES REPENTINAS.

El Ecsmo. é Ilmo. Sr. Obispo diocesano D. Juan José Diaz de Espada y Landa, concedió 40 dias de indulgencia á los fieles que con las debidas disposiciones hicieren oracion delante la imágen expresada.

ORACION Á LA SANTA.

Invicta sierva del Señor, gloriosísima virgen y mártir SANTA BÁRBARA, que por no faltar á la fidelidad de esposa de Jesus, os sacrificásteis, cual inocente cordero al cuchillo, pedidle á vuestro esposo me libre de muerte repentina, para que recibidos los Sacramentos de la iglesia, descanse en paz. Librame tambien de piedra, centellas, rayos y tempestades; y sobre todo de la mas terrible de mis pasiones, que por este medio y vuestra especialísima asistencia, segura tengo la mayor de todas las dichas, que es la Bienaventuranza. Amén.

LA MAGNIFICAT DE NUESTRA SEÑORA EN LATIN Y EN CASTELLANO.

Magnificat ánima mea Dóminum. Et exultavit spiritus meus* in Deo salutári meo.

Engrandece mi alma al Señor. Y se regocijó mi espíritu, en Dios mi Salvador.

Quia respéxit humilitatem ancillæ suæ: ecce enim ex hoc beatam me dicent omnes generationes.

Por que ha mirado la pequeñez de su sierva: hé aquí, que desde ahora me llamarán bienaventurada todas las generaciones.

Quia fecit mihi magna qui potens est :* & sanctum nomen ejus.

Pues ha hecho en mí grandes cosas el que es poderoso, y cuyo nombre es santo.

Et misericordia ejus á progenie in progenies,* timentibus eum.

Y su misericordia se extiende de familia en familia, á los que le temen.

Fecit potentiam in brachio suo:* dispersit superbos mente cordis sui.

Hizo valentía con su brazo: esparció á los soberbios del pensamiento de su corazon.

Depósuit potentes de sede,* & exáltavit húmiles.

Ha derribado del trono á los poderosos, y ensalzado á los abatidos.

Esurientes implévit bonis,* et divites dimísit inánes.

A los hambrientos hinchió de bienes, y envió vacíos á los ricos.

Suscépit Israël puerum suum,* recordatus misericordiæ suæ.

Recibió á Israël su siervo, acordándose de su misericordia.

Sicut locútus est ad patres nostros,* Abraham, & sémini ejus in sæcula.

Como prometió à nuestros padres, á Abrahan y à su descendencia para siempre. Gloria Patri &c.

☞ Se hallará en la oficina de D. Pedro Martinez de Almeida calle del Sol núm. 55.

FIGURE 5.1 Printed image of Santa Bárbara from Prieto's archive. ANC, CM 11/1, "S. Barbara," n.d., loose folio. Courtesy of the Archivo Nacional de Cuba.

"no determinate content but rather [safeguarded] a space for opposing hegemony."[7]

Just as his Lucumí ancestors had taught him in the eighteenth century, Camejo and Prieto followed colonial rules and regulations to generate sovereignty in a slave society. They proved their Christian devotion by participating in baptisms as godparents. The people they initiated at several churches in Havana were diverse and identified as Lucumí, Carabalí, and Creole.[8] Prieto participated in the baptisms of Juan and Jacobo, both of whom were liberated Africans (*emancipados*) from the condemned slave ship *Mágico*.[9] According to the ship register, these two men arrived from Little Popo, were "Lucumí Elló" (Ọ̀yọ́), and had the Yorùbá names "Allai" (Àjàyí) and "Cucudi" (Kukudi?).[10] Catholic initiations clearly influenced the structure of modern-day observations of the Lucumí religion. David Brown has observed how initiates join a "religious house" under the guidance of "godparents," whereby "the kinship relations of [a] sacred family augment and complement the kinship relations of one's natural and baptismal families."[11] Camejo and Prieto's "godchildren" were therefore the ritual descendants of a Lucumí spiritual family, which ultimately reinforced in Catholic terms Yorùbá concepts of the "house" (*ilé*) tied into an "ancestral place of origin" (*oríkì orílè*).

Camejo and Prieto lived in several residences always just a few blocks from the church in the neighborhood of Jesús, María y José. No matter where their home was located, it served as the Lucumí *cabildo* headquarters. Upon returning from Pensacola, records show they initially leased a property on Esperanza Street for three *pesos* and two *reales* per month.[12] By 1818, they relocated to Gloría Street, where they bought a small house from M. Guerrero for two hundred *pesos* (which cost less than the price of an adult slave).[13] For the next seventeen years, their home on Gloría Street served as the central meeting place and mutual aid society for Yorùbá speakers in Havana. While the number of their residence remains unknown, it was close to a district called El Manglar, which translates as "mangrove swamp."[14] This area referred to an underdeveloped tract of land near where a branch of the Zanja River emptied into the bay. From a patchwork of oral traditions, however, their Gloría Street home was likely situated close to the intersections of San Nicolás, Indio, and Florida.[15] It is not known who built Camejo and Prieto's house, but *cabildo* communities often purchased land and then constructed their own buildings collectively.[16]

Havana's multicultural society meant that Camejo and Prieto had to reposition their authority constantly. As a *cabildo* "queen" and "king," they nurtured a Lucumí kinship group in what likely became a relatively large

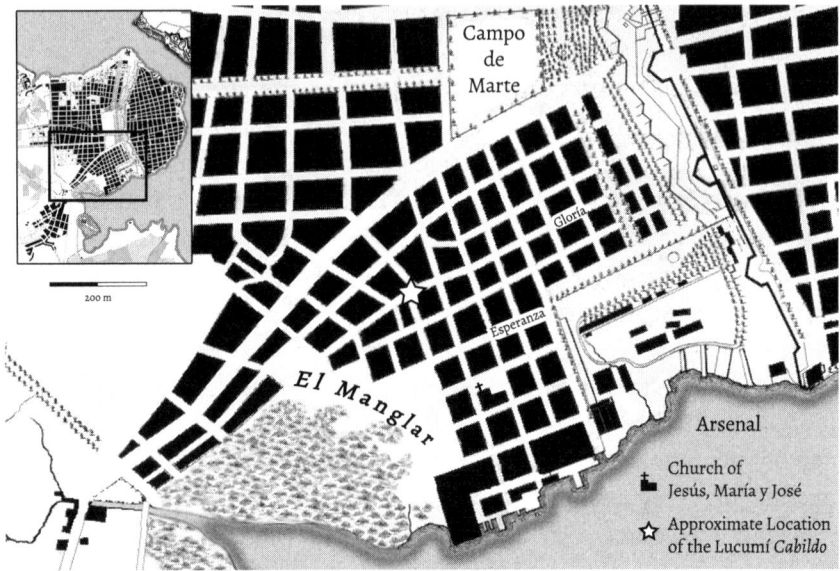

MAP 5.1 Neighborhood of Jesús, María y José, c. 1820.
Source: Henry B. Lovejoy, *African Diaspora Maps*, 2018.

compound in Jesús, María y José. Their Lucumí *ilé* paid tribute to the Catholic Church and the Spanish government in the form of taxes and other duties. Because they had one of the larger *cabildos* in the port city, adversaries likely challenged their relative power on a regular basis. This threat not only came internally via ranking members and new Lucumí from Africa, but also from non-Lucumí communities operating elsewhere in the same neighborhood and sometimes on the same street. At the largest peak of arrivals from Africa, Camejo and Prieto led one of fourteen other documented *cabildos* in Havana: ten were Carabali, two Congo, one Mandinga, and another Mina.[17]

Among the most devout, Ṣàngó embodied fire and required the payment of tributes, especially if the god "destroys property."[18] In 1827, Camejo and Prieto surely paid their dues when a fire burned a large section of Jesús, María y José, including their home on Gloría Street.[19] This disaster damaged documents from the *cabildo* archives and disrupted their revenue stream. Although Prieto and Camejo saved what they could, especially property records, they had to move to a temporary residence, which they rented on Chamorro Street in early 1828.[20] Over the next year, Camejo, Prieto, and the Lucumí community quickly rebuilt the house on Gloría Street. Afterward, they subsidized costs by renting and selling rooms to *cabildo* members.[21] With more land suddenly available (likely due to the fire), Prieto leased adjacent land from Domingo de Rivas for five *pesos* per year. This sizeable yard measured about seven meters in front and twenty-five to thirty meters in the back.[22] The extra land likely served well in the weekly gatherings and rituals, which authorities permitted by law on every Sunday and holidays.

As entrepreneurs, Camejo and Prieto contributed to the development of the island's capital city. Besides earning membership fees, they allowed their home and headquarters to function as a bank, which likely ran and operated saving and credit associations (*èsúsú* or *àjọ*).[23] They reinvested profits back into the community by arranging for the delivery and postpartum care of babies, posting bonds, interceding in work agreements, granting loans, and paying for baptisms.[24] According to receipts between 1819 and 1833, they helped emancipate people through *coartación* down payments, which varied between three and thirty-four *pesos*.[25] Most *cabildo* services cost money. Camejo and Prieto received traditional ritual tributes, which are known today as *derechos*.[26] Camejo and Prieto practiced herbalism and sold that knowledge. In his testimony, he explained how people came to the "business [to] consult him about an illness [after which he gave] them his remedy."[27] According to John Mason, Prieto's testimony strongly suggests he was "both a priest of Ṣàngó and Ọ̀sanyín, the *òrìṣà* of herbs and healing."[28]

African-style funerals were technically illegal according to colonial law from 1792 and reenacted in 1827, Camejo and Prieto organized elaborate burials probably for high-ranking *cabildo* members.[29] In 1827, Prieto persuaded authorities with a "greasing of silver" to organize a wake "with the husband, children and friends of the deceased María del Rosario Torres." In the same year, he also hosted a service for María Regla de Cárdenas, whereby he paid for all the funeral's ritual materials including "a bottle of arrowroot, 12 [bottles] of *aguardiente*, 4 vials of ginger, 12 bottles of dry wine, 6 [bottles] of *aguardiente* from the Island, 3 cheeses and other various effects."[30] Torres and Cárdenas might have been related to former leaders of the Lucumí *cabildos* documented in the 1780s.[31]

Even though financial records do not refer to María Francisca Camejo, women in Lucumí history require more prominence. Stereotypes neglect female spiritual power, political clout, financial savvy, and other central roles within seemingly male-dominated institutions. Scholars have argued that a woman's status in Yorùbá-speaking society and culture derived from economic independence "rather than from her husband's importance."[32] While Prieto performed ceremonies, he likely consulted his wife's deep ritual knowledge. Camejo likely administered schedules, kept track of the ritual family, organized purchases, received deliveries, booked musicians, organized masses, prepared sacrificial offerings and food, directed ritual sequences, and collected payments. As is the tradition in several modern-day house-temples, leadership typically revolve around women. Brown has shown that since the early twentieth century, many women founded some of the most influential branches of the Lucumí religion practiced in Cuba.[33] Through my experiences, this tradition has continued in some houses up until today.[34]

Beyond Santa Bárbara, this Lucumí community revered a cluster of saints made evident by a series of printed images of the Virgin Mary, including Nuestra Señora del Carmen, Nuestra Señora de los Remedios, and Nuestra Señora de Monserrate.[35] Worshipping more than one saint or òrìṣà was common in both West Africa and the New World. Unlike Ṣàngó and Santa Bárbara, links between these three Marian devotions and modern-day òrìṣà belief remain unclear. Differences in practices transformed over time, and historicizing such changes is not always easy to do.[36] At best, Nuestra Señora del Carmen descended from heaven to free human souls from purgatory. Images of people in chains, trapped in flames, and praying to Maria illustrated salvation through the worship of saints and òrìṣà.[37] She tentatively equates with Naná Burukú, who in Dahomey mythology created the universe but in Cuba (some believe) is the mother of the cemetery guardian, Babalú Ayé or San Lázaro.[38] Today, her following is considered to be "in decline."[39] Otherwise, Monserrate was a black Madonna known affectionately as the "little dark one" (*moreneta*); and Remedios is a devotion linked to both the reconquest of Spain and conquest of the Americas in 1492. Perhaps these three saints never equated with òrìṣà at all, but only with Spanish and Catholic traditions (figures 5.2–5.5).

Privileges entrusted to well-respected, free militiamen included permission to host annual festivals. Beginning in 1818, Camejo and Prieto organized elaborate processions devoted to Santa Bárbara held on 4 December. On 27 June 1824, he requested a license "to hold dances and diversions" honoring the patron saint in the *cabildo* house. Captain General Francisco Dionisio Vives granted this request, which demonstrated the high degree of trust that colonial authorities had for Camejo, Prieto, and their operations.[40] Unfortunately, the 1827 fire destroyed the original license, which Prieto quickly replaced after writing a letter to a Havana bishop. He stated how he had paid for masses and songs for the past "nine consecutive years" and had previously held a license permitting "forty days of indulgence to the faithful who make prayers before [Santa Bárbara's] image."[41] Receipts dated between 1824 and

NUESTRA SEÑORA DE LOS REMEDIOS.

Segun se venera por su Cofradía en la iglesia del convento de nuestro padre S. Francisco.

FIGURE 5.2 Printed image of Nuestra Señora de los Remedios from Prieto's archive. ANC, CM 11/1, "Nuestra Señora de los Remedios," n.d., loose folio. Courtesy of the Archivo Nacional de Cuba.

NUESTRA SRA. DEL CARMEN.

Se hallará ésta y otras várias en la imprenta de Boloña, calle de la Obra-pía número 37.

FIGURE 5.3 Printed image of Nuestra Señora del Carmen from Prieto's archive. ANC, CM 11/1, "Nuestra Señora del Carmen," n.d., loose folio. Courtesy of the Archivo Nacional de Cuba.

Pues sois de nuestro consuelo
El medio más poderoso,
Sed nuestro amparo amoroso
Madre de Dios del CARMELO.

FIGURE 5.4 Second printed image of Nuestra Señora del Carmen from Prieto's archive. ANC, CM 11/1, "Nuestra Señora del Carmen," n.d., loose folio. Courtesy of the Archivo Nacional de Cuba.

DECIMA.

A vos, sagrada SEÑORA,
Se acoje todo cristiano,
Y en sus dolores ufano
Rendidamente os implora:
El Altísimo atesora
Gracias en vos, por que os cuadre,
Y con ser Eterno Padre,
Quiso con modo prolijo,
Lo reconociese hijo
Del MONSERRATE la madre.

FIGURE 5.5 Printed image of Nuestra Señora de Monserrate from Prieto's archive. ANC, CM 11/1, "Nuestra Señora de Monserrate," n.d., loose folio. Courtesy of the Archivo Nacional de Cuba.

1834 show how Prieto used *cabildo* funds to pay for these festivals, which cost between six and thirteen *pesos* per event. The celebrations likely started inside the house on Gloría Street, where they held rituals with sacrifices of animals, plants, food, tobacco, alcohol, and other things. Respected members then proceeded to the church of Jesús, María y José, where they likely attended a Christian mass. The parade probably ended back at the *cabildo*. Over several weeks, the festival involved drumming, dancing, and singing in honor of the saints and òrìṣà.

Camejo and Prieto's month-and-a-half-long Ṣàngó festival incorporated several Catholic feast days into a celebration that publically displayed their Christian beliefs but also validated degrees of hegemony within the Spanish colony. In consideration of the complexity of òrìṣà mythology within Catholic traditions, or vice versa, the month of December and first weeks of January were one of the holiest times of the year. Santa Bárbara's feast day occurred on 4 December, which was followed by the Immaculate Conception and the twelve days of Christmas. The forty days of Ṣàngó festivities culminated during the Day of Kings festival. On 6 January, all of Havana's *cabildos*, whether Mandinga, Gangá, Mina, Arará, Lucumí, Carabali, or Congo, paraded through the streets and had permission to enter the inner-city walls. Therein, they sought alms from the upper classes, which observed the event from the safety of balconies and barred windows.[42] Conceivably, Camejo and Prieto received honorary tributes as Lucumí royalty from Havana's white, slave-owning class while simultaneously paying homage to the king of Spain as loyal subjects.

During the most revered feast days, *cabildo* "queens" and "kings" imitated the dress of the peninsular monarchy, military, church, and slave-owning classes. Prieto wore "long military coats, starched shirts, enormous ties, flamboyant double-peaked hats, gold braid and loud, wide sashes across the chest, decorations, swords on the belt, great staffs with silver points—a symbol of authority."[43] Camejo dressed in "puff-shouldered, flowing gowns with petticoats, jewelry, and large umbrellas."[44] The banners, umbrellas, clothes, and other royal regalia were symbolic of kingship in West Africa, and the tributes paid for by Havana's white, colonial elite demonstrated, in a certain sense, a recognition of dynastic claims. In West Africa, umbrellas symbolized the power and autonomy of kings, chiefs, and military leaders. During the processions, it would have been an honor for high-ranking members of the Lucumí *cabildo* to carry the parasol to shield Camejo and Prieto from the hot Caribbean sun. Musicians played horns, drums, bells, shakers, and other instruments, while announcing and singing their praises to their "queen" and "king."

FIGURE 5.6 *Cabildo* banner of "La Sociedad de Socorros
Mutuos Nacion Lucumi de Santa Bárbara, Año 1820."
Fernando Ortiz Collection, La Casa de Africa, Havana.
Photograph by John Mason, c. 1986. Red silk with
gold embroidered letters, 109 cm by 76 cm. Mason,
Aráàràárá, Fig. 79, n.p. Courtesy of John Mason, 2017.

At the head of these Lucumí processions, *cabildo* members carried a cross,
followed by a flag, and then an effigy of Santa Bárbara. Even though the 1792
code of slave laws prohibited *cabildos* from marching with flags, authorities
disregarded this law for certain organizations and occasions. Members of
Ṣàngó tẹ̀ dún carried a banner with the image of Santa Bárbara "in a golden
frame and carried on a pole."[45] This red banner with gold decorative motifs
representing Ṣàngó has survived in La Casa de África museum in Havana.[46]
The embroidered writing translates from Spanish as, "THE LUCUMI NATION

MUTUAL AID SOCIETY OF SANTA BÁRBARA, YEAR OF 1820." Unfortunately, the saint's image has faded away from the circular center over time.

Colonial holidays in Havana had special meaning for people of Yorùbá descent because they could have imitated regal annual festivals in West Africa. For example, the bẹrẹ festival in Ọ̀yọ́ marked the anniversary of the reign or the installation of a new king (aláàfin). On 22 February 1826, the British diplomat Hugh Clapperton was in Ọ̀yọ́ when he observed a pilgrimage to the capital for payments of annual tributes.[47] In West Africa, payments came in the form of grass (bẹrẹ), which was used to thatch roofs and feed the horses in the cavalry. During the bẹrẹ festival, people burned fields to stimulate growth and mark the start of the new agricultural year. Prieto's forty days of festivities coincided with the time of year when fields were set alight during Cuba's sugar cane harvest (zafra). People from Ọ̀yọ́ in Cuba, especially those lucky enough to participate in the Ṣàngó tẹ̀ dún celebrations, understood the processions as idioms of kingship, power, and sovereignty.[48] Some Yorùbá speakers in Havana might have even recognized Prieto as the symbolic embodiment of the aláàfin because he held legitimate authority over his Lucumí subjects and displayed autonomy from colonial rule.

Camejo and Prieto's Santa Bárbara festivals and other gatherings involved sacrifices. The animals used during in-house rituals included goats and a wide selection of birds, such as chickens, pigeons, and doves. At the time of Prieto's arrest, authorities described how the Ṣàngó shrine had "a sediment of blood on its chest." They also uncovered an iron pot with "skeletal remains of a young male goat and other carcasses."[49] In modern-day practices, male kids are the preferred but not exclusive animal of both Ṣàngó and ancestral spirits (egungun).[50] Plants, stones, smoke, alcohol, and other items were almost certainly sacrificed too. In Prieto's yard, there were "a large number of dolls in the shape of palitroques [stick figures] driven into the ground."[51] It is worth noting that this tradition has not survived in Cuba, as modern-day practitioners could not identify with this documented account.[52] Just outside Badagry in 1851, however, the missionary James Huber observed how "women came and bowed down before [a Ṣàngó shrine] . . . and gave their little sticks to one of the priests."[53] This quote suggests that the tradition of planting sticks into the ground existed in both West Africa and Cuba during Prieto's time, although the practice has apparently discontinued in Cuba.

Lucumí ceremonies in Havana involved music, drumming, and dancing. Instruments found in the cabildo included "a piece of elephant tusk with two faces engraved in it [that] serves as a small bell to call to God." The ivory bell suggests Ọbàtálá, or even Odùduwà. Besides the *"Opachangó"* Prieto identified, other items for the òrìṣà included a "stick with a white tail, adorned with various ribbons and beads [that] has no other importance other than praying for the health of every Christian . . . and is also useful to dance."[54] Ṣàngó's thunder axe, plus flywhisks (ìrukẹ̀) and a bell (agogo) for Ọbàtálá symbolized Camejo and Prieto's royal status among the Yorùbá-speaking community in Havana. Prieto's deposition also suggested his *cabildo* was in the process of manufacturing or repairing drums. He explained that "a patch of male goat leather [was] used in his drumming functions."[55] Whether or not the Lucumí community had been building a trio of double-headed, hourglass-shaped drums belonging to Ṣàngó is a matter of interpretation. Nevertheless, this reference relates to Lucumí oral traditions Ortiz collected in the 1940s surrounding *Ṣàngó tẹ̀ dún* and the consecration of *bàtá* in the 1830s.[56]

Within this complex fusion of Christianity and òrìṣà belief, Camejo and Prieto owned another shrine, which he described in his testimony as a "small wooden doll with a mirror in its belly."[57] Among modern-day practitioners in Cuba, many believers argued that mirrors are not typically found in the shrines dedicated to the òrìṣà. Through extensive discussions with modern-day practitioners, one priest thought the shrine might have been Ọ̀ṣọ́ọ̀sì (San Norberto) — god of law, justice, hunting and magic — who sometimes has mirrors displayed on the front and back of his head.[58] Another thought the mirror and its reflection could have also referred to Ìbejí, the òrìṣà of twins.[59] Even though Ìbejí dolls tend to come in pairs, Miguel Ramos has argued that "a single carving for Ìbejí is not at all odd [because] these figures are commissioned upon the death of a twin [and] if one dies, the survivor will pay homage to his or her sibling through this image, which is consecrated through a series of rituals."[60] While the debate over what this description of a shrine represented may never end, Camejo and Prieto's religious beliefs almost certainly extended beyond saints and òrìṣà.

Different cultural expressions from around the Atlantic world intersected in Havana and collided in convoluted ritualized scenarios. Most modern-day practitioners I consulted mostly thought the reference to a "small wooden doll with a mirror in its belly" referred to *nkisi* which is a term from the Bantu languages used to refer to any object or shrine that an ancestral spirit inhabits.[61] In West Central African belief systems, practitioners use shrines with mirrors to peer into metaphysical spiritual dimensions. Moreover, the references from Prieto's deposition related to stick figures (*palitroques*) stuck into the ground and animal carcasses in iron pots (*cazuelas*) might not relate to òrìṣà at all. Rather, they could be references to the receptacles in which *nkisi* reside, which are called *nganga* or *prenda* in the modern-day African-derived religion of Palo Monte. These shrines, over which sacrifices are spilled, are distinctive because bones, feathers, and sticks protrude out from an iron pot. The term *nganga* refers to a priest, herbalist, and spiritual healer. With his business in herbalism, Prieto could have just as easily been initiated into a proto-Palo Monte priesthood (*tata nganga*).[62]

The existence of West Central African contributions to the development of Lucumí culture should not be surprising. According to Lydia Cabrera, the powerful *nkisi* known as "Siete Rayos [Seven Lightning Bolts] is the same as Santa Bárbara: Chango."[63] To reinforce the plausible fusion of multiple forms of worship in this predominately Ṣàngó-centric Lucumí *cabildo*, Prieto testified to burying in his yard a "human cadaver, which is used to pray to the *muertos*."[64] The term *muertos* has multiple meanings related to Yorùbá and Kikongo words meaning "spirits of dead ancestors." It translates as *egungun* in Yorùbá meaning "bone, skeleton," or *egúngun* which are a "masquerade supposed to be a dead person returned to the earth, the worship of the spirits of the dead."[65] Even today, priests (*babalawo*) bury the skeletal remains of their ancestors in their compounds.[66] Throughout most of West Central Africa, human bones, called *nfumbe*, are fundamental in building *nganga* shrines.[67] Bones, most especially human bones, are spiritually charged ritual objects of the highest degree. Today, Catholics still revere the bones of deceased saints and martyrs often displayed in cathedrals and churches around the world. Who Prieto buried in his yard will forever remain unknown, but it could have been former *cabildo* royalty, or perhaps even María Francisca Camejo who passed away during the cholera epidemic of 1833.

During the entire history of the transatlantic slave trade to Cuba, people from West Central Africa were the majority of all arrivals, followed by people from the Bight of Biafra, and then from the Upper Guinea Coast.[68] Consequently, people from the Bight of Benin were a minority, and the disproportionate dominance of *òrìṣà* worship in Cuban culture continues to be an enigma for many anthropologists, historians, and sociologists.[69] In addition to the creolization of West Central African cultures, Ivor Miller, for example, has shown cross-cultural linkages among Abakuá societies, which originated from fraternal associations in the Cross River region of the Bight of Biafra hinterland.[70] Among other studies, Emma Christopher has documented musical connections between Gangá-Longobá groups in Cuba with the Upper Banta in the interior of the Upper Guinea Coast.[71] While the variety of transatlantic connections in Cuba are numerous and impossible to list in their entirety, the point remains that different cultures from around the world intersected in Cuba in myriad combinations. These brief examples only highlight Camejo and Prieto's influences on processes of creolization within *Ṣàngó tẹ̀ dún*, Cuba, and the Atlantic world more broadly.

No matter what transpired in this Lucumí *cabildo*, these surviving records demonstrate Camejo and Prieto's persuasion on what Stephan Palmié has called "culture formations."[72] Through countless combinations of undocumented interactions, Prieto's religious beliefs recorded through the bias of a colonial military court only amplify concepts, such as "syncretism," which Melville Herskovits defines as outwardly worshipping the masters' religion yet inwardly revering African gods.[73] Andrew Apter elaborates how the "re-fabrication" of African American culture transpired in ways in which the enslaved bridged African ethnic differences in "underlying values and cognitive orientations," while Christian domination twisted realities of "resistance, accommodation, and co-determination."[74] Many elements of Camejo and Prieto's beliefs and practices are recognizable in today's standards, yet some of their beliefs are not identifiable at all because the timeless process conveyed in creolization theory is, as John Thornton describes it, "as unbounded, non-dogmatic, and continuously revealed."[75] In my opinion, behind the walls of *Ṣàngó tẹ̀ dún*, Catholicism, *òrìṣà*, military culture, *nkisi*, and countless other traditions "transculturated," to borrow Ortiz's term, in its own unique way. Camejo and Prieto only illustrates the complicated intricacies of the entire process.

CHAPTER SIX

New Lucumí from Ọ̀yọ́

At the beginning of the nineteenth century, the Lucumí community in Havana mostly included a small, tightknit group revolving around free militiamen, their spouses, and a network of friends. Leading up to Prieto's arrest, however, that social dynamic changed drastically. Once Cuba's agricultural revolution hit full stride, the island's population exploded from about 270,000 inhabitants in the 1780s to over 700,000 people by the 1820s.[1] In the years Camejo and Prieto were *cabildo* leaders between 1818 and 1835, more than 300,000 enslaved Africans arrived at the island, which was twice as many more people than the previous thirty years. Throughout Prieto's military career, migrations from the Bight of Benin to Cuba had been relatively small, numbering about nine thousand individuals. During Ọ̀yọ́'s collapse between 1817 and 1836, however, an estimated 47,000 people landed on the island.[2] While most of the enslaved went to plantations, Havana's population grew, especially following the Anglo-Spanish antislave trade treaty of 1817, which resulted in the liberation of hundreds of men, women, and children who suddenly inhabited the city as a new class of individual called Liberated Africans (*emancipados*). Camejo and Prieto emerged as leaders during these overlapping yet coincidental circumstances, which resulted in a major demographic shift to the Yorùbá-speaking community in and around Havana, as well as transformations to what it meant to be "Lucumí."

The decline of Ọ̀yọ́ in West Africa began in 1817 when Àfọ̀njá, the commander-in-chief of the kingdom's provincial military at Ìlọrin, had ambitions of taking the throne from Májútú, who from 1802 to 1831 reigned in Ọ̀yọ́ as the "owner of the palace" (*aláàfin*). According to Paul Lovejoy, Àfọ̀njá's attempt to achieve autonomy "unintentionally released the forces of *jihād*."[3] In Hausa territory, 'Uthmān dan Fodio, a Fulbe teacher and writer living in Gobir, overthrew the established governments and aristocracies of the Hausa states with his brother and son, 'Abdullahi dan Fodio and Muḥammad Bello, respectively. Between 1804 and 1808, these educated, militant Muslims established the Sokoto Caliphate and then raised an army to invade the Borno kingdom near Lake Chad from 1808 until 1810 and followed by Nupé in 1811. At the same time Prieto was suppressing the Aponte Rebellion in

1812, Bello wrote his seminal study calling for *jihād* because Ọ̀yọ́ traders enslaved and sold Hausa people "from our country . . . to Christians"—that is, Europeans at the coast.[4] Many Muslims living in Ọ̀yọ́—such as pastoral Fulbe, Hausa, Nupé slaves, and Yorùbá-speaking Muslims—joined Àfọ̀njá's coup d'état because of promises of freedom and independence. However, Àfọ̀njá, who was not Muslim, miscalculated his allies and his ambitions faded as "power increasingly shift[ed] to the proponents of *jihād.*"[5]

Ọ̀yọ́'s constitutional crisis, independence movements, and spread of *jihād* resulted in uncontrollable slave raiding throughout the savannah of the Bight of Benin hinterland.[6] When ʿUthmān dan Fodio died in 1817, Bello became the sultan of Sokoto, and he named his uncle emir of Gwandu, a title that carried the responsibility for waging *jihād* into Ọ̀yọ́. Alimi Ṣāliḥ, a Muslim scholar who had been preaching in Ọ̀yọ́ since 1813, inspired bands of Fulbe and Hausa, many of whom were Ọ̀yọ́ slaves, to respond to the call to *jihād.* According to Robin Law, this Muslim uprising occurred in Ọ̀yọ́'s eastern provinces at first but soon spread west across the entire kingdom.[7] Afterward, many Yorùbá speakers loyal to Ọ̀yọ́ went to the coast, where hundreds of people boarded Spanish slave ships destined for Cuba on an annual basis. Once the survivors reached the island, authorities and slave owners classified these people as "Lucumí" because they came from the Bight of Benin hinterland and understood the Yorùbá language.

Through simple conversation, news traveled across the Atlantic, meaning Camejo and Prieto heard countless stories about the politics and wars in the midst of Ọ̀yọ́'s disintegration. Enslaved Africans arriving in Cuba remembered the conditions of their enslavement years later. For example, Lorenzo Clarke, whose Yorùbá name was documented as "Ocusona" (Òkúsọnọ̀), described how he had been enslaved "during a war between the native chiefs [when he] was brought from Lagos in the brig *Negrito.*" In December 1832, this ship arrived in Havana with over four hundred Lucumí Elló (Ọ̀yọ́) on board. British abolitionists in England recorded Clarke's story on his return trip to Lagos from Havana in the 1850s. While living in Cuba, he claimed to have heard about the family that he left behind in Africa "through some new slaves."[8] Likewise, Doloré Réal, who was also "a native of Lagos of the Lucomi tribe," was on her way back to Africa from Cuba with Lorenzo Clarke: "[She knows that] she shall find her mother and her three brothers when she gets back [because she too] heard of them . . . through some *Bozals,* newly-imported from Lagos."[9] Scholars have long recognized the influence of returnees from Brazil, Cuba, and Sierra Leone on the development of a global, pan-Yorùbá identity. Upon returning to the Bight of

Benin, they told stories about people who continued to worship òrìṣà in Havana, including people such as Camejo and Prieto.[10]

Of the tens of thousands of enslaved Africans arriving in Cuba, the vast majority never returned to Africa and only a few had their stories documented. For example, Carl Ritter, a Prussian diplomat and abolitionist, interviewed former slaves in Cuba in the 1850s. Triumfo Souchay, aka "Diola" (Adéọlá), explained to Ritter: "My tribe was captured in a war with Afhanga [Àfọnjá] . . . I might have been about 15 years old—[I] was sold as a slave to the West Indies. This is common there. Also, in my Lucumi tribe, the prisoners of war were either bought or killed. . . . My tribe has only one god, whom we call "Allong" [Allāh?]. . . . The sun and moon are not prayed to. Every year the tribe has a two or three-month long worship service, in which one abstains from all meals in the daytime [Ramaḍān?]."[11] Souchay was likely born in Ọ̀yọ́ around 1802, spoke Yorùbá, was raised Muslim, and enslaved during the *jihād* around 1817.[12] According to J. D. Y. Peel, the Islam practiced among Yorùbá speakers was "reconciled to social practices of an un-Islamic character." Due to cultural "mixing" within West Africa, òrìṣà worship involved the "inculturation [of Islam] into local systems of meaning."[13]

In Cuba, Yorùbá speakers of diverse backgrounds discussed the trauma of enslavement during the British abolition movement. After the passing of the act to abolish the Atlantic trade in 1807, the British Royal Navy instigated blockades off the coast of the Bight of Benin, most especially around Ouidah. Samuel Àjàyí Crowther described the destruction of his hometown, Òṣogùn, in 1821 and how he boarded a Portuguese ship, which the British navy captured during their suppression efforts. He was subsequently taken to Freetown, Sierra Leone, instead of Brazil. As an adult, he remembered his childhood and how for "some years, war had been carried on in Eyo Country [Ọ̀yọ́], which was always attended with much devastation and bloodshed." The army that had enslaved him was as large as twenty thousand soldiers and was "composed of Foulahs [Fulbe], Yorriba Mahommedans [Yorùbá-speaking Muslims] and slaves of every description."[14] Even though Camejo and Prieto never met Crowther, they listened to similar stories about *jihād*, slave routes, and a place called Freetown. Crowther, for example, headed north in the Bight of Benin hinterland before heading south, when he was sold and resold several times before being bought by Portuguese merchants at Lagos but then recaptured by the British and taken to Sierra Leone.

The British blockades disrupted the slave trade off Ouidah, and as a result, European trade shifted east toward Lagos. This commercial transition, in conjunction with inland warfare, meant Ọyọ́ steadily lost control of access to the coast. As Prieto had experienced in the 1780s, Ọyọ́ traders had historically funneled people out of Porto Novo through the Ẹgbádo corridor. By 1812, however, Ọyọ́ traders began taking people to the market town of Apòmù in Ifẹ territory, which was to the south of Ìlọrin. As Ọyọ́ disintegrated into civil war in response to *jihād*, a series of other wars among rival Yorùbá-speaking kingdoms erupted over control of the trade route between Apòmù and Lagos. Between 1818 and 1822, Ifẹ, Ìjẹbú, and Ìjẹ̀sà formed a coalition and waged a protracted and successful war against Ọyọ́'s main ally in the south, the kingdom of Òwu.[15]

Once the cleric Alimi Ṣāliḥ died in 1823, his son 'Abd al-Salām executed Àfọnjá and declared Ìlọrin an emirate within the Sokoto Caliphate. Thereafter, Ìlọrin, with support from Gwandu, steadily pursued the destruction of Ọyọ́.[16] In addition to *jihād* emanating from the north, more external pressures threatened the kingdom from the west. Since the eighteenth century, Dahomey had been paying tribute to Ọyọ́, but when Gezo ascended the Dahomey throne in 1818, he aimed for sovereignty, and to revive the slave trade at Ouidah despite British blockades. By 1823, Gezo officially asserted Dahomey independence by refusing to pay tributes to Ọyọ́ and by decisively attacking the sections of Mahi territory that had long been under Ọyọ́ control.[17] Through the 1820s and 1830s, Dahomey aggressively pushed into the Ọyọ́ regions of Ẹgbádo, Àwórí, and Ànàgó.[18] According to Hugh Clapperton in 1826, the attacks against Ọyọ́ took place on all fronts, and "many of its citizens were being enslaved and ending up as victims of the trade."[19]

The region destabilized further, and more warfare ensued following the declaration of Ìlọrin as an emirate, Dahomey independence, the Òwu wars, and British blockades. Clapperton, who traveled from Badagry to the Ọyọ́ capital, made observations of an Ìjẹbú-Ifẹ alliance systematically capturing many Ẹgbá towns.[20] He noted in his journal how war "is only now a few hours from us [and is] not a national war but a slaving one."[21] Joseph Wright, who was Ẹgbá and liberated at Freetown, explained:

> The enemies satisfied themselves with little children, little girls, young
> men and young women; they did not care about the aged and old
> people. They killed them without mercy. . . . Abundant heaps of
> bodies were in streets, and there were none to bury them . . . We
> came to the market. Many hundreds of slaves, we were put in rows, so
> that we all could be seen at one view by the buyers; and in about five

hours another trade man came and bought me. He put me in a canoe at once and we sailed all that night. Next morning, we came to another slave market by [the] name [of] Krodoo [Ikorudu on the northern shore of the Lagos Lagoon], and there we remained the whole day, for the man wanted to buy more slaves. At the time of evening, the canoe was loaded with slaves and we sailed for his home directly. We arrived about twelve o'clock in the night. The town where we had just arrived, by [the] name of Ikko [Èkó, i.e., Lagos].[22]

Although Camejo and Prieto did not meet Wright either, they were *cabildo* leaders during the Ẹ̀gbá crisis and heard similar accounts about how Yorùbá speakers were killing and enslaving one another. To Wright, this civil war was irrational: "We are all one nation speaking one language."[23] Under the Lucumí construct in Cuba, Camejo and Prieto reinforced solidarity among Yorùbá-speaking people in their mutual-aid society dedicated to Santa Bárbara.

By the early 1830s, the *cabildo* "queen" and "king" must have heard countless reports about the transforming politics and geography of the Bight of Benin hinterland. Even if Camejo never went to West Africa, she still knew more about the situation than colonial authorities and slave owners in Cuba. She had heard how tens of thousands of refugees displaced during the wars resettled in new urban centers. For example, Ẹ̀gbá, Òwu, and Ọ̀yọ́, as well as Ifẹ̀ and Ìjẹ̀bú, converged and founded Ìbàdàn by 1829. At first, Ifẹ̀ armies were the most dominant group there, but as many more Ọ̀yọ́ and Òwu refugees arrived, they eventually expelled the Ifẹ̀ chiefs. Thereafter, Ìbàdàn transformed into a predominately Ọ̀yọ́ town and consolidated into a powerful state concentrated on counterattacking Ìlọrin. Regardless, Ìbàdàn did not oppose Ifẹ̀ and Ìjẹ̀bú raiding Ẹ̀gbá territory and even traded with its rivals in exchange for European merchandise.[24] Most Ẹ̀gbá refugees, some of whom first tried to settle at Ìbàdàn, became embroiled in conflict, and under the leadership of Ṣódẹkẹ́, they withdrew along with some Òwu toward the west. By 1830, they had settled at Abẹ́òkúta, which grew into a major urban center and powerful state.[25]

Leading up to the fall of Májútú in 1831, Ọ̀yọ́ suzerainty was weakened beyond repair. The kingdom's civilians abandoned the northern savannah towns. Májútú's successor, Àmòdó, who ruled Ọ̀yọ́ from 1831 to 1833, attempted to resist Ìlọrin, which destroyed or subjugated many towns, including the Ọ̀yọ́ capital. A year after Prieto's arrest in 1835, Àmòdó's successor, who was in power from 1833 to 1836, also failed to reassert Ọ̀yọ́'s

TABLE 6.1 Estimated arrivals of slaves to Cuba from ports in the Bight of Benin by five-year periods, 1816–1835

Date	Little Popo	Ouidah	Porto Novo	Badagry	Lagos	Other Ports	Totals	Percent
1816–1820	200	2,200	600	1,000	3,900	200	8,100	17.2
1821–1825	300	3,500	1,200	700	6,800	300	12,800	27.2
1826–1830	800	2,100	500	0	4,600	200	8,200	17.4
1831–1835	400	3,900	700	600	12,100	300	18,000	38.2
Totals	1,700	11,700	3,000	2,300	27,400	1,000	47,100	
Percent	3.6	24.8	6.4	4.9	58.2	2.1		

Source: Percentages for port-by-port departures obtained from Eltis, "Diaspora of Yorùbá Speakers," 24 (Table 2.3). Percentages applied to estimates for the Bight of Benin migration to Cuba from Voyages (estimates: 1816–35, Bight of Benin to Cuba).

autonomy, which ultimately, Robin Law concludes, "led to the final destruction of the Ọ̀yọ́ kingdom and the abandonment of the capital."[26] This political void contributed to the displacement and enslavement of many more people, most of whom went to Ìbàdàn, Abẹ́òkúta, Cuba, Brazil, Sierra Leone, and other places. To illustrate the scale of resettlement, an estimated 123,000 people boarded slave ships at the ports of the Bight of Benin between 1817 and 1835.[27] This estimate, however, does not take into consideration the tens of thousands of other people who died, entered Africa's internal slave trade toward Sokoto, or migrated elsewhere inland.

Between 1818 and 1835, Camejo and Prieto were on the front lines of a major refugee crisis flowing into Cuba. The impact of the so-called Yorùbá diaspora meant that the Lucumí community underwent demographic transformations during the years of Camejo and Prieto's leadership. According to estimates, 47,000 individuals were involved in the branch of the transatlantic slave trade from the Bight of Benin to Cuba, where just over three thousand people arrived on average per year. The largest peaks, however, involved over seven thousand people in both 1825 and 1834, which aligned with the start of the Ẹgbá crisis and the destruction of Ọ̀yọ́'s northern towns.[28] Over 60 percent of this migration originated at Lagos, about one-quarter from Ouidah, and another 11 percent from Porto Novo, Epe, Apa, and Badagry combined.[29] Little Popo accounted for less than 5 percent of this population movement, while other embarkations occurred as far west as Keta and into the Niger Delta (table 6.1).

One major contingent of new Lucumí who remained in Havana were people liberated in Britain's suppression efforts in the Caribbean. Reclassified and labeled *emancipados*, Liberated Africans rescued from slave ships were technically "free," but then they were forced to serve lengthy apprenticeships under the authority of the colonial government. As godfather of two *emancipados*, Prieto clearly contemplated British abolitionism and the Anglo-Spanish antislave trade treaty of 1817.[30] After Great Britain paid £400,000 sterling "for Spanish assent to abolition," Spain agreed to this bilateral treaty and gradually allowed the foundation of the Havana Slave Trade Commission, which tried its first case in 1824.[31] With this bribe, Spain bought Russian warships to fight in the Spanish American Wars of Independence. By 1835, the Anglo-Spanish mixed commission had condemned thirty-four slave ships under international law and liberated over eight thousand people arriving from ports between the Upper Guinea Coast and West Central Africa—a pale comparison to the hundreds of thousands of people "illegally" arriving at the island and heading to the plantations.[32]

The Havana Slave Trade Commission produced detailed records related to the people involved and enslaved during Ọ̀yọ́'s collapse. According to procedure, court officials recorded the biographical information of Liberated Africans into large bound registers in order to keep track of their impending apprenticeships. The information in these detailed records included African names, assigned Christian names, age, sex, height, colonial perceptions of African nations, and a brief physical description for each individual. In Cuba, a Liberated African could be identified from his tin-tag necklace "tied about the neck . . . with his number engrave[d] on it."[33] Lucumí, however, amounted to over 2,500 of the eight thousand registered individuals before 1835. They mostly boarded ships at Little Popo, Ouidah, and Lagos, but also from River Brass, Elem Kalabari, and Bonny in the Bight of Biafra.[34] The largest cohort of Lucumí *emancipados* arrived between 1832 and 1835, which corresponds to a cholera epidemic that decimated Havana's population and likely took the life of María Francisca Camejo in 1833.[35] Since Cuban authorities had little interest in caring for *emancipados* in a slave society, Anglo-Spanish negotiations turned to the "removal" of Liberated Africans from Cuba to British colonies in the Caribbean. Between 1833 and 1835, nearly 1,200 *emancipados* resettled in Trinidad, many of whom were "Lucumí."[36] Policy stipulated that the number of males had to equal the number of females, meaning Lucumí *emancipados* who remained in the Spanish colony were by and large mostly male. These new Lucumí

TABLE 6.2 Registered Lucumí *emancipados* aboard condemned slave ships of the Havana Slave Trade Commission arriving from the Bight of Benin and Bight of Biafra, 1824–1835

TSTD ID	Ship Name	Port of Embarkation	Date of Capture	Date of Sentence	Date of Register	Lucumí on Ship	Ship Total	Percent of Lucumí on Ship
2374	Mágico	Little Popo	1826/01/22	1826/01/31	N/A	160	175	91.4
557	Orestes	Ouidah	1826/02/28	1826/03/05	N/A	207	212	97.6
756	Firme	Little Popo	1828/11/12	1828/12/12	1828/12/23	73	483	15.1
776	Voladora	Little Popo	1829/06/05	1829/06/30	1829/07/01	56	330	17.0
960	Santiago	River Brass	1830/04/09	1830/05/21	1830/05/28	16	100	16.0
963	Emilio	Elem Kalabari	1830/06/11	1830/06/28	1830/07/07	39	187	20.9
1250	Indagadora	Lagos	1832/06/25	1832/07/09	1832/07/16	134	134	100.0
1266	Negrito	Ouidah	1832/11/21	1832/12/20	1833/01/05	433	477	90.8
1295	Joaquina	Bonny	1833/11/10	1833/11/21	1833/12/03	13	318	4.1
1298	Manuelita	Lagos	1833/12/07	1833/12/17	1833/12/31	470	477	98.5
1307	Rosa	Ouidah	1833/12/25	1834/02/15	1834/02/17	281	289	97.2
1355	María	Bonny	1835/01/14	1835/01/26	1835/02/01	34	340	10.0
1361	Julita	Ouidah	1835/01/22	1835/02/21	1835/02/23	258	336	76.8
1383	Tita	Ouidah	1835/06/29	1835/07/14	1835/07/23	332	392	84.7
					Total	2,506	4,250	59.0

Source: NA, FO 313/56–62; "Registers of Liberated Africans: Implementation"; and H. Lovejoy, "Registers of Liberated Africans: Transcription."

TABLE 6.3 Distribution of *emancipados* who remained in Cuba by *nación* and gender, 1832–1835

Nación	Male	Female	Total	Percent
Lucumí	1,099	140	1,239	34.6
Congo	919	257	1,176	32.8
Carabali	582	100	682	19.0
Mandinga	134	80	214	5.9
Gangá	114	65	179	4.9
Arará	87	10	97	2.8
Mina	6	0	6	<0.1
Total	2,941	652	3,593	
Percent	81.9	18.1		

Source: NA, FO 313/56–62; "Registers of Liberated Africans: Implementation"; and H. Lovejoy, "Registers of Liberated Africans: Transcription."

men suddenly became a new majority within Havana's established Lucumí community (tables 6.2 and 6.3).

The registers of Liberated Africans provide a rare glimpse into the ethnolinguistic configuration of new Lucumí arriving in Havana through the 1820s and early 1830s. These records contain twenty-six different Lucumí subclassifications, most of which have been interpreted and plotted on a map in the first chapter (map 1.1). Many of these ethnonyms refer to Yorùbá-speaking kingdoms, confederations, cities, towns, and villages. Others, of course, refer to non-Yorùbá-speaking peoples in the region, such as Nupé, Hausa, Borgu, and Dahomey. Using methods created by Ugo Nwokeji and David Eltis, transliterations of documented African names can in some cases "provide a solid basis for identifying ethnicity."[37] An analysis of the Lucumí subclassifications associated with Yorùbá-speaking kingdoms and places indicates that over 75 percent had Yorùbá names, compared to less than 25 percent from other non-Yorùbá-speaking ethnonyms. This analysis confirms how the largest concentrations of Yorùbá speakers left Ouidah and Lagos, while non-Yorùbá-speaking groups generally departed to the east and west of those two ports.[38] Between 1816 and 1835, over 35,000 Yorùbá speakers arrived in Cuba, suggesting they could not amount to much more than 5 percent of the island's total population.[39] Although it is difficult to ascertain, the population of Yorùbá speakers in Havana must have been upwards of a couple thousand people through the 1820s and 1830s, which was

TABLE 6.4 Distribution, interpretation, and ports of embarkation for the Lucumí subclassifications of Liberated Africans associated with Yorùbá-speaking kingdoms and towns, 1826–1835

Lucumí Subgroups	Interpretations	Ports (Individuals)	Individuals
Elló (Eyó, Ayó, or Ayló)	Òyó	Ouidah (1,035), Lagos (106), Little Popo (93)	1,234
Ecumachó	Ẹkùmòṣọ, Ogbómòṣó	Lagos	470
Llabú (Yavú)	Ìjẹbú	Ouidah (40), Lagos (28)	68
Otá	Òtà	Ouidah	61
Evá (Ebá)	Ègbá	Ouidah (57), Elem Kalabari (2), Little Popo (1)	60
Layí (Llallí)	Ìjàyè	Ouidah	2
Dasá	Ìdáṣà	Ouidah	1
Efú	Efue	Ouidah	1
Llané	Ìjànnà	Ouidah	1
Pové	Pobé	Ouidah	1
Sabé	Ṣábẹ	Ouidah	1
		Total	1,902

Source: NA, FO 313/56–62; "Registers of Liberated Africans: Implementation"; and H. Lovejoy, "Registers of Liberated Africans: Transcription." Interpretations of Lucumí subgroups discussed in person, or via email and phone, with Andrew Apter, Robin Law, Paul Lovejoy, and Olatunji Ojo, 2008–17.

clearly a noticeable jump in population that Prieto had first encountered in the late eighteenth century (tables 6.4–6.8).[40]

Liberated Lucumí from Òyó were a conspicuous group. Upon arrival, they could not speak Spanish initially, and many adults had elaborate body markings, scarifications, and brandings. Emeterio Lucumí Ayló (Òyó), aka "Muro" (Morọ), had two scars "like palm trees from the nose to each cheek"; and Justo Lucumí Ayló (Òyó), aka "Dugu" (Ìdógu), had "three lines of his nation on the forehead."[41] Also, slave traders in West Africa branded people.[42] Many people on board the *Negrito*, including Lorenzo Clarke, aka Òkúsọnò, had a "P.V. on the right nipple," while others had a "burned mark O."[43] As soon as scholars create a comprehensive digital catalogue of ethnic scars and brandings, new perspectives about ethnicity, identity, and ownership in West Africa and Cuba will undoubtedly emerge. These identi-

TABLE 6.5 Distribution of the interpretation of African names for Lucumí subclassifications of Liberated Africans associated with Yorùbá-speaking kingdoms and towns, 1826–1835

Ethnolinguistic Group	Individuals	Percent
Yorùbá	1,422	74.8
Multiethnic	169	8.8
Not yet identified	144	7.6
Other	127	6.7
Muslim	40	2.1
Total	1,902	

Source: NA, FO 313/56–62; "Registers of Liberated Africans: Implementation"; H. Lovejoy, "Registers of Liberated Africans: Transcription"; and H. Lovejoy, "Old Oyo Influences," chap. 2. Interpretations of documented names conducted independently with Olatunji Ojo, 8 April–24 October 2011; Abubakar Babajo Sani, 10 July–10 October 2011; Umar Hussein, 10 September–20 September 2011. "Multiethnic" refers to common Yorùbá names also used in other non-Yorùbá-speaking groups. "Other" refers to names in Fon, Ewe, Twi, Edo, Igbo, Isoko, Warri, Igala, Jukun, Tiv, among other languages and dialects. "Muslim" includes names, such as Muḥammad.

fying marks could then lead to a better understanding about who these people were and where they came from inland.[44]

Ecclesiastical sources provide insight into family dynamics within the Lucumí community. Between 1808 and 1835, hundreds of Lucumí participated in Catholic rituals at Havana's churches in some capacity.[45] The information from baptism, death, and marriage records demonstrates the complexity of the spiritual family and biological relationships that took place in the New World. Forced to live in a foreign and oppressive environment, people of African descent formed new bonds and partnerships.[46] Ecclesiastical sources demonstrate the complexity of creolization through biological reproduction. Lucumí, Mandinga, Gangá, Mina, Arará, Carabalí, and Congo—as well as negros, blancos, pardos, criollos, and peninsulares—all had children with one another. For example, Camejo was born in Cuba, but as a Lucumí cabildo "queen," she clearly identified as both Lucumí and Creole. Likewise, José Isidro Congo and Maria de la Merced Torre Lucumí had a son together.[47] This family dynamic raises the question of whether this child was raised Lucumí, Congo, or Creole. In another example, María de las Nieves Lucumí had five children between 1821 and 1828. The father was listed as "unknown," but throughout this entire time her owner was Don Marcos Vidal, a native of Havana, who was legally married to Benigna López.[48] What was the

TABLE 6.6 Distribution, interpretation, and ports of embarkation for Lucumí subclassifications of Liberated Africans associated with non-Yorùbá-speaking kingdoms and towns, 1826–1835

Lucumí Subgroup	Interpretation	Ports (Individuals)	Individuals
Tapá	Nupé	Bonny (36), Ouidah (15), River Brass (13), Little Popo (12), Elem Kalabari (9)	85
Arará	Dahomey?	Little Popo	67
Chambá (Chamvá)	Tchámbà	Little Popo (61), Ouidah (1)	62
Agusá (Jausá)	Hausa	Little Popo (29), Elem Kalabari (3), River Brass (3), Ouidah (1)	36
Cacanda	Kàkàndá	Elem Kalabari (20), Bonny	21
Basa	Bassa	Bonny	9
Mosi	Mosi	Little Popo	3
Dagñame	Dahomey	Ouidah	2
Ecuá	Takwa?	Ouidah	2
Igara	Igala	Elem Kalabari	2
Bogú	Borgu	Ouidah	1
Egruá	Igala?	Elem Kalabari	1
Ellico	Isoko	Bonny	1
Guarí	Gwari	Elem Kalabari	1
Opu	Opu	Elem Kalabari	1
		Total	294

Source: NA, FO 313/56–62; "Registers of Liberated Africans: Implementation"; and H. Lovejoy, "Registers of Liberated Africans: Transcription." Interpretations of Lucumí subgroups discussed in person, or via email and phone, with Andrew Apter, Robin Law, Paul Lovejoy, and Olatunji Ojo, 2008–17.

race and ethnicity of these "fatherless" children? The answer is not so simple, because people in Cuba had a higher social status based on the color of their skin and might not have wanted to accept parenthood of their mixed-race children, which could occur though involuntary, adulterous relationships.

In West Africa and Cuba, slavery was widespread and common. The free population of African descent, especially militiamen, could own property, including slaves. People with enough capital were economically independent, and some bought, sold, and owned people from Africa. For example, Juan Francisco Lucumí, likely a Yorùbá speaker from Ọ̀yọ́, owned Feliciano Arará, who was possibly a Fon speaker from Dahomey.[49] Perhaps old ani-

TABLE 6.7 Distribution of the interpretation of African names for Lucumí subclassifications of Liberated Africans associated with non-Yorùbá-speaking kingdoms and towns, 1826–1835

Ethnolinguistic Group	Individuals	Percent
Yorùbá	60	20.6
Multiethnic	54	18.5
Not yet identified	96	32.8
Other	54	17.8
Muslim	30	10.3
Total	294	

Source: NA, FO 313/56–62; "Registers of Liberated Africans: Implementation"; H. Lovejoy, "Registers of Liberated Africans: Transcription"; and H. Lovejoy, "Old Oyo Influences," chap. 2. Interpretations of documented names conducted independently with Olatunji Ojo, 8 April–24 October 2011; Abubakar Babajo Sani 10 July–10 October 2011; Umar Hussein, 10 September–20 September 2011. "Multiethnic" refers to common Yorùbá names also used in other non-Yorùbá-speaking groups. "Other" refers to names in Fon, Ewe, Twi, Edo, Igbo, Isoko, Warri, Igala, Jukun, Tiv, among other languages and dialects. "Muslim" includes names, such as Muḥammad.

mosities between rival slave-trading states carried over from Africa in Cuba. Lucumí were enslaved not only by white, colonial elites and Creoles, but also by other people from Africa and their descendants in the Atlantic world. Camejo and Prieto likely did not own any slaves, although they could have because they had wealth. As public figures with a broad network of friends, they clearly associated with people who practiced slavery. Whether or not they were outspoken against the institution is a matter of interpretation. Given their status as *cabildo* leaders, they most likely opposed slavery, but they lived in a society where they could not easily question the *status quo*. Among themselves and their most trustworthy friends, however, Camejo and Prieto likely gossiped about Cuban slave society, probably criticized ironies in the social hierarchies, and perhaps contemplated ideologies of abolition, independence, and citizenship.

Participation in *cabildo* life in Havana was not necessarily reserved for Lucumí, but was restricted to the people admitted as members. Discrimination did not occur based on race or gender. In 1835, Prieto stated how "*blancos, mulatos* and *negros* of all sexes gather[ed] at his house."[50] Camejo and Prieto likely welcomed people they could trust, which would have required different levels of initiations into their spiritual family, whether Catholic, through

TABLE 6.8 Approximate distribution of estimated arrivals in Cuba from the Bight of Benin by ethnolinguistic group (in five-year periods), 1816–1835

Ethnolinguistic Group	1816–1820	1821–1825	1826–1830	1831–1835	Total	Percent
Yorùbá	6,100	9,500	6,300	13,500	35,400	75
Fon	500	700	500	1,100	2,800	6
Ewe	400	600	400	900	2,300	5
Mahi	300	500	300	700	1,800	4
Nupe	200	400	200	500	1,300	3
Asante-Fante-Akan	200	400	200	500	1,300	3
Gurma	200	300	100	400	1,000	2
Hausa	100	200	100	200	600	1
Other	100	200	100	200	600	1
Total	8,100	12,000	8,200	18,000	47,100	

Source: Applied ratios of the results of interpreted documented African names for people leaving the Bight of Benin as they relate to estimates of the total Bight of Benin migration to Cuba. Voyages (estimates: 1816–35, Bight of Benin to Cuba); and H. Lovejoy, "Old Oyo Influences," chap. 2.

òrìṣà worship, or otherwise. Secrecy prevailed above all else, and Prieto protected the identities of his associates, members, followers, and clients. He testified that he "could neither say the first nor last name of those who requested his council."[51]

In an authoritarian political system, Camejo and Prieto had to be selective about who they admitted into the *cabildo*. Fugitive slaves hid in and around Havana. Newspapers constantly warned the public about urban runaway slaves. For example, "a negro Lucumí . . . went astray in the vicinity of Jesús, María [y José]."[52] Camejo and Prieto probably denied access to people they might have considered dangerous or put their security in peril. As a military family, Camejo and Prieto understood the consequences of aiding and abetting runaway slaves or allowing a slave to participate in *cabildo* activities without explicit permission from the owner. Without membership rosters, it is impossible to know who went inside Camejo and Prieto's *cabildo*. Nevertheless, the public Santa Bárbara festivals attracted considerable interest from many curious onlookers, whether Lucumí or not, free or enslaved. Recruitment could have occurred anywhere at any time, and membership dues were an integral revenue stream.

During the years of Camejo and Prieto's leadership in the first third of the nineteenth century, the social dynamics of the Lucumí community in Havana transformed substantially due the influx of Yorùbá speakers to the island. According to one interpretation of *Ṣàngó tẹ̀ dún*, this god "arrived and planted," which perhaps refers to the Ọ̀yọ́ diaspora to Cuba.[53] It was during this period that major transformations in "Lucumí" identity occurred because people involved in Ọ̀yọ́'s collapse brought their culture across the Atlantic, whereby it fused into the socioreligious paradigms observed in Camejo and Prieto's Lucumí *cabildo*. For people from West Africa, the representation of Ṣàngó as Santa Bárbara could have confused some, or even seemed profane to others but regardless of what people thought about it then, it has continued to persist for over two hundred years.

CHAPTER SEVEN

Lucumí War

What impact did the major demographic transformation of Ọ̀yọ́'s collapse have on Prieto and his leadership of a *cabildo* in Havana? Most Yorùbá speakers who arrived in Cuba in the 1820s and 1830s had been involved in *jihād* and other warfare, and less than 30 percent of all new arrivals were female.[1] Among the estimated 35,000 Yorùbá speakers who reached Cuba during the years of Camejo and Prieto's leadership, upwards of 25,000 were men or boys. Among the people who boarded slave ships for Cuba, a major contingent had military training and worshipped the principal deity of Ọ̀yọ́. Sàngó's iconography—that is, red and white, thunder axes, or *bàtá* drums— became obvious symbols to target for enslavement in the Bight of Benin hinterland. From the perspective of Ọ̀yọ́'s rivals in West Africa, whether Muslim or not, the political restructuring was an opportunity to expel a dominant culture from the region. Upon reaching Cuba, Ọ̀yọ́ warriors and Sàngó devotees mostly went inland to the sugar, coffee, and tobacco plantations, where some then reorganized and participated in warfare. Colonial authorities, who lived in fear of independence and abolition, deliberated, discussed, and documented resistance to slavery especially after the Haitian Revolution and Aponte Rebellion.

Camejo and Prieto, who had heard about the ethnic cleansing taking place in the kingdom of Ọ̀yọ́ and its environs, likely anticipated Lucumí slave uprisings in rural Cuba. Havana was not an isolated port city. It not only served as a major hub to Atlantic networks, but also to the hundreds of plantations and hundreds of thousands of enslaved Africans inland. As scholars of slave resistance in Cuba have shown, the free and enslaved people who resided in the capital routinely went to the countryside to work, and rural slaves visited Havana on a regular basis.[2] Just as people brought news from Africa on slave ships, the slaves who delivered commodities to Havana carried news with them from the plantations across the island. Camejo and Prieto's home on Gloría Street was a beacon for *òrìṣà* worshipers and a pivotal location to learn about family and friends resettling across the Atlantic. For enslaved Yorùbá speakers, this Lucumí *cabildo* was a center of ethnic solidarity, and people knew it, including the white, slave-owning classes.

The political instability arising from the Spanish American Wars of Independence and British abolitionism provided a backdrop that threatened the success of any *cabildo*. As mainland colonies from Argentina to Mexico separated from the Spanish monarchy, by the early 1820s, Cuba, Puerto Rico, and the Philippines remained Spain's only colonial possessions. At the time Camejo and Prieto solidified their leadership in Havana, the island's inhabitants divided in support of and against colonial rule. When King Ferdinand VII abolished the 1812 constitution on 7 March 1823, he made his intentions clear to keep Cuba a part of Spain. To enforce compliance, the king appointed Francisco Dionisio Vives as captain general in May. Vives was a loyal subject who had fought gallantly against Napoleon in Europe. He favored foreign trade and the expansion of the plantation economy, while strongly opposing independence and abolition.

In one of the first orders of business, Vives investigated an independence conspiracy, called the *soles y rayos de Bolívar*, which had taken root in Cuba after 1822, if not earlier. Financed by independence advocates on the Spanish mainland, the leaders of Masonic lodges across the island held secret meetings to start a revolution with the support of African slaves in order to create the independent "Republic of Cubanacán."[3] As officials began rounding up suspects in 1823, many proindependence advocates fled the island to avoid persecution. News within Cuba traveled fast, and by August 1824, Lieutenant Gaspar Rodríguez instigated a military uprising in Matanzas. Manuel Barcia argues that this open dissent revealed "that the ever-loyal army was not free from turmoil and division," and "ideas of independence had not vanished from the island."[4]

As the government investigated more and more people, Vives mandated that Spain tighten control of the colony, and the king issued royal decrees granting the captain general unlimited dictatorial power. In 1825, Vives created the Military Commission, an autocratic court that held the authority to prosecute anyone without representation at any time.[5] Thereafter, Cuba's liberal, intellectual elite fled the island in distress. Camejo and Prieto did not have the resources to leave. As more and more enslaved Africans arrived, resistance to slavery increased. Under Vives's authority, the Military Commission actively strived to connect the pieces of a larger conspiracy. For example, a slave uprising involving over two hundred individuals occurred in Guamacaro, to the southeast of Matanzas, on 15 June 1825. In this case, diverse people from Africa united together to fight for their freedom. Barcia has shown that there was no conspiracy, and the Military Commission "failed to incriminate the free colored residents in the district, many of whom spent months in the provincial prison paying for crimes they likely did not commit."[6]

Throughout the period of his military dictatorship, Vives censored the press and forbade the possession of liberal literature, which circulated nonetheless. His dictatorship closely monitored commerce, travel, and even personal lives. As investigations into slave uprisings increased by the end of the 1820s, most judicial inquiries had much substance despite the belief that a revolution for Cuban independence was imminent.[7] Most slave owners, whether they supported Vives or not, continuously suspected the free black population because they embodied independence and abolitionism. In 1825, Manuel Ximenez Guarzo, a resident of Havana, expressed his anxieties: "If those who have redeemed themselves from slavery by their honor, or by their savings . . . are feared in the towns because of their excessive numbers compared to the whites, how much more are they to be feared if we add to them *negros bozales* who lack these qualities? And how much greater would be the danger if the incendiary spirit of independence is communicated to the slaves, making a common cause, following the example of those of Santo Domingo?"[8] The concern of slaves, *emancipados*, and free people fomenting revolution had more validity than Ximenez Guarzo may have realized because many men from the Bight of Benin hinterland had previous military training and combat experience. In 1830, Ferdinand VII, at the request of Vives, deployed thirty thousand troops from Spain to police the island, control the slave population, and fortify the coast from foreign invasion.[9]

Camejo and Prieto therefore operated a Lucumí *cabildo* in a precarious environment whereby any shift in perception would jeopardize their safety, security, and stability. They clearly understood that decades of loyal military service would not necessarily ensure protection, and they knew the implications when soliciting the replacement Santa Bárbara festival license from Vives in 1827. The captain general did everything under his authority to control the island, which suggests that the Lucumí *cabildo* thrived because Camejo and Prieto abided by colonial rules and regulations in the midst of the refugee crisis from Ọ̀yọ́. They never published or traveled. They paid their taxes to church and state. And when all else failed, they knew the right people who would turn a blind eye in exchange for a bribe. Camejo and Prieto understood the risks, and despite having no heirs or being recognized as Spanish citizens, they hired a lawyer to prepare their last will and testament. Their will demonstrates an elite status in the Lucumí community because they left money for three masses for each of their souls and proper burials in Havana's cemetery.[10]

After Vives stepped down, an aging Ferdinand VII appointed Mariano Ricafort as the next captain general on 12 May 1832. His tumultuous, two-year tenure included the death of Havana's longstanding archbishop, a cholera epidemic, and the emancipation of all slaves in the British Caribbean colonies.[11] As Ricafort responded to crisis after crisis, Cuba's more liberal thinkers, who had been in exile, began returning to the island, whereby they denounced government organizations in print despite the censorship. José Antonio Saco, one of Cuba's most prolific writers, became editor of a bi-monthly periodical initially commissioned by Vives to report on the island's economic activities, history, and literature. Saco openly criticized the Military Commission, which he noted consisted of only three people: "one notary who executes all of the preparatory acts of justice; one military lawyer who accuses, and just a judge who decides on the life and fortune of the citizens."[12] For Camejo and Prieto, this sudden transfer of both the church and state authority, in addition to more political opposition, created unprecedented uncertainty.

The sudden outbreak of cholera in late February 1833 decimated the island's population in a couple of months. A British official in the Havana Slave Trade Commission observed how the disease "raged with extraordinary malignity [so that] nearly half of the population fled from Havana."[13] Again, Camejo and Prieto had little options except to remain at their home. Saco and Ramon de la Sagra, who conducted independent population censuses in the 1820s, calculated how over eight thousand people died from cholera in Havana in the first three months of the epidemic. At least a thousand died in the impoverished neighborhood of Jesús, María y José because people shared contaminated water.[14] Meanwhile, white people sincerely believed people of African descent were spreading the disease and the prejudice pushed newfound levels of discrimination.[15] To assess the alleged African origins of cholera, Saco estimated deaths according to African *nación*, whereby several hundred Lucumí died in Havana alone.[16]

Before the outbreak, Camejo was "gravely ill," suggesting that she was prone to contract the disease, and by the time Prieto testified before the Military Commission in 1835, he was of "widowed status." As authorities dumped bodies in mass graves located on the city's periphery, Prieto probably did all he could to give his wife of "thirty-five or forty years" the proper burial outlined in their will.[17] He solicited support from his community, the church, the òrìṣà, and ancestral spirits (e.g., *egungun, nkisi*). After her death, Prieto owned images of Nuestra Señora del Carmen, who possibly equated with Naná Burukú, the mother of Babalú Ayé—guardian of the cemetery.[18]

Since authorities found human remains buried on the *cabildo* property in 1835, Prieto could have buried Camejo at their home.

Even with the belief that Africans were the carriers of cholera, massive inflows of enslaved Africans kept arriving at the island. For many slave owners, the health of slaves became a major concern because they wanted to protect their investments. By the summer of 1833, Don Francisco Santiago de Aguirre, a wealthy plantation owner and retired second lieutenant, had lost a number of slaves to the disease on one of his coffee plantations, called *San Salvador*, located about thirty kilometers west of Havana.[19] To replenish his workforce, Aguirre bought a ship full of healthy Lucumí a few miles from his plantation at a small, deep, and fortified inlet called the Boca de Banes (in reference to the mouth of the Banes River).[20] On 5 July 1833, the *Segunda Gallega* with 270 people on board arrived in Cuba from an unspecified port in the Bight of Benin.[21] At this time, ships avoided Havana not only because of the epidemic, but also due to increased British efforts to suppress the slave trade. The trends suggest that among the people on board this vessel, many likely were Ọ̀yọ́ males who had left Lagos and disembarked under the guard of ten soldiers stationed at the turret at the Boca de Banes.

Aguirre misjudged what it could mean to keep together a group that had been enslaved during Ọ̀yọ́'s collapse and then bonded together during the Middle Passage. The result of this miscalculation was precisely what Prieto and the established Lucumí community in Havana could have anticipated. By mid-August, this cohort overtook several plantations and captured the town of Banes in a matter of hours. But as quickly as it spread, the insurrection was suppressed. Afterward, the Military Commission traveled to Aguirre's plantation to investigate and conduct a trial. Court officials documented over three hundred people by *nación*, recorded testimonies with interpreters, listed Christian and African names, identified the leaders, exonerated dozens, tallied fifty-four dead, hunted for fugitives, and inflicted punishments.[22] Juan Iduate, who unraveled the hourly chronology of this slave revolt, explained that Lucumí overseers on the plantation had planned this rebellion but could not implement it until Aguirre had purchased a couple hundred Lucumí off of one slave ship.[23] While scholars have argued that slave revolts occurred in response to callous treatment, William Van Norman Jr. accurately contends that this incident involved "cultural calculations." These Lucumí viewed cholera as "proof of the malevolent power of their captors"; thus, they fought "against the evil that brought disease."[24] Additionally, Barcia has rightly asserted that this uprising represented a continuation of the conflict from the Bight of Benin hinterland on Cuban soil. In the trial records, court officials documented this event as a "black uprising," "riot," and "rebellion," and referred to the participants as "rebels" and "insurgents." Yet the Lucumí who testified via an interpreter probably used the Yorùbá word for "war" (*ogun*), which indicates "a conscious choice on their part to refer to their own actions as actions of war."[25] Hermenegildo Lucumí, aka "Olló" (Ojo), described quite frankly how the situation near Banes "was just as bad here as it was in Guinea."[26]

News of this Lucumí slave uprising traveled fast between the countryside and Havana, which undoubtedly caused concern among city residents. As a retired soldier, Prieto likely learned of events almost as fast as reports reached the capital, and once the details emerged, he was probably not the least bit alarmed. He knew more about the social dynamics of the people arriving from the Bight of Benin hinterland than Spanish and Cuban authorities could ever comprehend. The interpretations of documented African names of the people involved illustrate the ethnic component to the Lucumí unrest to the west of Havana. Of the alleged participants, 265 were Lucumí, and upwards of 75 percent had Yorùbá names, while the remainder were Ewe, Fon, Twi, Edo, Mende, and Muslim.[27] These percentages reconfirm estimates from the previous chapter that the majority were from Ọ̀yọ́ and its environs.

The evidence demonstrates how the Yorùbá language was a key component for the relative success of the Lucumí War. The plan, as it unfolded on 13 August, involved waiting until Aguirre went to Havana. In his absence, a group of male Lucumí overseers seized the plantation's "big house" around 8 P.M. Aguirre's mother moaned how she "was very scared when the *negros* entered the house and started breaking furniture." She told the court they were all "speaking Lucumí," which clearly meant Yorùbá.[28] During the trial, Diego Barreiro, a white overseer, testified that he heard voices in the barracks chanting "*Ho-Bé*," the meaning of which he misunderstood "to signify 'reunion' in the Lucumí language."[29] In Yorùbá, ọ̀bẹ means "knife," which the slaves shouted as they grabbed machetes. People speaking the same language did not preclude cooperation across ethnicities. Mandinga and Gangá fought alongside Lucumí, and many Lucumí refused to join the cause. Lucumí leaders attempted to recruit the reluctant, telling them "they were not the children of the whites." Most were like Prieto—the children of Odùduwà.

On Cuban plantations, domestic slaves held higher social status than field slaves. They had better living conditions, better clothing, more food, and generally access to more opportunity—perks they would not relinquish or endanger. Most new Lucumí from the Bight of Benin preferred war over slavery, if only for a moment. Some of the people who refused to unite were assaulted or murdered.[30] People arriving via Ọ̀yọ́ had already experienced much worse in West Africa before boarding a slave ship. During the Military Commission's investigation, Lucumí house slaves explained what they had seen, made accusations, and then were absolved from prosecution and punishment.

Once the big house on the plantation was set alight, the situation escalated. Likely from Ọ̀yọ́'s cavalry, Lucumí warriors rode horses to prevent news from spreading, which was futile. Under the cover of darkness, José Mina, a house slave, took a horse and rode it to the turret at Boca de Banes. The soldiers stationed there explained how "they could not send a single soldier because four went to Guanajay sick [from cholera,] and there were only four left to defend the fortification."[31] José Mina then got back on his horse and rode to warn other plantations in the vicinity, some of which were already under attack. A white overseer, Blas Hernández, ran to the Boca del Banes on foot, where the soldiers gave him a horse. After, he rode through the towns of Banes, Caimito, Guayabal, and Guanajay, which was home to a unit of over two hundred infantry soldiers.[32] Meanwhile, a town official in Banes known only as Tagle took his family to safety in Guanajay, and then he himself rode east to notify authorities in the capital.[33]

This war involving Lucumí in rural Cuba confirms how Ọ̀yọ́ soldiers and priests boarded slave ships and continued to fight overseas. Remarkably, this evidence reveals details about Ọ̀yọ́ military leadership and tactics. In the plundering, the Lucumí army acquired firearms, gunpowder, swords, machetes, wooden sticks, clothes, alcohol, food, and umbrellas. Gonzalo Mandingo, who fought alongside Lucumí, declared that "during the war they distinguished the principal leaders by the way in which each one carried an open parasol."[34] As cited in chapter 1, Lionel Abson, a British governor at the fort in Ouidah in the 1780s, described umbrellas in West African armies "and the generals under them."[35] In Cuba, the men riding horses were potentially ranking soldiers from Ọ̀yọ́ who had become overseers on Aguirre's plantation. Santiago Trujillo testified that one leader on horseback "carried a red parasol," and a "*negra* came by horse also with a red sash."[36] To most people on the scene, the color symbolized Ṣàngó.

The Lucumí army was well organized and contained a cavalry unit, and an infantry of nearly 250 men, women, and children.[37] The cavalry, led by Joaquín Lucumí, was composed of black overseers from the plantation. Fierabrás Lucumí or "Edú" (Edu/Edun), who carried the title "overseer of the raw

Africans" (*contramayoral de los bozales*), commanded the infantry.[38] According to testimonies, Luis Lucumí, also an overseer, was the "religious chief of the uprising."[39] He wore a "woman's white hat with feathers," which was emblematic of Ọbàtálá.[40] Acts of war demanded protection and strength from all the princial òrìṣà in the pantheon.

Ọ̀yọ́ military discipline and tactics involved rituals and sacrifices. Francisco Guiterrés, a white overseer, witnessed from a distance when Luis Lucumí entered an abandoned plantation on horseback. He described how he held in his hands

> peacock feathers tied together with a red string, with something from
> an animal, and a doll; this same King drew a sugarcane machete he
> was carrying, and singing the song of his people, hit a bell three times,
> [which was] the signal call of the overseer [to start working], and he
> saw that no one appeared [from the slave barracks.] All of his compan-
> ions, who arrived on horse, rode around the slave barracks and [when
> they] saw that they could not find anyone, [they] started to plunder the
> buildings. Soon after, another great number of *negros* arrived on foot
> and they started to sing and dance with three drums and various horns
> around the barracks; soon after they brought in some hens and they
> started to kill the birds and eat them raw; [then] they made a circle
> [around] the King and the Queen; [and] soon after the King mounted
> his horse and started to set fire to the big house.[41]

In this setting, a priest led the charge and sang out in Yorùbá to recruit more people. Once the cavalry and infantry arrived, they ransacked an empty plantation. Then the Lucumí army fed the òrìṣà in victory before marching onwards.

Music was an integral component in warfare pageantry in the Bight of Benin hinterland, and this dimension carried over across the Atlantic. The rhythms of the òrìṣà provided inspiration and raised morale. As the Lucumí army advanced, they did so to the sounds of "drums, horns, and war songs."[42] Musicians played "three drums."[43] The instruments were made on the plantation, but a trio suggests reiterations of Ṣàngó's bàtá drums. Horns signaled to field slaves when to start and stop working on plantations, but in battle they relayed military commands.[44] One witness, who did not join the Lucumí army, reported that he overhead a "song of war from their land . . . shouted in evil ways." The documented lyrics, "Orí ere osé," has multiple meanings in Yorùbá depending on tone, but the translation of this phrase could mean "Rise up without mishap," "Your head is good," or "Your destiny is great" (*orí rẹ àṣẹ*).[45] This Yorùbá phrase is quite possibly among one of the earliest documented in Cuba and the Atlantic world.

Between 9 and 11 P.M., witnesses observed how the Lucumí army systematically destroyed the coffee and sugar plantations of *San Salvador*, *Sandrino*, and *Fénix*, before looting the town of Banes. Afterward, the Lucumí warriors retreated and regrouped back at Aguirre's plantation. Before dawn, they marched around the other side of the Loma de Aguirre, likely to flank their opposition and gain position along some cliffs called Mesa de Anafre. Along the way, they destroyed three more plantations called *San José Germán*, *Catalina*, and *Coronela*. At the break of dawn, Spanish military reinforcements stationed at Guayabal arrived to protect the residents of Banes and its surroundings. Under its commander, Pedro Domenech, this small unit had a sergeant, a drummer, and twelve soldiers; in addition, there were townsfolk, plantation overseers, farmers, and house slaves already involved in suppressing the war. Around 7 A.M., this motley crew, who nevertheless knew the geography well, ambushed the Ọ̀yọ́ army in a passage between the base of a swamp and a hill. Domenech ordered "the soldiers in front and peasantry in the back." The Lucumí army held their ground as two soldiers died, another two were injured, and the remainder retreated to reclaim Banes. The casualties on the Lucumí side were minimal but significant. The priest, Luis Lucumí, was killed, as were all of the horses, which was a strategic focal point of the ambush. The Lucumí army also depleted most of its gunpowder and ammunition during the melee.[46]

Once the full regiment from Guanajay arrived, the Lucumí War ended. The final battle took place at the sugar plantation coincidently named after *San Juan Nepomuceno*. Around 9 A.M., Captain Don Joaquín Machado marched two hundred men armed with muskets and bayonets up the middle, while Domenech and his crew flanked the Lucumí army through the plantation fields. Three Cuban soldiers were killed, and another dozen or so were wounded. Due to the earlier ambush, however, there was little the Ọ̀yọ́ soldiers could do. The main leaders, along with another fifty men, were killed; several more committed suicide; and others tried to hide in the coffee plantation, the swamp, or up the cliffs of the Mesa de Anafre. By 16 August, when officials from the Military Commission arrived to survey the scene, the Spanish military had already captured ninety-two people, and over the next eleven days, they searched the region and rounded up over a hundred more.[47] Less than a week later, news of suppression efforts in the Banes region quickly circulated back to Havana and a report was immediately sent to Spain assuring the tranquility of the island (map 7.1).[48]

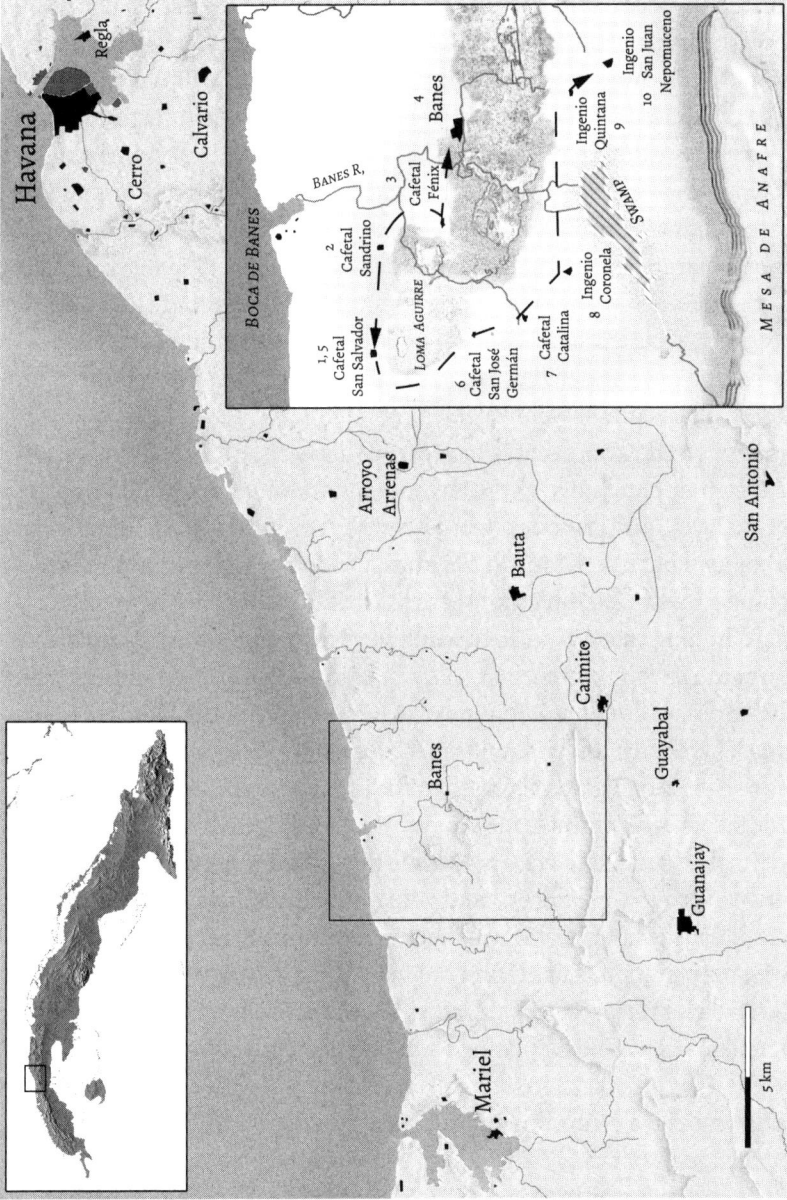

MAP 7.1 The Lucumí War, 1833.

Source: Henry B. Lovejoy, *African Diaspora Maps*, 2018.

On 19 August, military judge Tomás de Salazar listened to the testimonies of white witnesses first, starting with Aguirre and moving on to overseers and soldiers. He then heard from the enslaved who refused to participate. This ordering of witnesses was the *modus operandi* by which the court preestablished guilt. A white overseer, Diego Barreiro, claimed that one of the accused swung a machete at him yelling, "Bloody Hell! We want freedom! We are united with voices of liberty!"[49] Margarita Lucumí, a terrified house slave, revealed that the plan was simple: "to kill the whites and be free."[50] Once this tone was set, the accused defended themselves without formal representation through a Yorùbá-speaking interpreter, whom they did not choose. Nevertheless, some of the "rebels" incriminated themselves. Luis Gangá corroborated earlier testimony stating that "he wanted to be free."[51] Such testimony has led scholars to argue that liberation from slavery was all the motivation anyone needed, but in this case, Ọ̀yọ́'s collapse and the cholera epidemic played much bigger roles.

Prieto followed these events closely from his home on Gloría Street. Before the inquiry concluded, he knew judgments would be swift, theories would emerge, and rumors would swirl. As with other trials, the punishments—public executions, beatings, whippings, and imprisonment—were going to set an example and serve as a warning. It is not hard to imagine Prieto hoping that authorities would not set their sights on his *cabildo* because of the Lucumí connection. His anxiety must have hit an all-time high with the signing of Britain's Abolition of Slavery Act on 28 August 1833, which was a week before the military judge made his ruling. People in Havana knew that Prieto baptized Africans liberated by the Havana Slave Trade Commission. Once the surviving Lucumí leaders of the Banes affair marched into Havana to await final sentencing, Prieto must have instructed Havana's Lucumí community to keep a low profile to avoid being implicated in any way. Still, the most suspicious residents of Havana, whether Spanish or Cuban, must have been whispering Prieto's name and the *cabildo* Santa Bárbara.

When Salazar released his verdict on 4 September, he concluded that no larger conspiracy was being planned and that cholera was to blame:

> The disgraceful circumstances produced by cholera, which [had] produced many victims there and in other places . . . has led [owners] to gather their slaves in a healthy, isolated and comfortable place . . . and [the slaves of Aguirre's plantation were] given a nourishing diet most appropriate to protect them from the prevailing disease. . . . Ever

since they were born, these *negros* were used to the treatment of a hard slavery [and] they were not capable of knowing the beneficial value conferred upon them. They believed that they must then aspire to an absolute freedom without limits; and in order to obtain it they looked at and considered white people their enemies. They then went out with such great force, one after another, like ignorant barbarians to make war wherever they could find it.[52]

In reaching his judgment, Salazar never contemplated the Lucumí *cabildo* or the effects of Ọ̀yọ́'s collapse on Cuban slave society. Prieto and his friends probably heaved a huge sigh of relief.

A week later, a firing squad executed the convicted leaders of Cuba's Lucumí War. As an ongoing punishment, authorities made some of the other prisoners decapitate the heads and carry them to places around the region to hang in cages: near Banes, outside slave barracks at some plantations, along roads where the ambush occurred, and at the site of the final battle. Once they had finished this task, they began an eight-year prison term in Havana. Throughout this authoritarian display, the public demanded more answers because British emancipation increased speculation that abolition was imminent. To ease public fears, Antonio Lorenzo Baltanás, the secretary involved in the investigation, published an article in Havana's newspaper on 18 September. He estimated how 375 slaves had united "without any other purpose except to steal, destroy, burn, and kill." He wrote of this "horrible savagery" and emphasized how heroic soldiers killed "many barbarians."[53] As a final reassurance, the Spanish commissary judge of the Havana Slave Trade Commission, Claudio Martínez de Pinillos y Ceballos, endorsed the article to show how *emancipados* and British abolitionism had not influenced this case.[54]

The established Lucumí community in Havana must have returned to their daily lives with much more apprehension. Until his arrest and interrogation two years later, Prieto almost certainly worried that the authorities would formulate theories that he was conspiring to organize a revolution to topple the colonial regime. By 1833, Prieto was around sixty years old. His wife had died, and he probably hoped to live out his final days prosecution-free as a Lucumí "king." As a Yorùbá-speaking soldier loyal to the Spanish crown, Prieto must have been curious, and he undoubtedly compared Spanish and Ọ̀yọ́ military organization among his most trusted friends. Prieto clearly understood that this case could potentially upset his leadership in an instant.

The war raised awareness toward Lucumí among authorities, who would not soon forget but who could not fully comprehend the warfare in West Africa and the arrival of Ọ̀yọ́ warriors fighting on Cuban soil. Even though Prieto escaped prosecution, he probably could have guessed that it was a matter of time before *emancipados* or groups of Lucumí did something to jeopardize his respected social standing.

CHAPTER EIGHT

Prieto's Disappearance

A rigid dictatorship in fear of revolution mostly explains why fragments of Prieto's life were written down, his personal papers survived, and his story did not entirely vanish from historical record. As Captain General Mariano Ricafort reeled and reacted to the archbishop's death, the cholera epidemic, a Lucumí War, and British emancipation, King Ferdinand VII died on 29 September 1833. His succession led to civil war in Spain, because the king's fourth wife, María Cristina from the House of Bourbon, convinced the ailing king to abolish Salic law, which excluded females from acceding to the throne. With this change in traditions, María Cristina became queen regent on behalf of their daughter, María Isabel Luisa, who inherited the throne at the age of three. During the Carlist Wars, supporters of the infant queen fought against Ferdinand's brother, Carlos V, who challenged these claims on the basis of old customs. The divisions in Spain carried over to Cuba, and by early 1834, María Cristina appointed a new cabinet filled with her supporters. Her council concluded that Ricafort was misgoverning Cuba and should be immediately removed from office.[1] On 7 March 1834, Miguel Tacón, who supported Isabel II and led campaigns against independence movements in South America, became the next captain general. According to Juan Pérez de la Riva, Tacón imposed a regime "full of hate and prevention against the natives of the Americas."[2]

Prieto's arrest and interrogation relates to Tacón's more stringent control over Cuban society. On Sunday 12 July 1835, the Military Commission investigated an urban slave uprising, which was nothing more than a minor disturbance. Essentially, a couple dozen Lucumí got into a fight with white residents crossing a bridge between the neighborhoods of Jesús, María y José and El Horcón. Following the Lucumí War of 1833, the Military Commission investigated the situation carefully, and many free and enslaved Lucumí, as well as Lucumí *emancipados*, were arrested. Given Prieto's relative authority over a large Yorùbá-speaking community in Havana, it was a matter of time before officials pointed fingers at his *cabildo* and questioned his motives. Since the fracas occurred close to his home on Gloría Street, Prieto was guilty by association even though there was no credible evidence tying him to the alleged crime, if one occurred at all. Despite his longstanding service, which should have led to his immediate exoneration, he epitomized what colonial authorities feared, and he became a target. It was during this investigation that the Military Commission searched Prieto's home, seized his religious shrines, confiscated the *cabildo* archive, and recorded his testimony.

On top of being Lucumí, Prieto's implication revolved around the day of the week in which the disturbance occurred. On holidays and Sundays, *cabildos* could legally gather by law in Havana. Since the sixteenth century, Spanish law and Catholic traditions considered Sunday a festival day.[3] Accordingly, Prieto could legally hold weekly meetings from "ten in morning until twelve . . . and from three in the afternoon until eight at night." The laws mostly restricted these gatherings to inside the house, and alcohol was prohibited.[4] The many legal prescriptions allowed considerable scope for interpretation, but they amounted to degrees of freedom for people of African descent in Havana. José Antonio Saco disapproved of the tradition, arguing that fifty-two Sundays, plus other festivals, resulted in "pecuniary damages" to the island's economy due to "the loss of so many work days" in a given year.[5]

On that fateful Sunday in July, Prieto was likely holding a meeting at *Sàngó tẹ dún*. Meanwhile, in another part of town on Omoa Street in El Horcón, Hermenegildo Jáuregui Lucumí held a meeting in his home. This freeperson and sugar worker was better known as "Taita," which Deschamps Chapeaux defines as a respectful title meaning "father," "progenitor," or "male elder."[6] Taita Hermenegildo claimed that he "heard a lot of commotion in the street and some were saying that other *negros* had incited the *emancipados*"; to do what is not clear. He insisted that he "did not leave his house," but rather that the captain of El Horcón, along with twenty soldiers, suddenly showed up at his residence and "without saying a single word took him to prison."[7]

White witnesses, however, placed Taita Hermenegildo at the scene of the altercation at the Chávez Bridge, where a branch of the Zanja River emptied into the Bay of Havana.[8] Either Taita Hermenegildo and his friends were attacking, or they were being attacked. Due to conflicting testimonies in the trial proceedings, there is no way of knowing who initiated the conflict. Nonetheless, the situation spun out of control when a military unit dispatched from the Atarés Castle arrived on the scene. The soldiers killed four people while assaulting and arresting anyone who was black. The Military Commission took interest in this case because during the skirmish the soldiers confiscated machetes, and it was claimed that one person had "rifle bullets, enough powder for four shots, and a shaving razor."[9] Also, an unidentified Lucumí man apparently knocked José Gomez, a resident of Havana, off his horse and rode it to Calvario, five miles to the south of Havana.[10] Until he was killed, a white witness claimed that this unnamed Lucumí on horseback was apparently shouting that "armed blacks were coming, and they were hurting whites."[11] The report implied that the suspect was mobilizing people of African descent outside of Havana, for what purpose is not evident, although authorities presumed a much larger conspiracy was underway.

Many other white witnesses claimed they heard people shouting that the *emancipados* were the cause of the disturbance. In the same vicinity on that Sunday, an indentured work crew of nineteen men, most of whom were Lucumí *emancipados* "belonging to the Bergantine *Negrito*," were building or repairing the Cristina Bridge, which ran parallel and was within sight of the Chávez Bridge. As a result, court officials questioned whether or not British abolitionism might have been a motivating factor. Juan E. Castro, who was in charge of this crew, probably proved that they were not involved by submitting "a list of nineteen *negros Emancipados* belonging to this [public] work."[12] Several of these Lucumí men could be cross-referenced with the register of the *Negrito*, which arrived from Ouidah in late 1832. The majority were Lucumí Ayó (Ọ̀yọ́), had Yorùbá names, brandings of "P.V. on the right nipple," and facial scarifications.[13] Despite many testimonies that accused these *emancipados* of their involvement, neither Castro nor his crew testified because the Cuban government apprenticed these people to build Havana's infrastructure (map 8.1).

With the Lucumí *emancipados* exonerated from any wrongdoing, the commission's investigation focused on Taita Hermenegildo and his associates. The suspects were taken to prison at first, but due to the injuries they sustained during their violent arrest, they were moved to the military hospital. By Sunday, 12 July at 9 P.M., a court-appointed Yorùbá translator, Francisco de la Paz Lucumí, interpreted testimonies from their bedsides. Juan Bautista Velazques presided over the trial, while the secretary was none other than Antonio Lorenzo Baltanás, who had recorded the proceedings for the Lucumí War in August 1833. Under extreme duress, Taita Hermenegildo and his friends claimed that the police suddenly and without reason entered the house on Omoa Street. All suspects denied having in their possession weapons of any kind.[14] José Clemente Dávila Lucumí even suggested that authorities had planted evidence, claiming that only after his arrest had "they found the bullets at the hospital."[15]

On the following day, the soldiers dispatched from the Atarés Castle testified before the court. They first went to the hospital to identify the accused.

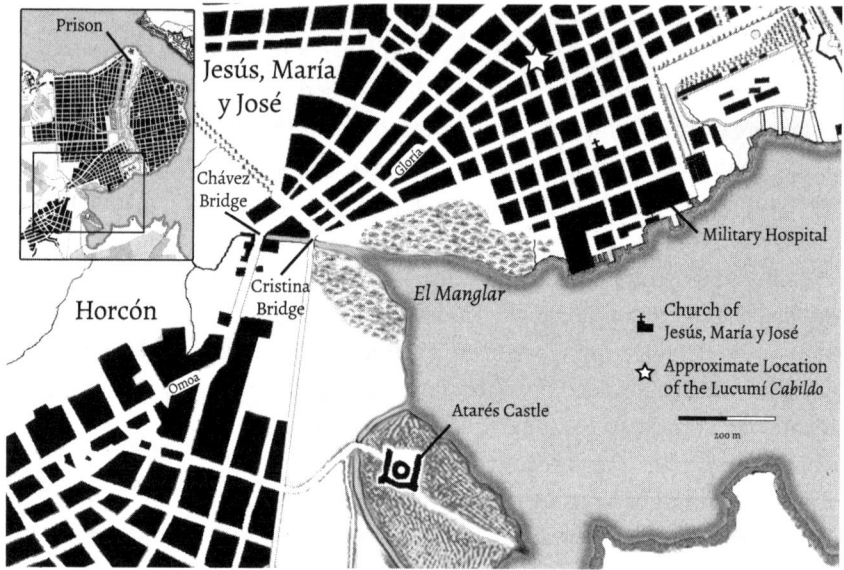

MAP 8.1 Key locations of the Lucumí disturbance in Havana, 1835.
Source: Henry B. Lovejoy, *African Diaspora Maps*, 2018.

Then they repeated the same story: Taita Hermenegildo and his friends had started attacking people on the bridge with machetes. One soldier, Narciso Serrano, claimed that he had heard these men shouting, *"Kill white, Havana mine!"*[16] On Tuesday, the court heard more testimonies from several white residents, who also went to the hospital for identification purposes. They too described how they heard shouting: *"Havana mine, kill white, white woman mine!"* or *"Long live my Havana, kill, kill!"*[17] After hearing these testimonies, which carried more weight, the military court gave the accused a second chance to confess their crimes and beg for salvation. The Lucumí men maintained their innocence, and in brief testimonies, they claimed that everything the soldiers and white witnesses were saying was total fabrication.[18]

More white witnesses described in detail the weapons Taita Hermenegildo was carrying before his arrest. Don Pedro Abreu, a sugar and tobacco trader, stated that he was "very certain" that he saw Taita Hermenegildo "with a staff in one hand, and a type of white tail in the other, and that he marched in front of a portion of *negros* all armed with machetes."[19] Moreover, the court secretary summarized many testimonies describing how most of the accused "wore white shirts and pants."[20] In terms of modern-day practices, the staff was likely the "beaded or painted dance wands—cutlasses, clubs, thunder-axes, fly whisks, and medicinal brooms—carried by priests in possession performances."[21] The white tail was almost certainly Ọbàtálá's horsehair fly whisk (*irukè*), which Prieto also had among his religious paraphernalia. These descriptions suggest this group had been involved in some sort of *òrìṣà*-based ritual. During initiation ceremonies today, David Brown explains how the initiate dresses in white for a full year to embody purity, obtain spiritual protection, and symbolize rebirth. These seven-day rituals that "Changó 'designed' [correspond to] initiatory seats for the arrival of kings, queens, and warriors."[22] Deschamps Chapeaux describes how a procession of people dressed in white "worked as a unifying power."[23] Although it is unclear what ritualized activities transpired that afternoon, the location around two bridges symbolized the *òrìṣà* where a crossroad (Ẹlẹ́gbára/Èṣù) met a river (Ọ̀ṣun) and the sea (Yẹmọja).

Throughout the initial investigation into the Sunday disturbance, Prieto's name was never mentioned in more than a hundred pages of accusations, testimonies, and denials. He was arrested two days after the incident on the bridge. The captain, Manuel de Moya, felt it necessary to conduct a deeper investigation into Prieto and his *cabildo*. To justify Prieto's arrest, Moya reported to the Military Commission that "various inhabitants" of the neighborhood

> suspected the *negro* Juan Nepomuceno Prieto *capataz* of the *nación*
> Lucumí Elló had participated in the conspiracy of the *negros* the
> afternoon of the twelfth; and who in it they saw leaving Prieto's house,
> shortly before the revolt broke out, about nineteen or twenty cleanly
> dressed *negros* of the Lucumí nation. And a short while afterwards, the
> aforementioned occurrence took place. And there is someone who
> asserts that from among the *negros* who were wounded, one of them in
> particular was among those who left the house of their *capatáz* . . .
> [They] had gone out killing *blancos* because their *capataz* influenced
> it. . . . Prieto is [also] reputed as being involved at some other time in
> a conspiracy movement against the *blancos* in the year of 1812, which
> demarcates the *C. of Aponte*. . . . Observing that at the time of making
> inspection of the house, and when Prieto resisted . . . I transported
> him to the disposition of Your Excellency. . . . And I enclose the
> papers that were in Prieto's house and extra articles of witchcraft with
> which he has tempted the gullible.[24]

Moya's report implied that the *cabildo* "king" had participated in the Aponte Rebellion of 1812, supported abolition, influenced Lucumí dissension in Havana, was spreading written propaganda, and practiced primitive idolatry.

It also suggested that the *emancipados* were involved, even though the court had already exonerated them.

On 15 July, the military judge submitted his sentence in a six-page report on the actual disturbance to Tacón. He described how "a handful of *negros* revolted, and thirsty for blood, they sacrificed some of those victims without consideration for class, sex, or age. Yes, Señor the referred afternoon of the twelfth will be a very painful memory about the ferocious acts that a group of armed *negros* did to disturb and shock public tranquility by the murders that they perpetrated with their own hands. . . . The horrendous crime that resulted in this intervention against the hideous and colored *negros* on the afternoon of Sunday the twelfth . . . [had] been very public and known by everyone."[25] This sentencing report expressed the fear and paranoia typical of Cuban slave society. Even the judge acknowledged "the truth" that the people involved were but "a small number." Since the report never referred to Prieto, the judge made it clear he would continue to investigate "by making new efforts to obtain clarification into the origin and ramifications that this [revolt] could have had" on public safety.[26]

On 16 July, a firing squad put to death six people, including Taita Hermenegildo. In a gruesome custom, their severed heads were mounted in cages on the Chávez and Cristina Bridges, and in Calvario, to serve as a warning to others. Some of the other suspects were sentenced to eight years in prison. The day after the execution, news reached the court of another Lucumí slave uprising in the *cafetales* near the town of Aguacate, located some thirty miles east of Havana. At six in the morning on 17 July, Tacón reported to Spain that about twenty "*negros* . . . all from the Lucumí nation" killed two white *mayorales* and another white man. As militia units from Jaruco and Matanzas arrived, "the rebels fled to the mountain, where [the authorities] found fourteen people who had hung themselves, and the six [people] who did not have time to do it were arrested."[27] This mass suicide only confirmed the court's suspicions of a larger conspiracy originating in Havana and tied into the Lucumí suspect on horseback who was killed in Calvario. The court immediately launched an investigation into Aguacate, which Juan Pérez de la Riva correctly argues did not have "any correlation with the rebellion in El Horcón."[28]

Due to two unrelated Lucumí disturbances in a matter of days, Tacón had to mitigate any rumors that might spread around the Atlantic world, especially after two of Havana's newspapers embellished the size of the uprising and motives of people involved.[29] The captain general sent duplicate letters to Spanish consulates in London, Paris, and Genoa explaining how "the distribution of checkpoints to take care of order particularly on festival days; [and] the vigilance of district commissioners, district judges, and other subordinate government agents . . . resulted in the dissolution of the riot that lasted a little more than an hour." Tacón further comforted foreign governments that "The anxiety and alarm were circumscribed to the narrow circle at the scene during the moments overcome with trying to finish off the rebels. The rest of the island equally enjoyed complete tranquility."[30] According to a report made by a French official stationed in Havana on the same day, "the papers maybe exaggerated this movement of negros which has taken place on the 12 of this month [July] in a suburb of Havana, [and] thanks to the tenacity and wisdom of the brave general Tacón, this movement of some drunk savages has been without consequence."[31]

Within all of the press and correspondence in circulation, Prieto's name was still never mentioned. Meanwhile, the military court continued interrogating people to determine the motives leading up to the disturbance. Don Clemente Dávila, the master of one of the executed Lucumí, was brought before the court to explain why a person whom he owned had bullets, gunpowder, and a razor in his pocket. To shift the blame away from himself, Dávila accused Manuel Lucumí, who was an *emancipado* from an unknown slave ship who sold potable water from a cart he pushed around town. Without mentioning Prieto's name, Dávila asserted that he saw Manuel frequently "talking in secret"—that is, in Yorùbá—with other Lucumí.[32] This slave owner also made no mention of Prieto or the Lucumí cabildo despite owning several Lucumí slaves, many of whom he had baptized.[33] Afterward, the court questioned the *emancipado*, Manuel Lucumí, who claimed in his defense that at the time of the disturbance he was in his house with the doors closed.[34] The judge "set the *negro* Manuel Lucumí free," likely because he worked for the government as an apprenticed laborer.[35]

As isolated incidents involving Lucumí occurred throughout Cuba in the immediate period leading up to Ọ̀yọ́'s final collapse, the Military Commission became more deeply committed to the idea of a conspiracy. Baltanás almost certainly reminded his superiors about the Lucumí War, if in fact they needed to be reminded. Prieto, who had been in Havana's prison for nearly four days, emerged as an obvious suspect. The court did everything in its power to put this issue to rest. At midnight on 18 July, witnesses were summoned to testify against the retired second sergeant. At this ridiculous hour, Don Juan Fernandez, a *criollo* butcher and resident of the neighborhood of Guadalupe, testified that he frequently visited his uncle, Secundino Fernandez, who lived across the street from Prieto on Gloría Street. On that Sunday, he claimed to have observed "at three in the afternoon . . . seventeen

to nineteen *negros* Lucumies leaving the house of the *Capataz* Juan Nepomuceno Prieto . . . all dressed in white pants and shirts."[36] Their departure from the Lucumí *cabildo* in white clothes preceded the disturbance and
therefore proved Prieto's involvement.

Afterward, Juan Fernandez recalled how he and his uncle armed themselves and helped suppress the disturbance. At the bridge, he saw the "dead
body of a *negro* who it seems [the soldiers] had just killed, and looking at it
with close attention, he knew him perfectly to be one of those persons he
saw leaving the house of the *negro* Juan Nepomuceno Prieto." Even though
there were more than a dozen people dressed in white still unaccounted for
in his testimony, the judge then asked Fernandez, "What conduct have you
observed about the indicated *Capataz* Nepomuceno?" Corroborating Moya's
accusation, Fernandez replied that Prieto's "conduct was nothing good . . .
[having] observed how [Prieto] had daily reunions of *negros* in his home."[37]
The *criollo* José de Feria, who owned a tobacco store in Jesús, María y José,
corroborated this testimony *verbatim*.[38] Hearsay evidence obtained from a
criollo butcher and a *criollo* tobacco merchant was all the Military Commission
needed to confirm their suspicions. Accordingly, Prieto masterminded this
conspiracy, which began in Havana and spread to Calvario, then Aguacate.

On the morning of 18 July, the judge and the secretary went into the prison
to interrogate the Lucumí leader. Prieto explained that he had arrived in Cuba
during Gálvez's time and identified himself as a *moreno libre* of the Lucumí
nation, a widower, and a retired second sergeant. Initially, the court asked
him, "For what reason were you arrested, in what place, with what weapons,
and who arrested you?" Prieto answered that he did not know the reason for
his detention, which occurred as he lay "in bed ill as he [had] been for a period of seven years, as the result of some fistulas that he [had] between both
passages, consequently without any weapon."[39] The court then asked if Prieto
knew Secundino and Juan Fernandez, both of whom Prieto denied knowing.
This response was likely untrue, since Secundino lived across the street, and
his nephew, Juan Fernandez, claimed to have visited Gloría Street frequently.

As the interrogation continued, court officials wanted to know where Prieto lived and with whom, as well as who owned his property. Prieto explained that he lived in his own house, which the secretary described with
an intent to incriminate, as being "in proximity of the [Chávez] bridge." Prieto explained that he lived with "the *negra* María Guillerma García . . . [who
cared] for him in his illness."[40] She was apprehended alongside Prieto, and
in her testimony, she denied knowing the reason for their arrests, the people
who testified against her, anything about the disturbance, anyone allegedly

involved, or the identity of the confiscated religious items from Prieto's home, some of which was almost certainly untrue.[41] There were other people arrested along with Prieto and García on 14 July, but they also denied having any knowledge or involvement in the disturbance.[42]

In reference to the events of 12 July, the court bluntly asked Prieto whether or not he knew the men who had been involved in the disturbance. Having lived in Havana for most of his life, Prieto knew better than to admit to associating with anybody who had recently been executed. He told the court that he had only heard about the riot from his bed when "Guillerma [García] shared the news with him [because] people in the street were shouting when the *negros emancipados* had rebelled, whereby they prepared to close the doors."[43] This explanation, which was the same one the *emancipado* Manuel Lucumí had used to prove his innocence, did nothing to exonerate Prieto.

The Military Commission probed deeper into Prieto's character. The judge asked whether or not he had been arrested on another occasion or had been involved in any other crime or conspiracy. The Lucumí leader stated that as a second sergeant he had "never been arrested, nor [had] he followed any cause which he [could] demonstrate with twenty-four years of service for the King [of Spain]." The direction of questioning arose from the arresting officer's accusation that Prieto had been involved in the Aponte Rebellion of 1812. When asked directly if he had participated, Prieto maintained that he had no connection, "neither as a witness nor as a criminal." This moment was when Prieto provided the name of the ship that took him to Pensacola, and the date when he left Havana for Florida.[44]

To confirm Prieto's service record, the court instructed a subinspector to search in Havana's military archive, whereby he found

the *moreno libre* of the *nación* Lucumí named Juan Nepomuceno Prieto had served as a soldier, 1st and 2nd Corporal, and retired in the class of 2nd Sergeant; [and] if on the twenty-sixth of June of 1812 was embarked on the Brigantine of War Juan Francisco de Borjas and went from the garrison in this city to the one in Pensacola, in which he survived for four years; and finally if there is some consistency, either in the relationships from other documents which justifies that the aforementioned Juan Nepomuceno had been included in the Conspiracy designed by the *negro* José Antonio Aponte and his cohort [in] the cited year of 1812 or in some other cause.[45]

Shipping records of the *Borjas* confirmed Prieto's departure from Havana to Florida at the specified date.[46] The subinspector would have also found

Prieto's name in muster rolls and hospital records from Pensacola.[47] In addition, the court would have noticed that the Lucumí leader provided an incorrect date for when he returned to Havana, which was after two years, not four.[48] And if they had time to go through the thousands of pages of trial records related to the Aponte Rebellion, which was unlikely, they would not have found Prieto's name documented therein.[49]

As this line of questioning unfolded, Prieto understood that his military privileges could do nothing to protect him. He knew that he was at the mercy of the court, which had the power to prosecute anyone perceived as acting against colonial rule. Officials ended this interrogation with questions about the religious items found in his home. At this moment, Prieto openly described his Ṣàngó shrines.[50] His candidness is puzzling. Why did he provide responses that were self-incriminating? He must have known he was guilty, and he could have answered this way because he was old, sick, and frustrated by oppression. Alternatively, it is entirely possible that Prieto had been worshipping Catholic saints alongside the òrìṣà for so long, and so openly, that there was nothing wrong with admitting the truth. Or perhaps he thought it would be better to explain the Ṣàngó/Santa Bárbara paradigm, then let the court make assumptions. After all, there were no real motives for him to organize a rebellion blocks from his house. He was a retired soldier. He was a *capatáz* who had had the support of the church and state for nearly two decades. His *cabildo* was profitable. His businesses as an herbalist and undertaker were successful. He paid taxes. And lots of people had trusted and respected his leadership until his arrest.

News of this small, Lucumí disturbance spread around the Atlantic world. While Prieto was being questioned, Tacón wrote to the Spanish government in Madrid to reassure that *"there has neither been nor any importance to the crimes of the negros of 12 [July] and that the Island of Cuba never enjoyed such complete peace and tranquility."*[51] But six days later, his tone changed as he bought into a conspiracy theory that the Havana disturbance was connected to Aguacate. In a second letter, Tacón outlined the links, and without any reference to Prieto, he embellished: "At four in the afternoon of 12 [July] . . . some fifty blacks robbed a warehouse or shop of machetes, and with such weapons and a little bit of gunfire, decided to murder white people. . . . At six in the morning [of 17 July,] twenty-two rebellious blacks killed two overseers and another man, all them white. . . . Those evildoers, all from the Lucumí nation . . . infringed upon the safety and desirable benefits that these happy inhabitants experience [in Cuba], under the wise laws that protect the security of their lives and interests." Tacón's second letter also praised the efficiency with which the Cuban militia units were able to "restore tranquility that [everyone] enjoys throughout the Island, [which was] now more secure than ever."[52]

On 31 August 1835, Tacón wrote yet another letter to Spain, whereby he explained how the so-called insurrection that had been caused by "a handful of *negros* . . . did not result in symptoms of division, even though it resulted in the propagation of dangerous principles among the people of color. The cause of this terrible dissemination [of ideas], can be found very near us. . . . Jamaica contains a numerous population of manumitted Africans, and Santo Domingo forms a Republic. Each and everyone of [African descent found] themselves imbued in exaggerated ideas of liberty and equality: everything that [the abolitionists] publish and issue . . . never loses sight of the precious island of Cuba, free until now of the horrors of a revolution."[53] Tacón explained that a group of men of African descent motivated the disturbance and that they were acting on behalf of abolitionist ideologies spreading rampantly throughout the Atlantic world. He probably inflated the significance of this disturbance to influence the Spanish government to continue supporting the institution of slavery, and to maintain the island under his despotic control.

Pro-slavery advocates in the United States repeated this narrative, likely to justify their slave-holding interests involved in cotton production. On 25 August 1835, the *Times* newspaper published an article called "'Insurrection in the Havana' on the 12th July to the Africans Emancipated by the Mixed Commission."[54] Once court officials from the Havana Slave Trade Commission obtained a copy of this article several months later, they too sent a report about the Lucumí disturbance to London to squash any misinformed claims. On 6 November 1835, William Macleay wrote to Viscount Palmerston, secretary of the Foreign Office:

We have the honor to assure your Lordship in the first place, that this riot which took place in the suburbs of the city [on Sunday, 12 July 1835] has been grossly exaggerated into an Insurrection, and secondly that the emancipated negroes had not the least concern with it whatever. It is true that the prejudice [that] prevails here against these poor people made them at first to be reported the authors of it, but it was soon found in reality that the rioters were some slaves and free negroes belonging to the tannery, who had got intoxicated in consequence of the holiday. The whole article in the "Times" is a tissue of misrepresentation, and evidently penned under the influence of that fear which too often produces in these slave colonies, first exaggeration, and then cruelty. We have ventured to address your Lordship on the subject because we know how anxious the supporters of the Slave Trade are for any facts whereon to found their arguments.[55]

Without references to òrìṣà rituals, the British perspective is likely the most accurate description of what actually transpired that day. This report further confirms that Prieto was a victim of fear, discrimination, and prejudice, not a conspirator in an attempt to overthrow the colonial regime.

There are no available records explaining what happened to Prieto after he gave his testimony in July 1835, which was when this Lucumí "king" disappeared from the historical record. The Military Commission did not provide any sentencing report or decision on what to do with him. In one possible outcome, the court had the authority to imprison Prieto off the record, and indeterminately. Saco described how Havana's penitentiary was a "horrible" place, where "men frequently [spent] years and years locked in the cells, [and] since [the authorities did] not give [prisoners] any activity, they [were] reduced to living in apathy."[56] If Prieto went to this unsanitary jail, he could have spent his last days in isolation, which suggests he died quickly given his advanced age and poor health. The church usually provided last rites to prisoners, and there is no clear evidence that Prieto received a Catholic burial or had, per his wishes, a burial in the city cemetery.

This dedicated soldier also believed in Christianity, but his admitted òrìṣà beliefs meant that he could also have been denied his last rites, with the guards disposing of his body unceremoniously. Alternatively, the authorities could have released Prieto from prison, destroyed his shrines, but still kept his personal papers, which still reside in Cuba's national archive. Without his *cabildo* house, and most likely banned from any association with a Catholic brotherhood, Prieto could have also died penniless and in relative obscurity. The presence of so many men from the Bight of Benin hinterland in Havana suggests that Prieto's downfall resulted in new Lucumí from Ọ̀yọ́ revising dynastic claims to establish a new order of Lucumí kingship in Havana.[57] However, I prefer to imagine an ending where his supporters gave him three masses and a proper burial beside Camejo with the money he left for himself in his will.

Conclusion

Prieto's Legacy

Juan Nepomuceno Prieto passed away as a free black man of the Lucumí nation, retired second sergeant of Havana's loyal black battalion, and "king" of a Lucumí *cabildo* dedicated to Santa Bárbara. He experienced a long life that started with his birth in the Bight of Benin hinterland around 1773. As the Ọ̀yọ́ kingdom consolidated control of trade to the coast, a Dahomey army enslaved him at Badagry in 1784. Sold to British traders, he crossed the Atlantic on board the *Golden Age*, and by early 1785, he was moved via the inter-Caribbean slave trade from Jamaica to Cuba. Shortly after the start of the St. Domingue uprising in 1791, he enlisted in the military, married María Francisca Camejo, and earned his freedom. His meritorious service included policing the arrival of enslaved Africans during Cuba's agricultural revolution, suppressing the Aponte Rebellion in 1812, and serving in Florida during the Napoleonic Wars. Once retired, Camejo and Prieto became leaders of Havana's most prestigious Lucumí *cabildo*, remembered among modern-day practitioners of Santería as *Ṣàngó tẹ̀ dún*. Their reign overlapped with the Spanish American Wars of Independence and the establishment of a diaspora of over 35,000 Yorùbá speakers in Cuba during the collapse of Ọ̀yọ́. He survived a cholera epidemic, which caused his wife's death and observed from afar the Lucumí War of 1833. After a disturbance in Havana involving a couple dozen Lucumí on a Sunday in July 1835, police arrested Prieto on suspicion of his involvement; during the investigation, his home was searched and his personal property seized, and he gave his testimony before a military court.

The responses Prieto made throughout the various stages of his life illustrate processes of creolization. He epitomized Ira Berlin's concept of "Atlantic Creole" as an individual with "cultural plasticity."[1] A native Yorùbá speaker, he became literate in Spanish but was also exposed to many other cultures by residing in Havana. Due to migrations to the island from around the Atlantic basin and beyond, Prieto lived in a multicultural society and was exposed to many languages, such as Fon, Twi, Hausa, Igbo, Kikongo, Lingala, Mende, Arabic, English, French, Portuguese, and German. The level of social agility that Prieto required to succeed within an oppressive environment demonstrates what Paul Lovejoy explains as a reliance on the familiar, all the while innovating out of necessity.[2] His open-mindedness ran counter to a slave society predicated on violence, oppression, and fear. Crucial to the creolization model, Andrew Apter describes "two fundamental axes of 'refabrication' in the making of African American culture." The vertical axis reflects the European domination over Africans, while the horizontal axis bridges diverse African ethnicities and cultures, resulting in historical discontinuities and continuities as well as invention and reinvention.[3] As exemplified in the case of Prieto's belief in Ṣàngó, this òrìṣà "fused" upward into the religion of the master as Santa Bárbara, yet the plausible presence of nkisi among Prieto's objects of worship illuminate how òrìṣà syncretized laterally across other African cosmologies.[4]

On a certain level, the creolization approach informs our understanding about the world in which Prieto lived. As Mintz and Price have argued, "Continuities between the Old World and New World must be established upon an understanding of the basic conditions under which migrations of Africans occurred."[5] With this point in mind, Prieto arrived in Cuba at the apex of Ọ̀yọ́ power but assumed leadership of a Lucumí cabildo during Ọ̀yọ́'s collapse. At the time he first joined a Lucumí cabildo in the 1780s, òrìṣà devotion had already been undergoing processes of change. Although impossible to date with any precision, the Ṣàngó/Santa Bárbara paradigm almost certainly existed before Prieto arrived in Cuba in the 1780s. It is not hard to consider that as soon as Yorùbá speakers from Africa joined the Spanish military, the òrìṣà of thunder, lightning, and war became equated with Spain's patron saint of the artillery. Prieto, who could have been initiated into Ṣàngó as a boy in West Africa, found a foreign community that was worshiping something equally familiar yet entirely different.

One major problem with creolization theory is the tendency to overlook processes of cultural change that began within African cultures. As scholars have long recognized, the development of Yorùbá culture involved historical discontinuities and continuities, as well as invention and reinvention, long before people crossed the Atlantic as slaves. J. D. Y. Peel argued that òrìṣà devotion emerged as a world religion due to the interaction of diverse peoples in West Africa involving influences from other cultures, Islam, and eventually Christianity.[6] The so-called Yorùbá diaspora in the Atlantic world, and the subsequent return of former slaves and Liberated Africans back to the Bight of Benin hinterland, ultimately had an impact on the development of a global pan-Yorùbá identity. Even though Prieto never returned to his place of birth, the people called "Yorùbá" today have been identified by various names throughout the history of the transatlantic slave trade. Ethnonyms and other identity markers documented in the Americas have always been slippery concepts because they changed over time. Different usages at various historical junctures raises questions as to historical meanings associated with other designations such as "Spanish," "British," "Cuban," "American," or even, "Creole."

Using biography to explore creolization requires incorporating and modifying Natalie Zemon Davis's methodology of historical imagination. Existing models fall short in not adequately explaining the trajectories of individual lives. This theoretical approach recognizes but oversimplifies the countless interactions of people who were making reasoned and informed decisions from individual experiences, which ultimately affected local responses to broader international events. As Jane Landers points out, Atlantic Creoles were "on the front lines" of revolutions, world economies, efforts to abolish slavery, and cultural change.[7] Take Prieto for example. How can anyone ever know for certain what fully happened in his life, especially when the great majority of people he interacted with were never documented? How can anyone fully grasp the infinite combinations of social interactions among millions of people who were forced into the Atlantic world without a little imagination? This microhistorical study only scratches the surface of reconstructing Prieto's life because there are simply too many silences, contradictions, and mysteries that can never be fully resolved.

After over a decade of research, I feel as if I know Prieto as much as it is possible. I like to think I understand the world in which he lived, the people he met, the places he went, the music he played, and the texts he read. If I have missed anything or omitted details in any way, it is only because there were too many possibilities to incorporate into a single monograph about this fascinating individual and his life in the Atlantic world during the Age of Revolutions. It is clear that Prieto understood shifting political currents in colonial Cuba and beyond. He successfully traversed the flows of change until he was wrongly accused of complicity. The way he identified himself transformed as his life progressed, and in most circumstances, he decided the way he wanted to be identified in different contexts. He often got to select when to be "African," "Lucumí," "Cuban," a soldier, or a king. He actively chose when to speak Yorùbá or Spanish. In the world he lived, nonetheless, choices were never his to make. He succeeded by learning when to submit and when to resist. Over the course of his life, his social dexterity enabled him to rise to a position of power, while so many of his compatriots could not.

WITH THIS BOOK, Camejo and Prieto's story and their involvement in the principal Lucumí *cabildo* of their day will retain a prominent place in the long history of African-derived religious practices in Cuba, and by extension elsewhere. If "the *cabildo* incontestably forms the starting point for the African *santaria* of Cuba," as Roger Bastide hypothesized, I still wonder why it has taken so long to situate Camejo and Prieto within *Ṣàngó tẹ̀ dún*?[8] I have found this silence especially strange. After all, *Ṣàngó tẹ̀ dún* has been glorified as "the most widely remembered and important Lucumí *cabildo* in Cuba's history."[9] Prieto testified that he revered "*Changó*, which is the same as saying King, or Santa Bárbara," which to me secures his place within the history of *Ṣàngó tẹ̀ dún* beyond any reasonable doubt.[10] The *cabildo* archives prove that Camejo and her husband owned property, won elections, negotiated festival licenses, revered Catholic saints as *òrìṣà* and *nkisi*, interceded in work agreements, raised capital, paid for people's freedom, became godparents, organized funerals, held social and religious meetings, played music, danced, and sang songs. Amazingly, they brought prestige to their house within a harsh political and cultural environment that aggressively oppressed cultures of people of African descent.

How much influence did Camejo and Prieto have on the development of the Lucumí religion into what is now known variously as La Regla de Ocha, La Regla de Ifá, and/or Santería? The answer may not seem obvious, because scholars have long debated the institutional origins of modern-day house-temples (*casa-templos*), which oftentimes have confusing chronologies of origin, operation, affiliation, and coexistence. In 1906, Ortiz envisioned how early twentieth century "sorcery temples" (*brujos templos*) had emerged after the abolition of slavery in 1886.[11] Jumping ahead to the 1980s, Joseph Murphy described how modern-day *òrìṣà* worship in Cuba "reformulated" after independence in 1902.[12] George Brandon has pushed the chronology back, adding that "the matrix out of which Early Santeria grew" occurred shortly after the 1860s through the "disintegration of old cultural ties, and the physical decimation of whole generations of Africans from the Bight of Benin."[13] Rafael L. López Valdés has theorized how independent and undocumented house-temples formed in the mid- to late- nineteenth century. While all the above arguments have validity, they do not go back far enough in recognizing what happened before the middle of the nineteenth century. I tend to agree with Brown who explains how "*cabildos* were formative in creating shared ways of surviving, organizing, ritualizing, and sometimes rebelling." But once the transatlantic slave trade ended and the African-born population began dying out, the next generation "selected patterns of the old-style *cabildo*" within a new legal framework of an independent Cuban Republic.[14]

In examining the "ethnogenesis" of Lucumí culture over time, Stephen Palmié raises yet another convincing counterpoint about how it would be "more fruitful—less nominalistic, more historical—to view the Lucumí *cabildos*, documented as they are . . . *not* as the incipient New World 'Yorùbá-enclaves' . . . of contemporary Yorùbá culture."[15] Prieto's socioreligious practices differed from the ways in which people observe and practice the Yorùbá religion in Cuba today. On one hand, Camejo and Prieto possessed images of Catholic saints, some of which have no clear associations with modern-day devotion. On the other, Santa Bárbara clearly does. Moreover, the rules and laws of the colonial slave society, which authoritarian dictators from Gálvez to Tacón enforced, affected how Prieto could worship the *òrìsà*. I agree with Palmié's insistence on the necessity to situate changes to "Lucumí identity" into varied and transforming historical contexts. And I support Andrew Apter most of all, who has recommended, "The best we can pursue is the historical anthropology of their representations, and of the emergent networks and apparatuses in which they have been entextualized, contested, objectified, and catalogued."[16] Fortunately, the surviving documentation has allowed for an examination of Camejo and Prieto's beliefs and practices within their particular historical context.

As far as I can determine from extant archival sources and the secondary literature at the time of this publication, Camejo and Prieto led the earliest documented Lucumí *cabildo* dedicated to Santa Bárbara on record.[17] However, the succession of Lucumí *cabildos* in Havana remains entirely imprecise, especially since collections of oral and written sources sometimes contradict one another. Quintín Lecón Lombillo, whom John Mason interviewed in 1986, stated that the "Society of Santa Bárbara was the oldest *cabildo* in Havana."[18] Archival evidence proves that Yorùbá speakers from the Bight of Benin hinterland began arriving in Cuba in the sixteenth century, yet the first known reference to a *cabildo* was in 1568, but it was not to one that was Lucumí.[19] Apparently, the earliest documented Lucumí *cabildo* dates to around 1728 from undocumented references in secondary sources, but not specifically to one associated with Santa Bárbara.[20] By 1755, records show at least two Lucumí *cabildos* existed in Havana, yet neither of their patron saints were Santa Bárbara.[21] As established in the third chapter, there were at least a half-dozen references to Lucumí *cabildos* between the 1770s and 1810, but still, Santa Bárbara is not explicitly documented in conjunction with any of those Lucumí *cabildos* either, although there were clear associations between *cabildo* leadership and the military.

I therefore want to be as bold as to revise the period as to when Yorùbá speakers consolidated Lucumí *cabildos* in Cuba. The chronology based on oral sources posits how a Lucumí society for Santa Bárbara "really became organized in the first decades of the eighteenth century."[22] However, this periodization seems a little too early for my liking. As this study shows, Ṣàngó equated as Santa Bárbara took root on the island during the Bourbon reforms and the militarization of the island, especially after the British occupation of Havana in 1762. Arguably, this particular òrìṣà/saint paradigm did not begin in hiding, but rather openly in the ranks of the military. Once black soldiers adopted the concept, New World òrìṣà traditions became widely accepted in Cuba's largest city. Camejo and Prieto were remarkable in this process because they learned from their *cabildo* mentors how to navigate the rules and regulations of a slave society in many cases for their own economic, political, and social benefit. As exemplified by the licensed annual Santa Bárbara festivals lasting forty days, the popularization of òrìṣà worship exploded and thrived publically.

My understanding emphasizes Camejo and Prieto's role as an example of how "Yorùbá" culture in the New World developed separately in different regions and periods. After all, the patron saints of Catholic brotherhoods in Brazil equate Ṣàngó with São Jerônimo in Bahia and Pernambuco, but São João in Rio de Janeiro and Rio Grande do Sul.[23] Those processes therefore need to be evaluated within their own varied historical contexts, which have definitive links back to Africa, most especially surrounding Ọ̀yọ́'s collapse. During British abolition efforts, the Yorùbá diaspora included destinations in Brazil, Sierra Leone, Cuba, and from Cuba to British Caribbean colonies. The influence of Ọ̀yọ́'s collapse on the history of the Atlantic world is most apparent due to the outward migration of Ọ̀yọ́ warriors who came to lead the Cuban Lucumí War of 1833 and the Malê Uprising in Brazil in 1835.[24]

DO MARÍA FRANCISCA CAMEJO and Juan Nepomuceno Prieto fit into the branches (*ramas*) of the Lucumí religion that have since spread from the island to many other places around the world? In my opinion, their legacy can be situated into one of the most famous Lucumí oral traditions related to the consecration of Cuba's "first" *bàtá* drums. In the 1940s, Fernando Ortiz recorded this oral history from interviews with Miguel Somodevilla who was "the oldest and most senior master *bàtá* drummer."[25] This oral tradition has circulated widely once Ortiz published it in *Los instrumentos de la música afrocubana* in the 1950s. Most modern-day practitioners have heard this story, and almost all *bàtá* drummers can recite variations of it. As the legend goes, "the *bàtá* sounded for the first time in a Havana Lucumí *cabildo* named Alakisá on Egido Street," which intersects with Gloría Street upon which Camejo and Prieto once lived. Two Lucumí friends, Filomeno García Àtàndá and Juan Àyànbí, "went to the Alakisá and knew immediately that the drums being played there were not orthodox, they were profane, and that no set of consecrated *ilú* [the largest *bàtá* drum] existed in Cuba. In about 1830, . . . the two friends constructed and consecrated a set of the hourglass-shaped *bàtá* drums."[26] This oral source therefore determines that the rituals used to build *bàtá* drums occurred toward the end of Camejo and Prieto's lives.[27]

Beyond a date and general location, this account relates to modern-day beliefs and practices for five main reasons: First, all *bàtá* drummers in Cuba honor the people who made and consecrated their instruments, as well as the names of their teachers. This deep ritual knowledge always starts with Àtàndá and Àyànbí.[28] Second, Àtàndá died around 1876. One of his grandsons was John Mason's informant, Quintín Lecón Lombillo, who died in 1999.[29] In the mid-1980s, this direct descendent of Àtàndá stated that his grandfather and his friend Àyànbí "were Ègbádo, and the Ègbádo were known for remaining loyal to the Aláááfin of Òyó."[30] Third, Àtàndá and Àyànbí cofounded another Lucumí *cabildo* with Remegio Herrera Adéṣíná, one of Cuba's most famous African-born priests (*babaláwo*). This new house formed shortly after "the creation of the *bàtá* drums," was located in Regla, and was dedicated to Nuestra Señora de Regla (Yẹmọja).[31] There is a photograph of Adéṣíná in Regla's municipal museum that show his facial scarifications of three diagonal lines on each cheek, likely revealing he came from Òyó.[32] Fourth, Adéṣíná's leadership of this *cabildo* continued under the direction of his daughter, Josefa "Pepa" Herrera, until her death in 1947. She knew Somodevilla and many scholars, such as Ortiz, Lydia Cabrera, and José Luciano Franco. Finally, in the *bàtá* traditions Ortiz recorded, he equated Ṣàngó tẹ̀ dún with "Alakisá," which translates as "ragged" (*ripiao*) in Spanish because in Yorùbá *alákisà* means "ragged person."[33]

My interpretation of Cuba's longstanding *bàtá* tradition—and mine is only one of many—specifically identifies Camejo and Prieto's *cabildo* with usages of the word *alákisà*. The reference to "ragged person" relates to the final years of Ọ̀yọ́'s collapse, during which time Camejo and Prieto's *Ṣàngó tẹ̀ dún* was in decline. Around 1833, Camejo, who probably administered the business and directed ritual activities in the *cabildo*, passed away. Meanwhile, Prieto was ill with fistulas, did not have any heirs, and was grieving the loss of his wife. The Yorùbá term *alákisà* described Prieto and his house because it was old, torn, and in tatters. Once Prieto was arrested, his disappearance left a political void in Havana's Lucumí community. During the transition of power, the new Lucumí from Ọ̀yọ́ stepped in to fill the leadership roles, much as Camejo and Prieto had once done themselves following the Aponte Rebellion in 1812. The new generation from Africa reconstituted dynastic claims to kingship by offering more "authentic" forms of *òrìṣà* worship from Africa; hence, the consecration of *bàtá* drums from Ọ̀yọ́ in Havana.

When Àtàndá, Àyànbí, and Adéṣíná came to Cuba from the Bight of Benin hinterland during Ọ̀yọ́'s collapse, they likely joined Camejo and Prieto's *Ṣàngó tẹ̀ dún*. Therein, they recognized a business opportunity to improve the drumming practices within the Lucumí community. Together, they negotiated how to consecrate a *bàtá* trio based on the skills they brought with them from Africa. According to Somodevilla via Ortiz, Filomeno García Àtàndá was a carver and *bàtá* drum master, while Juan Àyànbí was an Ifá diviner, herbalist, and *bàtá* drummer. In his 1835 testimony, Prieto described "a patch of male goat leather used in his drumming functions," which suggests drums were being made (or being repaired).[34] Arguably, the legendary *bàtá* drums sounded for "the first time" in Prieto's *cabildo*.[35] By the time of Prieto's legal troubles in 1835, Adéṣíná founded a new Lucumí *cabildo* on the other side of the bay in Regla. To etch out his own dynastic claims to kingship, Adéṣíná could have deliberately selected Nuestra Señora de Regla as the patron saint of his Regla *cabildo* because in most *òrìṣà* mythology Yẹmọja sits above Ṣàngó in the pantheon because she is his mother. As a result, Àtàndá and Àyànbí "made and consecrated a second set of *batá*."[36]

There is additional circumstantial evidence because during the trial, Prieto identified his nurse as María Guillerma García. She was also arrested on that fateful Sunday of the Lucumí disturbance in July 1835 and made to testify before the military court. She stated that she lived "two doors up from Juan Prieto" with her father and sister, Isidrio and Paula García, who were free blacks and *cabildo* members.[37] Did Àtàndá, aka Filomeno García, acquire his last name from the same García family? Unless ecclesiastical sources surface to prove otherwise, it cannot be known with any certainty what were the relationships, if any, surrounding this common Spanish surname.[38]

USING ORAL AND DOCUMENTARY EVIDENCE, it is possible to trace the legacy of Camejo and Prieto's Ṣàngó tẹ̀ dún dedicated to Santa Bárbara into the twentieth century. By 1843, colonial authorities recorded a Lucumí *cabildo* "Bragurá Santa Barbara" on 49 Monseratte Street, which was also on Egido Street.[39] A decade later, Swedish traveler Frederika Bremer observed the "Cabildo de Señora Santa Bárbara de la nación Lucumi Alagua" outside the city walls.[40] "Bragurá" and "Alagua" appear to be similar terms for a district in Ẹ̀gbá territory known as Gbàgùrà, which is "said to have been founded by immigrants from Ọ̀yọ́."[41] Alternatively, these ethnonyms could also mean "chairman" (*alága*); "an elder who commands respect" (*alàgba*); "the chief of the *egungun* worship" (*alágba*); "Ṣàngó's guide, or one who clears the path for Ṣàngó" (*ẹlẹ́gùn*); "a masquerader" (*eleegun*); the verb "to pray" (*gbàdúrà*); or even the òrìṣà of crossroads, Ẹlẹ́gbára.[42] Despite plausible variations in meaning, documented references to a Lucumí *cabildo* dedicated to Santa Bárbara in the same neighborhood after Camejo and Prieto disappeared from historical record prove the continuation of Ṣàngó tẹ̀ dún under different leadership.

By the start of Cuba's Ten Years' War in 1868 and the island's struggle for independence, colonial authorities documented the "Cabildo Lucumí Ayones [Ọ̀yọ́] Santa Bárbara."[43] This brotherhood relates to another oral tradition Lydia Cabrera recorded concerning the transfer of power in Ṣàngó tẹ̀ dún in the 1870s. Her contacts were José de Calazán Herrera and a woman known only as Teresa M., both of whom died in the 1950s. In this account, Cabrera reports an internal dispute between the older, conservative, African-born members (*viejos de nación*), and young Cuban-born members (*criollitos*) who "wanted to promise and boast of being progressive." According to her information, "around the [18]70s, the Changó Terddún occupied a house on Jesús Peregrino Street, and soon after, in Jesús María [on] Gloría between Indio and Florida."[44] This story revolves around the period when the transatlantic slave trade to Cuba stopped with the last voyage arriving in 1866. As a result, the African-born population began to die out and was being replaced by Cuban-born descendants. My interpretation of this oral source relates to another change of leadership in Ṣàngó tẹ̀ dún, which at this time was located on the same street Camejo and Prieto had once owned a home.

Surrounding Cuban independence at the turn of the twentieth century, other Lucumí *cabildos* dedicated to Santa Bárbara were documented. López Valdés argues that these "house-temples" were called *cabildos* but differed from the institutions in the early nineteenth-century.[45] In 1891, 1900, and 1910, the "Cabildo Lucumí Sociedad de Santa Bárbara," aka "Cabildo Africano Lucumí," officially presented to government authorities a membership roster and set of institutional rules and regulations, whose submission was mandatory for all *cabildos* of Africans and their descendants at this time.[46] One police inspector compared such sets of rules and laws to a "constitution," which "resembled that of a state."[47] By the turn of the twentieth century, membership of the Cabildo Africano Lucumí included "the most powerful and influential figures of the emerging *reglas* of Ocha and Ifá at this time. They were Africans and Creoles; they were ethnically and racially diverse; they belonged to two different sub-*reglas* of priesthood—La Regla de Ocha and La Regla de Ifá; they descended from different genealogical 'branches' (*ramas*) of these two sub-*reglas*; they also practiced the Congo-Cuban Palo Monte religion and belonged to the Abakuá society; and they were men and women." According to Brown, the Cabildo Africano Lucumí was the "reincarnation of the great Changó Tedún . . . a key, if not the key, institutional hub and cultural repository for the Lucumí religion in Havana, if not all of Cuba."[48]

Notable members of the Cabildo Africano Lucumí included the founders of "four of the five principal Ifá *ramas*:" Adéṣíná Remegio Herrera, Eulogio Rodrigues (Tata Gaitán), Bernabé Menocal, and Esteban F. Quiñones. This famous Lucumí house-temple also included "founders of the most influential Lucumí *ramas* of the Regla de Ocha," such as Caridad Argudín, Margarita Armenteros, Belén González, and the twins, Gumersindo and Perfecto. The last member worth noting is Quintín García, who was the son of the man who constructed the legendary *bàtá* drums, Àtàndá, and the father of Quintín Lecón Lombillo, Mason's informant. The amalgamation of so many notable leaders of the different branches (*ramas*) into the Cabildo Africano Lucumí occurred at the time police were targeting people who were practicing witchcraft (*brujería*). Camejo and Prieto's institutional legacy served as precedent to legitimize òrìṣà worship and avoid persecution in Cuba.

When members of the *cabildo* submitted their constitution to Cuban authorities in 1910, they claimed a direct line to the years of Camejo and Prieto's leadership of Ṣàngó tẹ̀ dún. As the second article stated, "The individuals who profess the Lucumí religious faith, find themselves socially and morally obliged to put themselves under the standard that maintains and guarantees the image of 'Santa Bárbara' as the religious faith of the African Lucumí cult since the year of 1820."[49] However, Camejo and Prieto's legacy extends further back to an even older generation that included notable Lucumí *cabildo* leaders such as Antonio Pimienta, Nicolás Palomino, Pedro Infazón, María Esperanza de Céspedes, Dolores Martínez, María Loreto Torres, Isidrio Cárdenas, and Joseph Antonio Aguilar.[50] Many of these people boarded slave ships at the Bight of Benin, arrived in Cuba during Ọ̀yọ́ expansion, and enlisted in the Spanish military during the Bourbon reforms. This early and relatively small but significant migration represents the period when a "proto-Lucumí" identity formed and consolidated in the mid-to-late eighteenth century.

Once the old African-born population started to die out in the 1860s, Lucumí identity and culture creolized once again and the Cuban-born generation consolidated into the Cabildo Africano Lucumí by the late nineteenth century. This biography therefore demonstrates three interlocking periods of creolization, one of which also might be called "Ọ̀yọ́-ization," in order to explain the long, historical development of Lucumí religion and culture in colonial Cuba from the Age of Revolutions to modern times.

Notes

Introduction

1. ANC, CM 11/1, "Capitania Pedaneo de Jesus Maria," 14 July 1835, fol. 211. For a complete transcription and translation of this document, see H. Lovejoy, "Arrest Report."

2. ANC, CM 11/1, "Capitania Pedaneo de Jesus Maria," 14 July 1835, fol. 211 (emphasis in original, which reads "*C. de Aponte.*" I have interpreted "C." to mean "conspiración").

3. See Childs, *1812 Aponte Rebellion*.

4. See Tomich, *Through the Prism*.

5. Voyages (estimates: 1775–1835, all embarkation regions to Cuba).

6. ANC, CM 11/1, "Declaración de Juan Prieto," 18 July 1835, fol. 220v. For a complete transcription and translation of this document, see H. Lovejoy, "Arrest Report."

7. Davis, *Trickster Travels*, 18–19.

8. Mintz and Price, *Birth of African-American Culture*, 44; and see also Mintz and Price, *An Anthropological Approach to the Afro-American Past*.

9. Berlin, *Many Thousands*, 94; see also Landers, *Atlantic Creoles*.

10. P. Lovejoy, "Identifying Enslaved Africans," 2.

11. Examples of select literature on cultural formation include Apter, "Herskovits's Heritage"; Herskovits, "African Gods"; Herskovits, "New World Negro"; Herskovits, *Acculturation*; Herskovits, *Myth of the Negro Past*; Ortiz, *Contrapunteo cubano*, 98; Peel, *Religious Encounter*; and A. Ramos, *As culturas negras*, chaps. 7 and 14.

12. See H. Lovejoy, "Santería."

13. See H. Lovejoy, "Proyecto Orunmila."

14. I was a research assistant for Jane Landers' British Library's Endangered Archive Program to document ecclesiastical sources in Cuba in 2002. See *Slave Societies Digital Archive*.

15. Studied under a drummer I have only ever known as André, who members of Proyecto Orunmila introduced me to in 2002 and 2004; Michael Marcuzzi (York University) in 2005; and Francisco Aguabella (University of California Los Angeles) in 2007.

16. See Du Bois, *Souls of Black Folk*; and Gilroy, *Black Atlantic*.

17. See Ajayi, "Samuel Ajayi Crowther of Oyo,"; Curtin, "Joseph Wright of the Egba"; and Lloyd, "Osifekunde of Ijebu."

18. Examples of select biographies of enslaved Africans include Carvalho Soares, *Devotas da cor*; Fuentes, *Dispossessed Lives*; Landers, *Atlantic Creoles*; Law and P. Lovejoy, *Mahommah Gardo Baquaqua*; Reis, *Domingos Sodré*; Scott and Hébrard, *Freedom Papers*; Sparks, *Two Princes*; Sweet, *Domingos Álvares*; Sweet and Lindsay, *Biography and the Black Atlantic*; Warner-Lewis, *Archibald Monteath*; and see also *Dictionary of Caribbean and Afro-Latin American Biography*.

19. See A. Ramos, *As culturas negras*, chaps. 7 and 14; and Herskovits, "African Gods."

20. D. Brown, *Santería Enthroned*, 3.

21. Bastide, *Les amériques noires*, 101.

22. Examples of select literature on *cabildos* include D. Brown, *Santería Enthroned*; Carmen Barcia, *Los ilustres apellidos*; Deschamps Chapeaux, "Cabildos"; Childs, "Defects of Being a Black Creole"; Howard, *Changing History*; López Valdés, *Componentes africanos*; Moreno, *La antigua hermandad*; Ortiz, *Los cabildos*; Pichardo, *Diccionario provincial*, 37; and Pike, *Aristocrats and Traders*, 172–74.

23. Ortiz, "Los 'batá,'" 315–16.

24. Cabrera, *El Monte*, 24 and 25n3.

25. D. Brown, *Santería Enthroned*, 70.

26. ANC, CM 11/1, "Declaración de Juan Prieto," 18 July 1835, fol. 225v.

27. D. Brown, "Garden in the Machine," 20n16.

28. Mason, *Aráàràárá*, 154.

29. Franco, *La conspiración*, 25; and Franco, *Las conspiraciones*, 13.

30. Geggus, "Slavery, War, and Revolution," 15; Hall, *African Ethnicities*, 119–20; Howard, *Changing History*, 73–78; and Paquette, *Sugar Is Made*, 123–25.

31. Palmié, *Wizards and Scientists*, 90 (emphasis in original).

32. Childs, *1812 Aponte Rebellion*, 144–45.

33. Carmen Barcia, *Los ilustres apellidos*, 390–427.

34. See Brubaker and Cooper, "Beyond 'Identity.'"

35. Saco, "Examen de las tablas," 343.

36. P. Lovejoy, "Identifying Enslaved Africans," 1–2.

37. Peel, *Religious Encounter*, 190.

38. See Castellanos, *La brujería*; Dumont, *Antropología y patología*; Roche y Monteagudo, *Las policías*; and Trujillo y Monagas, *Los criminales*.

39. Ortiz, *Hampa afro-cubana*, 26.

40. See Baba, *Mi'râj al-Su'ûd*; P. Lovejoy, "Context of Enslavement"; and email with Yacine Daddi Addoun, 27 August 2012.

41. See H. Lovejoy and Ojo, "'Lucumí and 'Terranova.'"

42. See Law, "Ethnicity and the Slave Trade."

43. See Law, *Ọyọ Empire*; and P. Lovejoy, *Caravans of Kola*.

44. Law, *Ọyọ Empire*, 81–90; and Lloyd, "Political Development," 13.

45. See Childs and Falola, "Yoruba Diaspora"; Eltis, "Diaspora of Yoruba Speakers"; P. Lovejoy, "Yoruba Factor"; and Voyages (estimates: 1501–1866, Bight of Benin to all disembarkation regions).

46. See chap. 6, especially Table 6.8.

Chapter One

1. See Crowther, *Dictionary of Yoruba Language*.

2. See Herskovits, "New World Negro"; Mintz and Price, *Anthropological Approach*; and Ortiz, *Contrapunteo cubano*.

3. ANC, CM 11/1, "Declaración de Juan Prieto," 18 July 1835, fol. 220v.

4. José de Gálvez led Spain's *Consejo de las Indias* and implemented the Bourbon reforms. His brother, Matías, was captain general of Guatemala and then viceroy of New Spain. Matías's son, Bernardo, was a naval leader during the American Revolution, governor of Louisiana and Cuba, and viceroy of New Spain until his death in 1786. See Caughey, *Bernardo de Gálvez*; and Chávez, *Spain and the Independence*.

5. ANC, CM 11/1, "Testamento de Juan Prieto," 10 October 1834, fol. 220.

6. Law, *Ouidah*, 2.

7. Akinjogbin, *Dahomey and Its Neighbors*, 166; and Law, "Lagoonside Port," 48.

8. ANC, CM 11/1, "Capitania Pedaneo de Jesus Maria," 14 July 1835, fol. 211.

9. ANC, CM 11/1, "Declaración de Juan Prieto," 18 July 1835, fol. 225v.

10. Barber, *I Could Speak*, 339.

11. Barber, 109 and 135.

12. McIntosh, *Yoruba Women*, 79.

13. See Samuel Johnson, *History of the Yorùbás*; and Ogundiran, "Living in the Shadow."

14. Stilwell, *Slavery and Slaving*, 20.

15. Samuel Johnson, *History of the Yorùbás*, 77.

16. Andrew Apter translated this phrase by email, 15 August 2012.

17. Oduyoye, *Yoruba Names*, 3.

18. Samuel Johnson, *History of the Yorùbás*, 81; see also Akinnaso, "Sociolinguistic Basis"; and Akinnaso, "Yoruba Names."

19. Clapperton, *Hugh Clapperton*, 99–100.

20. Olódùmarè has other names, such as Ọlọrun and Olófin. D. Brown, *Santería Enthroned*, 121.

21. Examples of select literature on òrìṣà worship include Bolívar Aróstegui, *Los Orishas en Cuba*; D. Brown, *Santería Enthroned*; Falola and Genova, *Òrìṣà*; Gleason, *Orisha*; Olupona and Rey, *Òrìṣà Devotion*; Ortiz, *Hampa afro-cubana*; and Verger, *Orisha*.

22. Akinjogbin, *Cradle of a Race*, 44–48.

23. Falola and Akinyemi, *Encyclopedia of the Yorùbá*, 84.

24. Pemberton, "Sacred Symbols," 5.

25. CMS, O 87, 7 July 1852; cf. McKenzie, *Hail Orisha*, 75.

26. In Yorùbá, the word ọ̀pá means "stick, staff, or pole." ANC, CM 11/1, "Declaración de Juan Prieto," 18 July 1835, fol. 225v (emphasis in original).

27. Wescott and Morton-Williams, "Symbolism and Ritual Context," 23.

28. CMS, O 51A, 9 Nov. 1851; cf. McKenzie, *Hail Orisha*, 82.

29. ANC, CM 11/1, "Declaración de Prieto," 18 July 1835, fol. 225v.

30. See Thieme, "Descriptive Catalogue."

31. Examples of select literature on *bàtá* drums include Bascom, *Drums of the Yoruba*; Bencomo, "Sacred Bata Drums"; D. Brown, *Santería Enthroned*, 64; Hagedorn, *Divine Utterances*; Klein, *Yorùbá Bàtá*; Lacerda, *Yoruba Drums*; H. Lovejoy, "Drums of Ṣàngó"; Marcuzzi, "Bàtá Drumming"; Ortiz, "Los 'bàtá,'" 315–16; Thieme, "Descriptive Catalogue"; Timi de Ede, "Los Tambores"; and Sublette, *Cuba and Its Music*. I also interviewed Francisco Aguabella, 14 May 2007; and Michael Marcuzzi, February 2005.

32. Thieme, "Descriptive Catalogue."

33. Samuel Johnson, *History of the Yorùbás*, 149–52.

34. Apter, "On African Origins," 236; see also Thompson, "Divine King"; and Thompson, "Aesthetic of the Cool."

35. ANC, CM 11/1, "Declaración de Prieto," 18 July 1835, fol. 225v.

36. Peel, *Religious Encounter*, 114.

37. Matory, *Sex and the Empire*, 189.

38. CMS, O 31, 25 June 1846; cf. McKenzie, *Hail Orisha*, 179.

39. CMS, O 67, 25 June 1847; cf. McKenzie, *Hail Orisha*.

40. CMS, O 76, 15 January 1870; cf. McKenzie, *Hail Orisha*, 180–82.

41. Discrepancies of traditions from Benin describe how Ọranmiyàn was not an Ifẹ prince sent to Benin but an exiled Benin prince who reclaimed his ancestral throne. D. Brown, *Santería Enthroned*, 144–46; Egharevba, *Short History of Benin*, 7; Samuel Johnson, *History of the Yorùbás*, 143–48; and interview with Ernesto Valdés Jané, 12 July 2002.

42. ANC, CM 11/1, "Declaración de Juan Prieto," 18 July 1835, fol. 225v (emphasis in original).

43. Matory uses the term "Age of Sango" in *Sex and the Empire*, 8–13.

44. Law, *Ọyọ Empire*, 94–96.

45. Apter, "Herskovits's Heritage," 22.

46. Beier, "Yoruba Enclave," 238–40; and Law, "Ethnicity and the Slave Trade," 205–19.

47. Thornton, *Africa and the Africans*, 190.

48. H. Lovejoy and Ojo, "'Lucumí' and 'Terranova,'" 364.

49. NA, ADM 7/830, "Description des Côte d'Afrique . . . by Jean Barbot," 1688; and Barbot, *Description of the Coasts*, 352.

50. Eltis, "Diaspora of Yoruba Speakers," 27.

51. Law, *Ọyọ Empire*, 85–90; see also Law, "West African Cavalry State"; and Law, *Horse in West African History*.

52. Examples of select literature on Dahomey include Akinjogbin, *Dahomey and Its Neighbours*; Bay, *Wives of the Leopard*; Law, *Kingdom of Allada*; Law, "Dahomey and the Slave Trade"; Law, "Ideologies of Royal Power"; Law, "Dahomey and the North-West"; Law, "Slave-Raiders and Middlemen"; Polanyi, *Dahomey and the Slave Trade*; Pollis, "Pre-Colonial Polity"; Ronen, "African Role"; and Ross, "Dahomean Middleman System."

53. Law, *Slave Coast*, 24; and Law, "Slave-Raiders and Middlemen," 54–55.

54. Adams, *Remarks on the Country*, 82–83.

55. Law, "Ouidah as a Multiethnic Community," 43; see also Law, *Ouidah*.

56. Voyages (database: 1777–85, principal place of slave purchase Bight of Benin).

57. ANP, C 6/26, "Letter of Ollivier de Montaguère," 6 October 1777; cf. Law, *Contemporary Source Material*, 40–41.

58. ANP, C 6/26, "Letter of Ollivier de Montaguère," 30 December 1780; cf. Law, *Contemporary Source Material*, 42.

59. ANP, C 6/26, "Letter of Ollivier de Montaguère," 24 November 1781; cf. Law, *Contemporary Source Material*, 42.

60. Law, "Lagoonside Port," 48.

61. NA, T 70/1546, "Letter of Lionel Abson," 26 September 1783; cf. Law, *Contemporary Source Material*, 43.

62. According to Borgu traditions, Kaiama was founded about 1750, and "some years afterwards the Yourbas [i.e., Ọ̀yọ́] invaded Kaiama." Later, Ọ̀yọ́ was "driven back with the loss of their chief men." Duff, *Gazetteer of the Kontagora Province*, 28; and see also Law, *Ọyọ Empire*, chap. 8.

63. NA, T 70/1546, "Letter of Lionel Abson," 26 September 1783; cf. Law, *Contemporary Source Material*, 43.

64. Voyages (database: 1777–85, principal place of slave purchase Bight of Benin).

65. Dalzel, *History of Dahomy*, 179–81.

66. Akinjogbin, *Dahomey and Its Neighbors*, 166.

67. Law, "Lagoonside Port," 47–49.

68. Lambert, *Sessional Papers*, vol. 68, "JOSEPH FAYRER was called," 21 May 1792, 143–48.

69. Akinjogbin, *Dahomey and Its Neighbors*, 166; and Law, "Lagoonside Port," 48.

70. Dalzel, *History of Dahomy*, 182–85.

71. Lambert, *Sessional Papers*, vol. 69, "View of the Evidence," 11 February 1788, 17.

72. Lambert, *Sessional Papers*, vol. 68, "JOSEPH FAYRER was called," 21 May 1792, 148.

73. "JOSEPH FAYRER was called," 148.

74. Glélé, *Le Danxome*, 80.

75. Dalzel, *History of Dahomy*, 146; and Law, "My Head," 402.

76. Yoder, "Fly and Elephant Parties," 418.

77. See Avoseh, *Short History of Badagry*; Falola and Avoseh, "Minor Works"; and Sorensen-Gilmour, "Badagry 1784–1863," 94–95.

78. Law, *Ọyọ Empire*, 84–96; and Morton-Williams, "Oyo Yoruba," 31.

79. Norris, *Memoirs of the Reign*, 15.

80. Dalzel, *History of Dahomy*, 187.

81. Isert, *Letters on West Africa*, 133.

82. Voyages (database: 1784, principal place of slave purchase Bight of Benin); and Voyages (ID 81606).

Chapter Two

1. See *Liberated Africans*.

2. Voyages (estimates and database: 1782–85).

3. Voyages (database: 1782–85, Bight of Benin to Caribbean).

4. Voyages (estimates: 1700–91, all embarkation regions to Cuba).

5. Blackburn, *Overthrow of Colonial Slavery*, 335–36; Knight, *Slave Society*, 89; Franco, *Comercio clandestino*, 14–60; García Rodríguez, "El mercado," 124–48; Murray, *Odious Commerce*, 4; Schneider, "African Slavery," 17; and see also Tomich, *Through the Prism*.

6. After the British occupied Havana, the slave trade to Cuba developed via British networks, which laid the foundation for Prieto's arrival. From 1763 to 1775, the Compañía Gaditana introduced over 23,000 people, mostly from Jamaica. In 1776, this company dissolved, and British inter-island trade to Cuba disappeared. Once France allied with Spain, St. Domingue sent over 5,500 people to Cuba in 1777 and 1778, and from the firms of Chauvel & Fils, Leconten & Co., Marion & Romberg, and Luis Rey

of French/Spanish heritage. Amores, *Cuba en la época*, 129n13; and Torres Ramirez, *La Compañía*, 171–78.

7. Murray, *Odious Commerce*, 8–9; and O'Malley, *Final Passages*, 89.

8. Voyages (database: 1782–85, Bight of Benin to Spanish Mainland Americas and Caribbean).

9. Discussions with David Eltis from January to December 2013.

10. Voyages (ID 81606); Voyages (database: 1782–85, Bight of Benin to Spanish Mainland Americas and Caribbean); discussions with David Eltis, 2013–14; emails with Steven Behrendt, Paul Lovejoy, Gregory O'Malley, Nicholas Radburn, David Richardson, and Suzanne Schwarz, 2014–16.

11. Average time to cross the Atlantic obtained from available dates in Voyages (database: 1782–85, Bight of Benin to Spanish Mainland Americas and Caribbean); and see also P. Lovejoy, "Middle Passage."

12. Beatson, *Naval and Military Memoirs*, 536; and see also Harbron, *Trafalgar and the Spanish Navy*, 164–73.

13. *Liverpool Plantation Registers*, 115, "Nancy," 2 June 1783; *Liverpool General Advertiser*, 10 July 1783; and email with Steve Behrendt, 28 October 2014.

14. Estimated percentages invested in this voyage: Parke & Heywood, 25 percent; Tarleton & Backhouse, 19 percent; Thomas & William Earle, 13 percent; Thomas Hinde, 19 percent; Thomas Leyland, 13 percent; and Jolly and Fayrer, 6 percent. ULL, DP, MS.10.48, "Tradesmen Notes & Disbursements on Ship Golden Age's Outfitt," 1783, fols. 24–26.

15. Behrendt, "Captains in the British Slave Trade," 79–140; Bennett, *Voice of Liverpool Business*, Tables A.1, A.2, A.3; and see also Elder, "Liverpool Slave Trade."

16. ULL, DP, MS.10.48, "Tradesmen Notes," 1783, fol. 23.

17. *Liverpool Plantation Registers*, 115, "Golden Age," 24 September 1783; *Lloyd's Register 1783*, G393; *Lloyd's Register 1784*, G98; MMM, Subsidiary Register Books, C/EX/L/5, vol. 1, *"Golden Age,"* 6 June 1787; and Voyages (ID 81606).

18. Lambert, *Sessional Papers*, vol. 68, "Mr. MATTHEWS called," 12 June 1788, 41.

19. ULL, DP, MS.10.48, "Invoice of Merchandize Shipped," 1783, fols. 1–15; and Morgan, "Liverpool's Dominance," 21.

20. Based on calculations from available departure and arrival dates in Voyages (database: 1775–1807, Liverpool to Ouidah).

21. Lambert, *Sessional Papers*, vol. 69, "Evidence of ROBERT NORRIS," 25 April 1789, 119.

22. Rediker, *Slave Ship*, 6.

23. ULL, DP, MS.10.48, "List of People," 1783, fols. 17–18.

24. Haggerty and Haggerty, "Visual Analytics," 17.

25. Elder, "Liverpool," 130–31; Voyages (database: Captain's name Joseph Fayrer).

26. Lambert, *Sessional Papers*, vol. 68, "JOSEPH FAYRER was called," 21 May 1792, 149.

27. "JOSEPH FAYRER was called," 144.

28. "JOSEPH FAYRER was called," 149.

29. The *grand cabess*, used for counting cowries, equaled four thousand shells and weighed about 10 pounds. Between 1777 and 1787, an adult male cost between forty-

four and fifty-two *grand cabess*; a boy was slightly less. Hogendorn and Johnson, *Shell Money*, 86–88; and Law, *Ouidah*, 130.

30. ULL, DP, MS.10.48, "Invoice of Merchandize," 1783, fol. 4.

31. "Invoice of Merchandize," fols. 1–15.

32. Archeological evidence shows that Atlantic exchanges such as corn, tobacco, cowries, and imported metals had reached as far as 50 kilometers northeast of Ilè Ifẹ by the seventeenth century. D. Brown, *Santería Enthroned*, chaps. 4 and 5; and Ogundiran, "Living in the Shadow," 97–98.

33. Law, *Ouidah*, 32 and 127–28.

34. Lambert, *Sessional Papers*, vol. 68, "Robert Norris, a Carolina Merchant," 2 June 1788, 5–12; and Lambert, *Sessional Papers*, vol. 69, "Evidence of Robert Norris," 25 April 1789, 118.

35. Isert, *Letters on West Africa*, 133.

36. Voyages (ID 81606).

37. Eltis, "Volume, Age/Sex Ratios," 489.

38. In 1776, an adult male cost 13 trade ounces valued at £32; in 1777, 11.5 to 12 trade ounces was £25; and in 1789, 13 to 14 trade ounces was £30. The average for these three valuations is calculated as follows: (1) £32 ÷ 13 oz. = £2.46 per oz.; (2) 25 ÷ ([11.5 oz. + 12 oz.] ÷ 2) = £2.13 per oz.; and (3) £30 ÷ ([13 oz. + 14 oz.] ÷ 2) = £2.22 per oz.; thus (£2.46 + £2.12 + £2.22) ÷ 3 = £2.27 per oz. In 1777, one trade ounce was "half the value of an ounce of gold . . . [at] £4 sterling"; hence, roughly £2 per trade ounce. *Journal of the Commissioners*, 131; M. Johnson, "Ounce in Eighteenth-Century West African Trade," 204 and 212–13.

39. P. Lovejoy and Richardson, "Competing Markets," 279; and P. Lovejoy and Richardson, "British Abolition," 108.

40. Rudé, *Hanoverian London*, 58; and Schwarz, *London in the Age of Industrialisation*, 52.

41. Lambert, *Sessional Papers*, vol. 69, "Evidence of Robert Norris," 25 April 1789, 121.

42. On average, African males were five feet, five inches tall; women were five feet, two inches, and children were under four feet, four inches. Lambert, *Sessional Papers*, vol. 68, "Robert Norris, a Carolina Merchant," 2 June 1788, 6; and Eltis, "Nutritional Trends," 459.

43. Lambert, *Sessional Papers*, vol. 68, "Robert Norris, a Carolina Merchant," 2 June 1788, 6–17.

44. Stanfield, *Observations on a Guinea Voyage*, 30 (emphasis in original).

45. Lambert, *Sessional Papers*, vol. 68, "Archibald Dalziel called in," 3 June 1788, 31; and Lambert, *Sessional Papers*, vol. 69, "Evidence of Archibald Dazell," 25 April 1789, 121.

46. Lambert, *Sessional Papers*, vol. 68, "Robert Norris, a Carolina Merchant," 2 June 1788, 9 and 16–17.

47. Stanfield, *Observations on a Guinea Voyage*, 35.

48. Christopher, *Slave Ship Sailors*, 52.

49. Smallwood, *Saltwater Slavery*, 122.

50. See Rediker, *Slave Ship*, chap. 9; and Richardson, "Shipboard Revolts."

51. See Christopher, *Slave Ship Sailors*, chap. 5; and Smallwood, *Saltwater Slavery*, 123.

52. Rediker, *Slave Ship*, 7–8.

53. See Handler, "Material Culture."

54. Lambert, *Sessional Papers*, vol. 69, "Evidence of ROBERT NORRIS," 25 April 1789, 119.

55. "Evidence of ROBERT NORRIS," 119.

56. Fabre, "Slave Ship Dance," 43–44.

57. Lambert, *Sessional Papers*, vol. 69, "Evidence of ROBERT NORRIS," 25 April 1789, 119.

58. Bascom, *Sixteen Cowries*, 3–6.

59. Greene, "Cultural Zones," 93.

60. See P. Lovejoy, "Middle Passage."

61. Lambert, *Sessional Papers*, vol. 68, "ROBERT NORRIS, a Carolina Merchant," 2 June 1788, 12.

62. Stanfield, *Observations on a Guinea Voyage*, 13 and 25.

63. *Lloyd's List*, no. 1643, "Barbadoes—arrived from Africa—Golden Age, Fayrer and gone to Jamaica," 1 February 1785; and *Lloyd's List*, no. 1645, "Jamaica—arrived from Africa—Golden Age, Farrer," 8 February 1785.

64. ULL, DP, MS.10.48, "List of People," 1783, fol. 17; and Lambert, *Sessional Papers*, vol. 68, "ROBERT NORRIS, a Carolina Merchant," 2 June 1788, 6.

65. Stanfield, *Observations on a Guinea Voyage*, 25–26.

66. See Behrendt, "Crew Mortality"; Christopher, *Slave Ship Sailors*; Kiple, *Caribbean Slave*; Rediker, *Slave Ship*; and Smallwood, *Saltwater Slavery*.

67. There appears to be a discrepancy between 503 and 513 survivors between ULL, DP, MS.10.48, "Sales of 503 Slaves," 2–3 Dec. 1784, fols. 27–28; and Voyages (ID 81606).

68. V. Brown, *Reaper's Garden*, 132–33.

69. ULL, DP, MS.10.48, "Disbursements to Rainford, Blundell & Rainford," 10 December 1784, fol. 29.

70. Rediker, *Slave Ship*, 152–53; and Stanfield, *Observations on a Guinea Voyage*, vi and 34–35.

71. *Nautical Magazine*, 6; Chenoweth, *18th Century Climate*, 133–35; and see also Pérez, *Winds of Change*.

72. ULL, DP, MS.10.48, "Sales of 503 Slaves," 2–3 December 1784, fols. 27–28.

73. The thirteen merchants were Thomas Archer, Edward Brailsford, John Brown, Edward East, Charles Graham, John Hall, Andrew Johnstone, Richard Lake, Alexandre Lindo, Richard Martin, Robert Moss, and Robert Thomson, as well as the firm Bond & Clark. ULL, DP, MS.10.48, "Sales of 503 Slaves," fols. 27–28.

74. See Ranston, *Lindo Legacy*, chap 2; and *Legacies of British Slave-ownership*.

75. ULL, DP, MS.10.48, "Sales of 503 Slaves," 2–3 December 1784, fols. 27–28.

76. Amores, *Cuba en la época*, 128.

77. Amores, 129.

78. Franco, *Comercio clandestino*, 55.

79. In 1784 and 1785, 182 documented slave ships with over 59,000 individuals went to the British Caribbean from all of Africa. Of this total, only seven documented voyages, including the *Golden Age*, originated at the Bight of Benin. Voyages (database:

1784–85, British flag to Spanish mainland Americas and Caribbean); and Voyages (database: 1782–85, Bight of Benin to Spanish Mainland Americas and Caribbean).

80. From January to June 1784, the Spanish government issued licenses to the following Spanish-born merchants: Francisco Fernández de Rábago (Cádiz), José Antonio de Campos (San Sebastián), and Juan López (Madrid). It also issued licenses to the following Cuban-born merchants: Marqués de Socorro, Marqués de la Real Proclamación, and María Candelaria González del Alamo. Due to hurricanes and other reasons, it appears as if none of these merchants were able to bring slaves to Cuba. AGI, PC 1410, "Licencias concedidas a varios individuos . . . ," 1784–85; AGI, SD 1473, "Expediente suscitado por Da. María Candelaria González del Alamo," 7 August 1788; cf. Amores, *Cuba en la época*, 129–31n13–17.

81. AGI, PC 1400, "Expediente sobre D. Miguel Antonio de Herrera," 19 August 1786; AGI, IG 2821, "Certificación de los derechos que pagó . . . ," 16 March 1785; AGI, SD 1665, "Urriza and Gálvez," 5 July 1785; cf. Amores, *Cuba en la época*, 130–31n16; AGI, PC 1356, "Licencia de Herrera," 12 September 1784; cf. Sherry Johnson, *Climate and Catastrophe*, 259n58; and see also Hall and Higman, *Slave Society*.

82. Elder, "Liverpool Slave Trade," 126–31; and see also *Legacies of British Slave-ownership*.

83. Amores, *Cuba en la época*, 130.

84. AGI, IG 2821, "Copia de contrata de [Eduardo Barry]," 13 February 1784; cf. Amores, *Cuba en la época*, 131–32 and n19.

85. ANC, IG 1052/23, "Relación de los negros bozales entrados en este puerto desde el año 1764 hasta 1810," 16 February 1835, fol. 39; cf. Amores, *Cuba en la época*, 131–32.

86. Voyages (database: 1784–85 vessel owners Peter Baker).

87. Parry, "Eliphalet Fitch," 85–86; Torres Ramírez, *La Compañía*, 72–73; and see also Lewis, "Anglo-American Entrepreneurs."

88. José Manuel Lorenzo was the acting Spanish captain for the Blair brothers. Amores, *Cuba en la época*, 130.

89. ANC, GG 510/26350, "Documento sobre un cargamento de Negros que condujo a la Isla de Trinidad D. Eduardo Barri," 1785–86, fols. 1–24.

90. ULL, DP, MS.10.48, "Invoice of Merchandize shipped onboard the Golden Age for Liverpool," 29 January 1784, fols. 31–35.

91. ULL, DP, MS.10.48, "First Insett," 1785, fols. 39–40.

92. ULL, DP, MS.10.48, "Owners of Golden Age 2nd & final Insett," 27 February 1786, fol. 42.

93. Elder, "Liverpool Slave Trade," 119–37.

94. Voyages (ID 81606).

95. ULL, DP, MS.10.48, "Sales of 503 Slaves imported in the Ship Golden Age," 2–3 December 1784, fols. 27–28; ULL, DP, MS.10.48, "Invoice of Merchandize shipped onboard the Golden Age for Liverpool," 29 January 1785, fols. 31–33; Haggerty, *Merely for Money*, 179–88; Haggerty and Haggerty, "Visual Analytics," 5–6; and *Legacies of British Slave-ownership*.

96. Parry, "Eliphalet Fitch," 94–95.

97. Radburn, "Guinea Factors," 253–83; and Ranston, *Lindo Legacy*, 50–63.

98. SKA, Wills 10110/15, "James Blair witness for William Julius' last testament," 5 June 1779; cf. *Kings Candle Sticks*; and Smith, *Wealth of Nations*, 2:165.

99. Ayisi, *Saint Eustatius*, 196; Morgan and Rushton, *Banishment in the Early Atlantic World*, 216; see also Barka, "Citizens of St. Eustatius"; Enthoven, "Abominable Nest of Pirates"; and Jameson, "St. Eustatius."

100. On St. Kitts, John Satterwaite & Co. were known associates with investors of the *Golden Age*. Elder, "Liverpool Slave Trader," 129–31.

101. Draper, *Price of Emancipation*, 188; and Rodgers, *Ireland, Slavery, and Anti-Slavery*, 94.

102. Amores, *Cuba en la época*, 131.

103. Licensees included Teresa Ambulodi, Bárbara Estrada, Pedro Tomás de Azanza, Roberto Madan, Rafael Morales, Pedro Julián de Morales, José Manuel López Lanuza, Conde de Montavalo, Conde de Vallellano, and Marqués de Real Agrada. Amores, *Cuba en la época*, 132–33n19–23; and see also González Quintana, "María Teresa de Ambulodi."

104. For Baker and Dawson contracts, see AGI, IG 2821, "Conde de Gálvez a José de Gálvez," 30 April 1785; AGI, IG 2821, "Conde de Gálvez a José de Gálvez," 5 April–10 May 1785; AGI, IG 2823, "Real Cédula," 28 February 1789; cf. Amores, *Cuba en la época*, 132–33n21–23.

105. Voyages (database: 1785–95, vessel owner John Dawson).

106. Voyages (ID 81247).

Chapter Three

1. Knight, *Slave Society*, 82.

2. Examples of select literature about the role of Havana in Spanish imperial history include Ely, *La economía*; Lufríu, *El impulso inicial*; Masó y Velázquez, *Historia de Cuba*; Parry, *Spanish Seaborne Empire*; Pérez, *Cuba*; and Pino-Santos, *Historia de Cuba*.

3. See de la Fuente, *Havana and the Atlantic*; Jennings, "State Enslavement"; Sherry Johnson, "Home Front"; Kuethe, *Cuba, 1753–1815*; and Landers, *Black Society*.

4. Fraginals, *El ingenio*, 65; Sherry Johnson, *Social Transformation*, 11–13; Knight, "Origins of Wealth," 231–53; Kuethe, *Cuba, 1753–1815*, 174; Kuethe and Andrien, *Spanish Atlantic World*, 5–6; and Wheat, *Atlantic Africa*, 151–56.

5. Hunt, *Inventing Human Rights*, 259.

6. R. Scott, *Slave Emancipation*.

7. Tomich and Zeuske, "Second Slavery," 91 and 94.

8. *Real cédula*.

9. Fraginals, *El ingenio*, 8; and Knight, *Slave Society*, 15–17.

10. Knight, *Slave Society*, 11–13; see also Ferrer, *Freedom's Mirror*; Ferrer, "Noticias de Haití"; Franco, *Historia de la revolución*; Geggus, *Impact of the Haitian Revolution*; Genovese, *From Rebellion*; and González-Ripoll et al., *El rumor de Haití*.

11. Voyages (estimates: 1500–1790 for Cuba; 1791–1840 for Cuba).

12. Arango y Parreño, "Representación manifestando las ventajas de una absoluta libertad en la introducción de negros . . . ," 10 May 1791, in *Obras del Excmo. Señor D. Francisco*, 31.

13. Humboldt, *Political Essay*, 33; see also Kiple, *Blacks in Colonial Cuba*.

14. Humboldt, *Political Essay*, 26–27.

15. Humboldt, 35.

16. Kuethe, "Havana in the Eighteenth Century," 18.

17. De la Fuente, *Havana and the Atlantic*, 225.

18. Examples of select literature on *castas* include Chance and Taylor, "Estate and Class"; Chance and Taylor, "A Reply"; Kuznesof, "Ethnic and Gender Influences"; Kuznesof, "More Conversation"; McCaa, Schwartz, and Grubessich, "Race and Class"; Poot-Herrera, "Los criollos"; and Schwartz, "Colonial Identities."

19. Taylor, *Magistrates of the Sacred*, 26.

20. De la Fuente, *Havana and the Atlantic*, 225.

21. H. Lovejoy, "Registers of Liberated Africans: Implementation," 7–8.

22. SSDA, ES, Bautismos de Pardos y Morenos (BPM), vol. 16, "Manuel Adulto de nación Inglesa," 8 September 1786, fol. 5v, entry 24.

23. Extensive searches related to the Prieto family conducted on *Cuban Genealogy Center*; see also Atienza y Navajas, *Nobiliario español*, 634 and 1102.

24. AGI, CC 5506 3/15, "Expediente de información y licencia de pasajero a Indias de José Prieto de la Fuerte, a La Habana," 12 December 1766.

25. AGI, PC 1470, 29 October 1790; cf. Sherry Johnson, *Social Transformation*, 86.

26. AGI, CC 5517 1/37, "Joseph Prieto canónigo de la iglesia cathedral y auxillio," 29 May 1772.

27. Juan Prieto was the Guarda-almacén of New Orleans from the late 1770s into the 1790s. See AGI, PC 471, 483, 603, and 700; and Arthur et al., *Old Families*, 396.

28. Email with Juan Bosco Amores, 24 October 2014.

29. Gárate, *Comercio ultramarino*, 36 and 269.

30. See Kirsch, "St. John Nepomucene."

31. See Anon., "Patronazgo del Cuerpo."

32. M. García, *El Español*, 227; and Harbron, *Trafalgar and the Spanish Navy*, 43 and 170.

33. ANC, CM 11/1, "Declaración de Juan Prieto," 18 July 1835, fol. 220v.

34. Tens of thousands of baptism records were surveyed carefully, some of which are illegible in both their original and digital formats. Moreover, entire volumes of baptism records are missing. It is therefore possible that Prieto's baptism record could surface in the future and such invaluable information could change this narrative to some degree. SSDA, JMJ, BPM, vols. 1, 3–9, 1773–98, 1808–44 (vol. 2 missing); SSDA, ES, BPM, vols. 16, 21, 22, 29, and 30, 1773–77, 1786–89, 1797–1800, and 1807–9 (vols. 12–15, 17–20, and 23–28 missing); SSDA, NSAG, BPM, vols. 5–6, 8–15, 1762–89, 1801–46 (vol. 7 missing); SSDA, NSR, BPM, vols. 1–4, 1805–48 (no vols. before 1805); SSDA, SAC, BPM, vols. 13–23, 1800–1840 (no vols. before 1800); SSDA, SCBV, BPM, vol. 23, 1801–3 (no vols. 1765–1801 and after 1803); SSDA, SCM, BPM, vols. 3–18, 1782–1841 (vol. 2 missing).

35. See Díaz, *Virgin King*.

36. Examples of select literature on the definition of *cabildos* include D. Brown, *Santería Enthroned*; Carmen Barcia, *Los ilustres apellidos*; Deschamps Chapeaux, "Cabildos"; Childs, "Black Creole"; Howard, *Changing History*; López Valdés, *Componentes africanos*; Moreno, *La antigua*; Ortiz, *Los cabildos*; Pichardo, *Diccionario provincial*, 37; and Pike, *Aristocrats and Traders*, 172–74.

37. Childs, "Black Creole," 210.

38. Landers, *Atlantic Creoles*, 145.

39. Carmen Barcia, *Los ilustres apellidos*; and Moliner Castañeda, *Los cabildos*.

40. In 1755, public notaries surveyed *cabildos* inside the city walls, including five Carabali, five Congo, four Mina, two Lucumí, two Arará, two Gangá, and one Mandinga. Seven of these *cabildos* were situated in La Sabana, which was the name given to the intersection at Calle Bayona and Calle Conde; another three *cabildos* were located on Calle Monserrate. AGI, SD 515/51, "Inventario de los cabildos," 1755.

41. Landers, "Catholic Conspirators," 497–500.

42. Deschamps Chapeaux, "Cabildos," 50.

43. López Valdés, *Componentes africanos*, 9–10.

44. D. Brown, "Afro-Cuban Festival," 55.

45. John Mason interviewed the *babaláwo* Quintín Lecón Lombillo in the Havana neighborhoods of Juanelo and Regla in 1986. He was the grandson of Filomeno García Àtàndá (c. 1799–1876), who came from Africa in the early 1830s and was credited with consecrating Cuba's first *bàtá* drums. Mason, *Aráàràrá*, 152–54; and interviews with John Mason, 4 February 2017.

46. Although evidence exists of people from the Bight of Benin arriving to Havana and becoming involved in the church in the sixteenth century, the earliest known documented record of *cabildos* founded by people from the Bight of Benin was Arará Magino *cabildo* in 1691. See Carmen Barcia, *Los ilustres apellidos*, 391–427. López Valdés refers to a "Cabildo Lucumí Amanga" in 1728 but does not provide a reference to the source or patron saint see *Africanos de Cuba*, 189. The 1755 Lucumí *cabildos* were dedicated to Nuestra Señora del Rosario and Nuestra Señora de las Nieves see AGI, SD 515/51, "Inventario de los cabildos," 1755.

47. Between 1783 and 1788, the leaders (and members) of the Lucumí *cabildo* on Jesús María included Isidro de Cárdenas, Joseph Antonio Aguilar, Alberto Aparicio (and Antonio Pérez, Joseph Antonio Ribero, Agustín Zaisa, Domingo Echevarria, Joseph Aguilar, and Joseph María Santalla). Fernando Acosta, Miguel Valdés, María de Jesús Valdés, and María Esperanza de Céspedes apparently founded the Lucumí *cabildo* on Villegas earlier in the century. In 1783, the leaders were Antonio Pimienta Lucumí Tembú, Nicolás Palomino, Pedro Infanzón, Dolores Martínez Lucumí Allom, and María Loreto Torres Lucumí Ibanya. ANC, EV 105/20394, "Cabildo Lucumí," 1783 and 1788; ANC, EG 277/5, "Cabildo de la Nación Lucumí," 1783 and 1790; cf. Carmen Barcia, *Los ilustres apellidos*, 415–17; see also Wetohossou, "Las migraciones," 172n60. The ethnonyms "Allom" likely referred to Ọ̀yọ́, "Ibanya" to Ìgbómìnà or Ìjànnà, and "Tembú" almost certainly referred to Tchámbà, that is, Konkomba. Variations of "Tembú" appear on plantation reports elsewhere in the Americas from 1769 onward. Curtin, *Atlantic Slave Trade*, 187; Richard and Debien, "Les origines," 5 and 24; Debien, "Les origines," 259; Froelich and Alexandre, "Histoire traditionnelle," 230; Froelich et al., *Les populations*, 14; and emails with Robin Law and Paul E. Lovejoy, 5–7 March 2012.

48. Rushing, "Afro-Cuban Social Organization," 181–82.

49. Law, *Ọyọ Empire*, 64.

50. Childs, *1812 Aponte Rebellion*, 104–5 and 110; and Deschamps Chapeaux, *Los batallones*, 54.

51. ANC, EC 147/1, "Manuel Blanco," fol. 53v; cf. Childs, *1812 Aponte Rebellion*, 105 and 239n172; Childs, "Black Creole," 219–22; Palmié, *Cooking of History*, 43; and Wetohossou, "Las migraciones," 172n60.

52. Childs, *1812 Aponte Rebellion*, 105–10.

53. "Nangas" is comparable to the "Nagô" ethnonym commonly found in Brazil. People in West Africa speaking the Gbe languages, including Fon, refer to Yoruba speakers as *anagonu*, which is a term derived from the Yoruba-speaking subgroup Ànàgó. "Barbaes" apparently refers to the Bàrìbá located in Borgu to the north of Oyo. "Chabas" appears to refer to the Konkomba (Tchámbà) from the Gurma cluster of peoples near the Atakora Mountains. Those identified as "Bambaras" probably did not refer to the Bambara (i.e., Bamana of Mali), but rather to Wangara, which was a corporate name for Muslims in Borgu. Wangara included people of western Juula and/or Dendi origin who had moved into Borgu and the Hausa states following their commercial interests in long-distance trade from the middle Volta basin through the Atakora Mountains and Hausaland and into Borno as far as Lake Chad. For more information related to these ethnonyms see Curtin, *Atlantic Slave Trade*, 186–87; Law, "Ethnicity and the Slave Trade," 212; Law and P. Lovejoy, "Borgu in the Atlantic Slave Trade," 69–92; H. Lovejoy, "Old Oyo Influences," chap. 3; and P. Lovejoy, "Role of the Wangara," 176n16.

54. ANC, EC 147/1, "Manuel Blanco," fol. 54v; cf. Childs, *1812 Aponte Rebellion*, 110 and 240n205.

55. Childs, "Black Creole," 222; Childs, "Gendering the African Diaspora," 243; and Hanger, *Bounded Lives*, chap. 4.

56. Deschamps Chapeaux, *La Habana*, 19.

57. Carmen Barcia, *Los ilustres apellidos*; and Landers, *Atlantic Creoles*, 148.

58. In 1805, Feliciano del Rey was *capatáz* of the Cabildo Lucumí Nuestra Señora de Regla. In modern-day practices, this patron saint is more closely associated with Yẹmọja. ANC, EG 123/15, "Cabildo Lucumi Nuestra Señora de Regla," 1805; cf. Carmen Barcia, *Los ilustres apellidos*, 417. Between 1807 and 1810, members of the *cabildo* Lucumí Llané were involved in a civil trial, whereby the leaders, Juan Nepomuceno Montiel and Rafael Aristeguy, accused two other members, Agustín Zaiza and Antonio Ribero, of stealing 500 pesos from the *cabildo* treasury to purchase a slave. The two accused were members of the late eighteenth-century Lucumí *cabildo* led by Isidro de Cárdenas and Joseph Antonio Aguilar. The ethnonym "Llané" could refer to the Ègbádo town of Ìjànnà, or less likely, a distortion of "Ayonu" (Ọ̀yọ́). ANC, EC 64/6, "Juan Nepomuceno Montiel y Rafael Aristeguy como apoderados de la nación Lucumí Llané contra Agustín Zaiza y Antonio Ribero sobre la estación hicieron de la caja de esta nación," 1807–10.

59. Manuel Blanco was a captain in the black militia. See Childs, *1812 Aponte Rebellion*, 110 and 240n205. The documentation from the Lucumí *cabildo* on Jesús María describes the leaders as "militiamen in charge" (*milicianos capataces*). ANC, EV 105/20394, "Cabildo Lucumí," 1783 and 1788. The documented Lucumí *cabildo* leader, Nicolás Palomino, from 1783 was listed in the muster roll as a Lieutenant from AGI, SD 2093, "Batallón de Milicias Morenos Libres," 28 December 1761; and Pedro Infanzón was listed in the muster roll as a Corporal from AGI, PC, 1368A, "Compañia de Morenos Zapadores," 10 December 1782.

60. Howard, *Changing History*, chaps. 2 and 3.

61. See Ortiz, *Los cabildos*; and Deschamps Chapeaux, "Cabildos."

62. Carmen Barcia, *Los ilustres apellidos*, 84.

63. Childs, "Gendering the African Diaspora," 232.

64. ANC, CM 11/1, "Declaración de Juan Prieto," 18 July 1835, fol. 224.

65. Kuethe, *Cuba, 1753–1815*, 40–41.

66. Jennings, "State Enslavement," 171–72.

67. Sherry Johnson, *Social Transformation*, 63 (my emphasis).

68. *Colección de documentos*, "Sobre preemencias de oficiales y soldados milicianos," 16 September 1708, 80; *Colección de documentos*, "Reglamento para las milicias y infantería y caballería de la isla de Cuba," 19 January 1769, 351–58; see also Carmen Barcia, *Los ilustres apellidos*; Childs, *1812 Aponte Rebellion*, 83; Deschamps Chapeaux, *Los batallones*, 21–22; H. Klein, "Colored Militia," 17; Kuethe, *Cuba, 1753–1815*; Kuethe, *Military Reform*, 8–27, 38–39; Landers, *Atlantic Creoles*, 139; McAlister, *Fuero Militar*; Sánchez, "African Freedmen"; and Zúñiga, *Entre esclavos*.

69. Deschamps Chapeaux, *El negro en la economía*, 47–86; see also Duharte, *El negro en la sociedad*, 91–115; and Landers, *Atlantic Creoles*, 140–42.

70. Deschamps Chapeaux, *Los batallones*, 56–57.

71. *Reglamento para las milicias*, 72–73; see also Carmen Barcia, *La otra familia*; Perera Díaz and Meriñi Fuentes, *Esclavitud, familia y parroquia*; and Stolke, *Marriage, Class, and Colour*.

72. The location of Prieto and Camejo's marriage was stated in ANC, CM 11/1, "Testamento de Juan Prieto," 10 October 1834, fol. 220v. Extensive searches for their marriage certificate conducted in SSDA, JMJ, Indices de Matrimonios, vol. 1 (no date); SSDA, JMJ, Matrimonios de Pardos y Morenos (MPM), vols. 1–2, 1773–1861; SSDA, NSAG, MPM, vols. 3–4, 1762–1859; SSDA, SAC, MPM, vols. 2 and 4, 1770–92 and 1812–39 (vol. 3 missing); SSDA, SCBV, MPM, vols. 6–8, 1785–1854; SSDA, SCBV, Expedientes de Matrimonios, 4 vols., 1803–29.

73. Extensive searches related to the Camejo family conducted on *Cuban Genealogy Center*; see also Platero Fernández, "Los apellidos," 12–15; and Knight, *Slave Society*, 13.

74. ANC, CM 11/1, "Testamento de Juan Prieto," 10 October 1834, fol. 220v; and SSDA, JMJ, BPM, vol. 3, fols. 108v–109, entry 806.

75. One or both of Camejo's parents may have been among small groups of people that arrived in Cuba from the Bight of Benin. Between 1700 and 1770, there were only two documented slave ships arriving in Havana directly from the Bight of Benin—one from Ouidah in 1718 and another from Little Popo in 1764. Voyages (database: 1700–75, Bight of Benin to Cuba).

76. Sherry Johnson, "Home Front," 206; see also Franklin, *Women and Slavery*, 130–32; Lavrin, "Colonial Woman," 23–59; Morrison, *Cuba's Racial Crucible*; and Morrison, "Slave Mothers."

77. Sherry Johnson, "Home Front," 207.

78. Deschamps Chapeaux, *Los batallones*, 65–67.

79. Landers, "Transforming Bondsmen," 120; see also Goveia, "West Indian Slave Laws"; Landers, *Black Society*, chaps. 3 and 10; and Watson, *Slave Law*.

80. Humboldt, *Political Essay*, 79.

81. Sherry Johnson, "Home Front," 212.

82. Bergad et al., *Cuban Slave Market*, 122. Examples of select literature on *coartación* include de la Fuente, "Slaves and the Creation"; Lucuena Salmoral, "El derecho"; Obrando Andrade, "Manumisión"; and Varella, "Price of 'Coartación.'"

83. Bergad et al., *Cuban Slave Market*, 73.

84. Deschamps Chapeaux, *Los batallones*, 65–67.

85. Drewal and Drewal, *Gẹlẹdẹ*, 10; see also Lloyd, "Status of the Yoruba Wife," 39; Lloyd, *Power and Independence*, 38.

86. Fadipe, *Sociology of the Yoruba*, 257.

87. McIntosh, *Yoruba Women*, 211.

88. Camejo and Prieto might have attended and supported Captain Gabriel Dorotea Barba's school for people of African descent, which by 1833, consisted of two buildings, "one for boys and another for girls." Barba held "evening classes . . . to teach the Christian doctrine." Landers, *Atlantic Creoles*, 154.

89. Cornelius, "Learned to Read," 171; see also Bly, "Pretends He Can Read"; Cardoso Morais, "Ler e escrever"; Cornelius, *When I Can Read*; and Richards, "Samuel Davies."

Chapter Four

1. Sherry Johnson, *Social Transformation*, 63.

2. *Reglamento para las milicias*, 37–38.

3. Deschamps Chapeaux, *Los batallones*, 67.

4. Kuethe, *Cuba, 1753–1815*, 44.

5. Sherry Johnson, *Social Transformation*, 64; and Kuethe, *Cuba, 1753–1815*, 44.

6. Sherry Johnson, "Home Front," 209.

7. Childs, *1812 Aponte Rebellion*, 87–88.

8. Kuethe, *Cuba, 1753–1815*, 41–43.

9. Deschamps Chapeaux, *Los batallones*, 68.

10. *Reglamento para las milicias*, 43.

11. Sherry Johnson, *Social Transformation*, 64.

12. ANC, EGu, "Cadet José López de Soto to Nicolás de Villa, proxy power of attorney," 27 March 1782; cf. Sherry Johnson, "Home Front," 207.

13. Deschamps Chapeaux, *Los batallones*, 74.

14. Email with Jane Landers, 12 October 2017.

15. De la Fuente, *Havana and the Atlantic*, 168–69.

16. ANC, CM 11/1, "NUESTRA SEÑORA DE LOS REMEDIOS," undated, loose paper; see also Carmen Barcia, *Los ilustres apellidos*, 61n56; and Landers, *Atlantic Creoles*, 171.

17. ANC, CM 11/1, "S. BARBARA GLORIOSA VIRGEN Y MARTIR, PATRONA DEL REAL CUERPO DE ARTILLERÍA," undated, loose paper.

18. During the island's wars of independence in the second half of the nineteenth century, the Virgen de la Caridad del Cobre emerged as Cuba's patron saint. She is often portrayed as a mixed-race female and heavily associated with Ọ̀ṣun in modern-day observations of the Lucumí religion. By the 1895 war, Cuba's freedom fighters, collectively known as *mambises*, sewed images of this Marian devotion on their

military uniforms. Examples of select literature on this saint include Arrom, "La Virgen del Cobre"; Díaz, "Rethinking Tradition"; Díaz, *Royal Slaves of El Cobre*; Dillon, "La Virgen de la Caridad del Cobre"; Lachatañeré, "La religión santera"; Murphy and Mei-Mei Sanford, *Ọṣun across the Waters*; Ortiz, "La semi luna"; Ortiz and Matos Arévalo, *La Virgen de la Caridad del Cobre*; and Portuondo Zúñiga, *La Virgen de la Caridad*.

19. See Artola, *La España*; Artola and Morán, *Las cortes*; Chandler, *Campaigns of Napoleon*; Esdaile, *Peninsular War*; Gandarias and Prieto, *Crónicas parlamentarias*; L. García, *Liberty under Siege*; Lovett, *Napoleon and the Birth*; and Suárez, *Las cortes*.

20. Childs, *1812 Aponte Rebellion*, 90–91.

21. Landers, *Atlantic Creoles*, 156.

22. *Diario de sesiones*, "El Sr. Gordoa," 4 September 1811, 1766.

23. Sartorius, *Ever Faithful*, 24; see also Sartorius, "Free-Colored Militias."

24. Landers, *Atlantic Creoles*, 155–57.

25. See Rodríguez, *Independence of Spanish America*; Langley, *Americas in the Age of Revolution*; and P. Lovejoy, *Jihād in West Africa*.

26. Childs, *1812 Aponte Rebellion*, 91.

27. Knight, *Slave Society*, 15.

28. ANC, CM 11/1, "Declaración de Juan Prieto," 18 July 1835, fol. 224.

29. See Childs, *1812 Aponte Rebellion*; Franco, *La conspiración*; and Franco, *Las conspiraciones*.

30. Childs, *1812 Aponte Rebellion*, 138–47.

31. Childs, 138–47.

32. Deschamps Chapeaux, *Los batallones*, 52.

33. Landers, *Black Society*, 199–200; see also *Diario de las operaciones*, "Carta al Gobernador Chester," 12 May 1781, 1–32.

34. Scholars have yet to find Aponte's book of drawings. Childs, *1812 Aponte Rebellion*, 3–4.

35. Childs, 6; and email with Matt D. Childs, June 2012.

36. Childs, 125.

37. Childs, 94–96.

38. Landers, *Atlantic Creoles*, 148.

39. See the introduction for a discussion on historiographical problems related to Ṣàngó tẹ̀ dún.

40. ANC, AP 12/24, "Bando del Capitán General de la Isla," 7 April 1812; cf. Childs, *1812 Aponte Rebellion*, 4.

41. Landers, *Black Society*, 199–200; see also *Diario de las operaciones*, "Carta al Gobernador Chester," 12 May 1781, 1–32.

42. Landers, *Atlantic Creoles*, 120.

43. DuVal, *Independence Lost*, 236.

44. ANC, AP, 10/13, "Real Orden, Cádiz," 18 June 1812; see also Patrick, *Florida Fiasco*; and Cusick, *Other War*.

45. ANC, FL 21/83, "El Intendente da cuente de haber salido de la Habana al de Pensacola las tropas auxiliares," 28 June 1812.

46. ANC, CM 11/1, "Declaración de Juan Prieto," 18 July 1835, fols. 224–224v.

47. ANC, FL 21/84, "El intendent participa que por disposición del Capitán General están para salir a Pensacola y San Agustín dos compañías mas de morenos," 4 September 1812.

48. AGI, PC 256B, "1ª Compañia de Morenos de la Habana," 13 January 1814; AGI, PC 256B, "2ª Compañia de Morenos de la Habana," 13 January 1814; AGI, PC 256B, "Cuerpo Artillería Nacional Compañía de Morenos de la Habana," 5 March 1814. It is unlikely that Second Sergeant León Monzón, one of Prieto's superiors in Florida, was the same person as Captain León Monzón, who was sentenced to four years in prison following the Aponte Rebellion. They might have been related, however, since one of the two participated in other rebellions in 1839 and 1844. See also Deschamps Chapeaux, *Los batallones*, 79–83; and Childs, *1812 Aponte Rebellion*, 176.

49. AGI, PC 256B, "Primera Compañia de Morenos de la Habana," 13 January–5 August 1814. No muster rolls have been located between 1811 and 1813.

50. ANC, FL 21/85, "El intendente acompaña relación de los barriles de harina introducidas en el puerto de La Habana procedente de Pensacola," 16 October 1812.

51. ANC, FL 9/24, "Relativo a la construcción de obras de defensa en la plaza de Pensacola," 29 August 1799; ANC, FL 9/44, "Copia de lo determinado por la Junta de Guerra sobre las defensas de la Plaza de Pensacola," 26 August 1799.

52. According to Saunt, "The Spanish borrowed words from indigenous groups to identify residents on the Chattahoochee-Flint rivers as 'Uchizes,' and those on the Coosa-Tallapoosa as 'Talapusas.' Hitchiti speakers who lived in the Deep South used 'Uchize,' meaning 'people of another language,' to refer to Muskogee. 'Talapusa' is apparently a Muskogee term that means 'stranger,' suggesting that Indians on the Coosa and Tallapoosa did not give it to themselves. To distinguish the inhabitants of the Coosa and Tallapoosa Rivers from those of the Chattahoochee and Flint, the British called them 'Upper' and 'Lower' Creeks. The term 'Creek' itself was an English term denoting indigenous groups living on Ochese Creek, a tributary of the upper Ocmulgee River in Georgia. Traders began applying it to every indigenous group of the Deep South. In the late eighteenth century, Native Americans in the region would adopt it as their own, along with another name imposed from without, 'Muskogulge' or 'Muskogee,' meaning 'people of the swampy ground,' a word of Algonkian origin." Saunt, *New Order*, 13–14.

53. Millett, "Defining Freedom," 378; see also Coker and Parker, "Second Spanish Period"; Coker and Inglis, *Spanish Censuses*; Holmes, "West Florida"; and McAlister, "Pensacola during the Second Spanish Period."

54. Saunt, *New Order*, 7.

55. Saunt, 3.

56. Ethridge, *Creek Country*, 31.

57. Saunt, *New Order*, 34–35.

58. Thrower, "Casualties and Consequences," 12–13.

59. LBH, 2/591, "Benjamin Hawkins to William Eustis," 21 September 1811; cf. Saunt, *New Order*, 211.

60. Thrower, "Casualties and Consequences," 10; and Saunt, *New Order*, 249.

61. Saunt, *New Order*, 256–57; and see also Braund, "Red Skins."

62. Bunn and Williams, *Battle for the Southern Frontier*, 25.

63. LOC, ASP, Indian Affairs, vol. 1, Senate, 13th Congress, 3rd Session, "Hawkins to Armstrong," 23 August 1813, 851–52.

64. Saunt, *New Order*, 256–57.

65. Adams, *History of the United States*, 228.

66. AGI, PC 1794/1417, Mateo González Manrique to Juan Ruíz Apodaca," 23 July 1813; cf. Saunt, *New Order*, 262.

67. Adams, *History of the United States*, 229.

68. Green, *Politics of Indian Removal*, 42.

69. Abram, "Cherokees in the Creek War."

70. See Jensen, "Horseshoe Bend."

71. Ethridge, *Creek Country*, 240.

72. Ethridge, 240.

73. AGI, PC 250, "Hospital Militar Compañia de Morenos de la Habana," 31 May 1814.

74. Landers, *Atlantic Creoles*, 121–28.

75. Marshall, *Royal Naval Biography*, "Letter from William Henry Percy to Alexander Cochrane, commander in chief on the North American Station," 9 September 1814, 65.

76. AGI, PC 256B, "Batallón de Morenos: Lista de los Individuos se embarcaron para la Habana en la Corbeta de la Real Armada la Diana," 8 September 1814. Prieto's name does not appear on monthly muster rolls from Pensacola thereafter. See AGI, PC 256B, "1ª Compañia de Morenos de la Habana," 8 September 1814; AGI, PC 256B, "1ª Compañia de Morenos de la Habana," 5 October 1814.

77. Eaton, *Major General Andrew Jackson*, 142.

78. Eaton, 152.

79. Millett, "Occupation of Pensacola," 233.

80. See Braund, *Deerskins and Duffels*; Coker, *Indian Traders*, chap. 15; Covington, "Negro Fort"; Dowd, *Spirited Resistance*, 185–90; Fisher, "Surrender of Pensacola," 326–29; Landers, *Atlantic Creoles*, chap 3; Martin, *Sacred Revolt*; Millett, "Defining Freedom"; Milligan, "Slave Rebelliousness," 11; Porter, "Negroes and the Seminole War"; and Wright, "First Seminole War."

81. Kuethe, *Cuba, 1753–1815*, 43.

Chapter Five

1. Childs, "Gendering the African Diaspora," 243; Childs, "Black Creole," 223–26.

2. ANC, CM 11/1, "S. Bárbara," n.d., loose folio. Image originally printed at the oficina de D. Pedro Martinez de Almeida, Calle del Sol, no. 55.

3. According to hagiography, Barbara was the daughter of a rich pagan from Heliopolis named Dioscorus. To protect Barbara from the evils of the world, Dioscorus locked his daughter in a tower and tried to arrange a marriage, which she rejected because she had secretly become Christian. After she acknowledged her faith, Dioscorus tried to kill her, but through prayer an opening in the tower appeared, and she was miraculously transported to a mountain. Her father eventually found her on the mountain and brought her back to the city, where she was imprisoned and tortured to make her renounce her faith. At night in the prison, God comforted her and healed

her wounds. Dioscorus could not make Barbara renounce her faith, so he decapitated her, after which the Lord struck him dead with fire and lightning sent from heaven. See Williams, "Old French Lives," 156–57.

4. ANC, CM 11/1, "Declaración de Juan Prieto," 18 July 1835, fol. 224v.

5. ANC, CM 11/1, "Declaración de Juan Prieto," 18 July 1835, fol. 225v (emphasis in original document).

6. See Bolívar Aróstegui and López Cepero, *Sincretismo Religioso*, 58–80.

7. Apter, "Herskovits's Heritage," 22.

8. SSDA, JMJ, Bautismos de Pardos y Morenos (BPM), vol. 3, "José del Rosario hijo legitimo de Cayetano Orta Lucumí y Maria Dolores Arianza Criolla, madrina Maria Francisca Camejo Morena Criolla," 26 March 1813, fols. 108v–109, entry 806; SSDA, JMJ, BPM, vol. 3, "José Escolastico hijo legitimo de Antonio Angel Carabali esclavo de Don Antonio Palomino y Maria de los Dolores Ballayana morena libre, padrino Juan Nepomuceno Prieto," 17 February 1816, fol. 197v, entry 1409; SSDA, JMJ, BPM, vol. 5, "José Justo adulto Lucumí esclavo de Doña María Padron, padrino Juan Nepomuceno Prieto," 19 May 1822, fol. 107v, entry 584; and SSDA, JMJ, BPM, vol. 7, "José de los Dolores adulto Lucumí esclavo de D. José Ramos, padrino Juan Nepomuceno Prieto," 2 November 1828, fols. 8–8v, entry 91.

9. SSDA, SAC, BPM, vol. 19, "Juan Lucumí adulto de los emancipados del Bergantin Goleta Maxico mercante y entregado por disposicion de Exmo. Sr. gobernador y capitan general à D. Aniceto Almenteros, padrino Juan Nepomuceno Prieto," 10 September 1828, fol. 185, entry 973; SSDA, SAC, BPM, vol. 19, "Jacobo adulto de los emancipados del Bergantin Goleta Maxico entregado por disposicion de Exmo. Sr. gobernador y capitan general à Doña Maria Ignasia Ayala, padrino Juan Nepomuceno Prieto," 21 September 1828, fol. 186, entry 978; see also Landers, *Atlantic Creoles*, 170–72; and Landers, "Catholic Conspirators," 517n55.

10. NA, FO 313/56, "Negros de Bergantin Goleta español el Mágico," 31 January 1826, fol. 23, entry 110 "Allai/Juan" and entry 111 "Cucudi/Jacobo"; see also Voyages (ID 2374); and *Liberated Africans*.

11. D. Brown, *Santería Enthroned*, 71–73.

12. ANC, CM 11/1, "Recebé de José María Guerrero," 9 May 1818, fol. 276.

13. ANC, CM 11/1, "M. Guerrero vendió a Juan Prieto una logia," 9 May 1818, fol. 278; Bergad et al., *Slave Market*, 279.

14. ANC, CM 11/1, "Declaración de Juan Prieto," 18 July 1835, fol. 276.

15. Most references to Lucumí *cabildos* after 1835 revolve around Gloría Street. An oral tradition about the 1870s described how a Lucumí *cabildo* named "Changó Teddum" moved from "Calle Jesús Peregrino back to Calle Gloría and in between Calle Indio and Calle Florida." Cabrera, *El Monte*, 34 and 35n3. Also, in the articles and regulations from the *Cabildo Africano Lucumi*, there was an address for San Nicolás 302. See ANC, AH 228/1, "Reglamentos por el Cabildo Africano Lucumi," 25 April 1910. For a deeper interpretation of the location of Camejo and Prieto's *cabildo*, see H. Lovejoy, "Old Oyo," 223–29.

16. Rushing, "Afro-Cuban Social Organization," 181.

17. There does not appear to be any record for Arará and Gangá *cabildos*, which likely existed despite a lack of documentation. See Carmen Barcia, *Los ilustres apellidos*.

18. McKenzie, *Hail Orisha*, 32.

19. McKenzie, 184–85.

20. ANC, CM 11/1, "Recebé al moreno libre Juan Prieto 14p a Alquiler de la casa que habita en barrio Jesús María calle que titular Chamorro," 1 January 1828, fol. 279.

21. Howard, *Changing History*, chap. 2 and 3; Landers, *Atlantic Creoles*, 170–72; and Landers, "Catholic Conspirators," 515n33.

22. The deed mentions "seven *varas* in the front and thirty in the back." One *vara* (rod or pole) was about 80 cm to 108 cm. ANC, CM 11/1, "Recibi de Juan Prieto cinco pesos por la renta del terreno," 1 December 1828, fol. 355.

23. By definition, *èsúsú* is a rotating credit and savings association where contributors had to wait for their turn in a payment rotation, while *àjọ* operated where members paid a fixed sum of money to a collector at regular intervals and could withdraw money at short notice. See Bascom, "*Esusu*"; and Falola and Adebayo, *Culture, Politics, and Money*, chap. 6.

24. Landers, *Atlantic Creoles*, chap. 4; see also Reis, *Death is a Festival*.

25. ANC, CM 11/1, untitled and loose documents.

26. D. Brown, *Santería Enthroned*, 131.

27. ANC, CM 11/1, "Declaración de Juan Prieto," 18 July 1835, fol. 276.

28. Interview with John Mason, 4 February 2017. In another interview on 16 August 2004, Ernesto Valdés Jané made a similar statement.

29. Carmen Barcia, *Los ilustres apellidos*, 186.

30. ANC, EV 250/18, "Sobre el velorio de Maria Regla de Cárdenas," 18 February 1827, no folio numbers; cf. Carmen Barcia, *Los ilustres apellidos*, 186.

31. Isidro de Cárdenas was *capatáz* of the Lucumí *cabildo* on Jesús María Street, while María Loreto Torres Lucumí Ibanya was *matrona* of the *cabildo* on Villegas Street. ANC, EV 105/20394, "Cabildo Lucumí," 1783 and 1788; ANC, EG 277/5, "Cabildo de la Nación Lucumí," 1783 and 1790; cf. Carmen Barcia, *Los ilustres apellidos*, 415–17; and see also chapter three.

32. Drewal and Drewal, *Gẹlẹdẹ*, 182; see also Apter, "Blood of Mothers"; Apter, "Embodiment of Power"; Lloyd, "Status of the Yoruba Wife," 39; and McIntosh, *Yoruba Women*.

33. Refer to Caridad Argudín, Apoto Belén González, Margarita Armenteros, Rosalía Efuche, Timotea Albear Ayayi La Tuan, and Aurora Lamar in D. Brown, *Santería Enthroned*, 69–74, and 102–4.

34. In Santiago de las Vegas, Ana Clara Tamayo of the Pimienta *rama* organized, administered, and managed all ritual activities. I personally observed how male priests and practitioners would seek out her ritual knowledge, and during ceremonies, she frequently corrected procedures midritual, demonstrating authority over all others in her house.

35. ANC, CM, 11/1, "Nuestra Señora de los Remedios," "Nuestra Señora de Monserrate," and "Nuestra Señora del Carmen," n.d., loose folios. These images were printed at the imprenta de Boloña on Calle Obrapía, no. 37; see also Carmen Barcía, *Los ilustres apellidos*, 181–83.

36. I have shown elsewhere that the syncretization of the *mulata* stereotype, the Virgen de la Caridad del Cobre, and Ọ̀ṣun occurred during the anticolonial wars of the late nineteenth century. See H. Lovejoy, "Ọ̀ṣun Becomes Cuban."

37. See Anon., "Our Lady"; Deschamps Chapeaux, *Los batallones*; and Hilgers, "Sabbatine Privilege."

38. Some of the more typical, modern-day òrìṣà/saint paradigms include Ẹlégbára/Èṣù who is generally associated with San Antonio; Ògún with San Pedro; Òṣun with the Virgen de la Caridad del Cobre; Yẹmọja with the Virgen de Regla; and Ọbàtálá with the Virgen de la Mercedes. See D. Brown, *Santería Enthroned*, 305. Variations occur over time and location. See also Bolívar Aróstegui, *Orishas*; and Ortiz, *Hampa afro-cubana*.

39. Bolívar Aróstegui, *Orishas*, 139–41.

40. ANC, CM 11/1, "Carta de Juan Prieto al Francisco Dionisio Vives," 27 June 1824, fol. 322.

41. ANC, CM 11/1, "Carta de Juan Prieto al Obispo," 11 November 1828, fol. 410; see also Carmen Barcia, *Los ilustres apellidos*, 184–85.

42. Ortiz, "Cabildos," 5.

43. Ortiz, "Cabildos," 6–9; and D. Brown, *Santería Enthroned*, 39.

44. D. Brown, *Santería Enthroned*, 40.

45. D. Brown, 37–38.

46. For discussions related to this Lucumí banner see D. Brown, *Santería Enthroned*, 37–38; Deschamps Chapeaux, "Cabildos," 51; and Mason, *Ááàràárá*, fig. 79a.

47. Clapperton, *Hugh Clapperton*, 160.

48. See H. Lovejoy, "Yoruba Annual Festivals."

49. ANC, CM 11/1, "Declaración de Juan Prieto," 18 July 1835, fols. 224–25v.

50. I underwent a ritual called "feeding a goat to the earth for the spirits" (*dar un chivo a la tierra para los muertos*). This ceremony involved digging a grave, pouring the goat's blood into the grave, and burying the animal carcass. During incantations to the ancestors, initiates cleaned themselves with various food items, such as bean, rice, fruit and alcohol, and then discarding the food on top of the dead goat. Afterward, everyone took turns shoveling dirt into the grave until the animal was buried. This ceremony was completed in Santiago de las Vegas in December 2012.

51. ANC, CM 11/1, "Declaración de Juan Prieto," 18 July 1835, fols. 224–25v.

52. Interviews with John Mason, 4 February 2017; Joaquín Segara Echevarría, 13 April 2012; Alexander L. Ramirez, 14 March 2012; Ana Clara Tamayo, 8 December 2011; Ernesto Valdés Jané, 12 March 2011; and Ismael Villa 10 December 2011.

53. CMS, O51A, 9 November 1851; cf. McKenzie, *Hail Orisha*, 159n25.

54. ANC, CM 11/1, "Declaración de Juan Prieto," 18 July 1835, fols. 224–25v.

55. "Declaración de Juan Prieto," fols. 224–25v.

56. Refer to the conclusion for my interpretation of the Ṣàngó tẹ̀ dún oral traditions obtained from Ortiz, "Los 'batá,'" 315–16.

57. ANC, CM 11/1, "Declaración de Juan Prieto," 18 July 1835, fols. 224–25v.

58. Interview with Joaquín Segara Echevarría, 13 April 2012.

59. Interview with Ernesto Valdés Jané, 12 March 2011.

60. M. Ramos, "Lucumí (Yoruba) Culture," 74.

61. Interviews with Ernesto Valdés Jané, 12 March 2011; Ana Clara Tamayo, 8 December 2011; Ismael Villa, 8 December 2011; Alexander L. Ramirez, 14 March 2012;

Joaquín Segara Echevarría, 13 April 2012; and John Mason, 4 February 2017; see also Landers, *Atlantic Creoles*, 172.

62. Examples of select literature on *nkisi* and *nganga* include Cabrera, *El Monte*; Cabrera, *La regla kimbisa*; Figarola, *La brujería*; MacGaffey, *Kongo Political Culture*; Ochoa, *Society of the Dead*; Vansina, *How Societies Are Born*, 51; and Vansina, *Paths in the Rainforests*, 146. Examples of select literature on migrations from West Central Africa to the Americas include Candido, *African Slaving Port*; Ferreira, *Cross-Cultural Exchange*; Heywood, *Central Africans*; and J. Miller, *Way of Death*.

63. Cabrera, *La regla Kimbisa*, 5.

64. ANC, CM 11/1, "Declaración de Juan Prieto," 18 July 1835, fols. 224–25v.

65. Crowther, *Dictionary of the Yoruba Language*, 68–69.

66. When I visited the house temple called Orichaoko in the neighborhood of Parraga, Havana, Enrique Villalba, the head *babalawo*, proudly showed me where he had buried the remains of his ancestors. Interview with Villalba, 30 March 2011.

67. Examples of select literature on *nfumbe* include Cabrera, *El Monte*; Figarola, *La brujería*; MacGaffey, *Kongo Political Culture*; Ochoa, *Society of the Dead*; and also an interview with Alexander L. Ramirez, 15 March 2012.

68. Voyages (estimates: 1501–1866, all of Africa to Cuba).

69. Childs and Falola, "Yoruba Diaspora," 7; Eltis, "Diaspora of Yoruba Speakers," 34; P. Lovejoy, "Yoruba Factor," 45; see also Dodson, *Sacred Spaces*; and Verger, *Trade Relations*.

70. Examples of select literature on Abakuá in Cuba include P. Lovejoy, "Departure from Calabar"; I. Miller, "Calabar on the Cross"; I. Miller, "Relationship between Early Forms of Literacy"; I. Miller, *Voice of the Leopard*; and Ortiz, "La 'tragedia' de los ñáñigos."

71. See Christopher, *They Are We*.

72. Palmié, *Wizards and Scientists*, 155.

73. Herskovits, "African Gods," 640–41.

74. Apter, "Blood of Mothers," 80.

75. Email with John Thornton, 14 June 2016.

Chapter Six

1. "Census of 1774," "Census of 1817," and "Census of 1827," in Kiple, *Blacks in Colonial Cuba*, 25–30, 34–46, and the appendix.

2. Between 1786 and 1815, the inter-Caribbean slave trade to Cuba involved an estimated 52,725 people; the total Bight of Benin migration to the entire Caribbean, minus Cuba, was 71,881 people; and the total slave trade from all of Africa to the Caribbean, minus Cuba, was 970,656 people. Therefore $71,881 \div 970,656 = 0.074$, or 7.4 percent—the percentage of the Bight of Benin migration to the Caribbean minus Cuba. I divided that percentage by the estimated number of arrivals to Cuba via the inter-American slave trade, then added that result to the direct Bight of Benin migration to Cuba: $0.074 * 52,725 = 3,901 + 4,757 = 8,658$. Therefore, total arrivals from the Bight of Benin to Cuba in this thirty-year period could not have exceeded 9,000 individuals.

Inter-Caribbean slave trade data mostly derives from Eltis, "interAmertoSpanAmer database"; and O'Malley, "inter-Caribbean database." See also Borucki et al., "Atlantic History"; García Rodríguez, "El mercado"; Lambert, *Sessional Papers*, vol. 72, "AN ACCOUNT OF THE NUMBER of Negroes imported into, and exported from, the Island of Jamaica [1773–1787]," 12 May, 1789, 239–40; Lambert, *Sessional Papers*, vol. 72, "IMPORT and EXPORT of Negroes, and Negroes retained in the Island, for 49 Years, viz. 1739–1787, both inclusive; distinguishing the Years of War from those of Peace," 1790, 207–9; O'Malley, *Final Passages*; Torres Ramirez, *La Compañía Gaditana*. See also Voyages (estimates: 1785–1816, all embarkation regions to Cuba); Voyages (estimates: 1816–35, all embarkation regions to Cuba); Voyages (estimates: 1785–1816, Bight of Benin to Cuba); *Voyages* (estimates: 1816–1835, Bight of Benin to Cuba).

3. P. Lovejoy, *Jihād in West Africa*, 10.

4. Bello, *Infāq al-Maysūr*, 69–72; see also Quadri, "Appraisal of Muhammad Bello's *Infâq al-Maysûr*."

5. P. Lovejoy, *Jihād in West Africa*, 10.

6. Clapperton, *Hugh Clapperton*, 40–45.

7. Law, *Ọyọ Empire*, 255–60.

8. Lorenzo Clarke stated that "his name was entered into a book." In the *Negrito's* register, Clarke's African name was "Ocusono." Independently from one another, Andrew Apter, Toyin Falola, Olatunji Ojo, and Ademola Omobewaji Dasylva all agreed that Òkúsọnọ̀ was a Yorùbá name common among Ìjẹ̀bú and Ẹ̀gbá dialects. The name's meaning is "Death has brought about adornment/beauty" and "Death has created beauty." See NA, FO 313/58, "Cargamento del Bergantin Mercante Español Negrito," 5 January 1833, fol. 135, entry 185; and "Cuban Slaves in England," 234–35; and see also H. Lovejoy, "Old Oyo," chaps. 2 and 6.

9. "Cuban Slaves in England," 237.

10. See Ajayi, "Samuel Ajayi Crowther"; Guran, *Agudás*; Matory, *Black Atlantic Religion*; Matory, "English Professors"; Otero, *Afro-Cuban Diasporas*; Sarracino, *Los que volvieron*; and Verger, "America Latina."

11. Ritter, "Mittheilungen über einige westafricanische Stämme," 12–16.

12. Barcia, "West African Islam," 300; see also Gomez, *Black Crescent*; and P. Lovejoy, *Jihād in West Africa*.

13. Peel, *Religious Encounter*, 23 and 189.

14. Ajayi, "Samuel Ajayi Crowther," 299 and 299n20.

15. Historians have debated the chronology of the Òwu war, which some argue began as late as 1820 and ended in 1827. I have used Law's dating of between c. 1818 and c. 1822. See Ajayi and Smith, *Yoruba Warfare*; Ajisafe, *History of Abeokuta*, 49; Akinjogbin, "Yoruba Civil Wars," 43–46; Biobaku, *Egba and Their Neighbors*, 13; Samuel Johnson, *History of the Yorùbás*, 206–8; Law, *Ọyọ Empire*, chap. 12; and Mabogunje and Omer-Cooper, *Owu in Yoruba History*.

16. See Law, *Ọyọ Empire*, chap. 12; P. Lovejoy, *Jihād in West Africa*, 10; and O'Hear, *Power Relations*.

17. Akinjogbin, *Dahomey*; and Law, "Oyo-Dahomey," 18.

18. Law, *Ọyọ Empire*, chap. 13.

19. Clapperton, *Hugh Clapperton*, 42.

20. Biobaku, *Egba and Their Neighbors*, 19–23; Folayan, "Egbado to 1832," 31; Samuel Johnson, *History of the Yorùbás*, 249; and Law, "Career of Adele," 35.

21. Clapperton, *Hugh Clapperton*, 141.

22. Curtin, "Joseph Wright," 323–25.

23. Curtin, 328.

24. Ajisafe, *History of Abeokuta*, 49, Biobaku, *Egba and Their Neighbours*, 13–15, Falola, "Warfare and Trade Relations," 26; Samuel Johnson, *History of the Yorùbás*, 206–8; and Law, *Ọyọ Empire*, 275–76.

25. Falola, *Ìbàdàn*, 337–40.

26. Law, *Ọyọ Empire*, 291–92.

27. See H. Lovejoy, "Mapping the Collapse of Oyo"; and Voyages (estimates: 1816–35, Bight of Benin to all disembarkation regions).

28. Voyages (estimates: 1816–35, Bight of Benin to Cuba).

29. See Law, *Ouidah*; and Mann, *Slavery and the Birth*, chap. 1.

30. *Parliamentary Debates*, "Copy of the Treaty with Spain for Preventing the Slave Trade," 23 September 1817, 67–80.

31. Eltis, *Economic Growth*, 110.

32. H. Lovejoy, "Registers of Liberated Africans: Implementation," 26–27.

33. NA, FO 84/29, "Letter from Kilbee to the Captain General of Cuba," 28 December 1824, fols. 323–24.

34. Lucumí leaving the Bights of Benin and Bifra were registered as Mina, Arará, Mandinga, and Carabali. See Adderley, *New Negroes*; Eltis, *Economic Growth*; H. Lovejoy, "Registers of Liberated Africans: Implementation"; H. Lovejoy, "Registers of Liberated Africans: Transcription"; Murray, *Odious Commerce*; Roldán de Montaud, "En los borrosos"; and Roldán de Montaud, "La diplomacia."

35. For more information on the cholera epidemic, see chap. 7.

36. H. Lovejoy, "Registers of Liberated Africans: Implementation," 26–27.

37. Nwokeji and Eltis, "Roots of the African Diaspora," 368.

38. This author coordinated independent interpretations with Olatunji Ojo, Abubakar Babajo Sani, and Umar Hussein of over 3,500 documented African names recorded in Cuba between 1826 and 1841. Refer to tables 6.7–6.8. See also H. Lovejoy, "Old Oyo Influences," chap. 2.

39. By applying ratios from the regional distribution of the transatlantic slave trade to population censuses in 1817 and 1827, it is possible to estimate, albeit tentatively, the Yorùbá-speaking population in Cuba. Of the total transatlantic slave trade to Cuba between 1816 and 1835, the Bight of Benin migration was approximately 15 percent, and upwards of 75 percent of that migration were Yorùbá speakers (see table 6.8); hence, $0.75 \times 0.15 = 0.1125$. Cuba's total population in 1817 was 553,033 and in 1827 was 704,487. In these census years, the "free colored" and "slave" population was 313,203 and 393,436 people, respectively; hence $0.1125 \times 313,203 = 35,235$; $35,235 \div 553,033 = 0.064$; and $0.1125 \times 393,496 = 44,268$; $44,268 \div 704,487 = 0.062$. However, these early population censuses did not take into account differences between people born in Africa and Cuba, whether free or enslaved, which suggests that Yorùbá speakers could not amount to what I estimate was "much more than 5 percent of the island's total population."

40. My estimate of "upwards of a couple thousand Lucumí in Havana" involved creating a database of baptism records from the church of Jesús, María y José between 1808 and 1836. There were over six hundred baptisms involving at least one Lucumí in some capacity. However, some baptisms involved more than one Lucumí, and sometimes two or more baptisms involved the same Lucumí person. Moreover, this survey involved only one church, suggesting records from other churches involved hundreds of other records involving Lucumí. Factoring in over 1,200 Lucumí *emancipados*, there had to be at least two thousand Lucumí residing in Havana in the 1820s and 1830s. Compiling all of Havana's baptism records into a database will undoubtedly lead to monumental results about the overall demographics of Havana's population of African descent. See SSDA, JMJ, BPM, vols. 3–7, 1808–1836; and *Slave Society Digital Archive*.

41. NA, FO 313/58, "Cargamento de la Goleta Mercante Española Indagadora," 16 July 1832, fols. 103 and 116, entry 46 and 117.

42. Law, *Ouidah*, 142.

43. NA, FO 313/58–59, "Cargamento del Bergantin Mercante Español Negrito," 5 January 1833, fols. 117–36 and 1–29; and some examples of brandings include entry 29, 44, 46, 47, 61, 83, 135, 163, and 167.

44. See Samuel Johnson, *History of the Yorùbás*, 104–9; Keefer, "Scarification and Identity"; and P. Lovejoy, "Scarification and the Loss."

45. SSDA, JMJ, BPM, vols. 3–7, 1808–36.

46. See Carmen Barcia, *La otra familia*; Perera Díaz and Meriño Fuentes, *Esclavitud, familia y parroquia*; and Stolcke, *Marriage, Class, and Colour*.

47. SSDA, JMJ, BPM, vol. 7, "José de Transito hijo legitimo de José Isidro Congo moreno libre y Maria de la Merced Torre Lucumí esclava de Nicolas Sequeria," 29 August 1831, fol. 76, entry 824.

48. SSDA, JMJ, BPM, vol. 5, "Victoria Bonventura hija ilegitima de padre no conocido y Maria de la Nieves Lucumí esclava de Don Marcos Vidal y Doña Benigna Lopez," 28 March 1821, fol. 22, entry 119; SSDA, JMJ, BPM, vol. 5, "Juan Vidal hijo ilegitimo de padre no conocido y Maria de la Nieves Lucumí esclava de Don Marcos Vidal y Doña Benigna Lopez," 20 June 1822, fol. 115v, entry 624; SSDA, JMJ, BPM, vol. 6, "Maria Serafina hija ilegitima de padre no conocido y Maria de la Nieves Lucumí esclava de Don Marcos Vidal y Doña Benigna Lopez," 29 August 1823, fol. 41, entry 327; SSDA, JMJ, BPM, vol. 6, "Clara del Carmen Bonventura hija ilegitima de padre no conocido y Maria de la Nieves Lucumí esclava de Don Marcos Vidal y Doña Benigna Lopez," 29 August 1825, fol. 126, entry 1025; SSDA, JMJ, BPM, vol. 6, "José Benbenuto hijo ilegitimo de padre no conocido y Maria de la Nieves Lucumí esclava de Don Marcos Vidal y Doña Benigna Lopez," 22 March 1828, fol. 224v, entry 1854.

49. SSDA, JMJ, BPM, vol. 3, "Tiabel hijo ilegitimo de Patricio [*sic*] y Feliciana Arará esclava de Juan Francisco Lucumí Libre," 14 July 1814, fol. 139, entry 1050.

50. ANC, CM 11/1, "Declaración de Juan Prieto," 18 July 1835, fol. 223.

51. "Declaración de Juan Prieto," fol. 223.

52. *Diario del Gobierno de la Habana*, 16 January 1819.

53. Mason, *Aráàràárá*, 154.

Chapter Seven

1. See "Summary Statistics" in Voyages (database: 1817–35, Bight of Benin to Cuba).

2. Examples of select literature on slave rebellion in Cuba include Barcia, *Great African Slave Revolt*; Barcia, *Seeds of Insurrection*; Childs, *1812 Aponte Rebellion*; Finch, *Rethinking Slave Rebellion*; Gloría Garcia, *Conspiraciones y revueltas*; Gloría Garcia, *La esclavitud*; Garcia Rodríguez, "A propósito"; Iduate, "Noticias sobre sublevaciones"; Landers, *Atlantic Creoles*; Llaverías, *La comisión militar*, 8–11; Paquette, *Sugar Is Made*; and Reid-Vasquez, *Year of the Lash*.

3. The main leaders of this conspiracy included José Francisco Lemus, José Fernández la Madrid, Vicente Rocafuerte, Manuel Lorenzo Vidaurre, and José A. Miralla, *Historia documentada*, vol. 2, Juan Francisco Cascales, "Parecer fiscal en la causa seguida por conspiración de los 'Soles de Bolívar,'" 14 January 1824, 226–27.

4. Barcia, *Great African Slave Revolt*, 1.

5. Examples of select literature related to the Military Commission include Barcia, *Great African Slave Revolt*; Barcia, *Seeds of Insurrection*; Childs, *1812 Aponte Rebellion*; Finch, *Rethinking Slave Rebellion*; Gloría Garcia, *Conspiraciones y revueltas*; Gloría Garcia, *La esclavitud*; Garcia Rodríguez, "A propósito"; Iduate, "Noticias sobre sublevaciones"; Landers, *Atlantic Creoles*; Llaverías, *La comisión militar*, 8–11; Paquette, *Sugar Is Made*; and Reid-Vasquez, *Year of the Lash*.

6. Barcia, *Great African Slave Revolt*, 150.

7. Between 1827 and 1830, the Military Commission began investigating yet another conspiracy, which came to be known as the "Grand Legion of the Black Eagle." In fits of paranoia, colonial officials believed exiled members of the *soles y rayos de Bolívar* conspiracy, among other independence advocates from Colombia, Mexico, and Central America, were sending undercover agents to infiltrate Cuban society. Despite extensive investigations, authorities never determined who the leaders were or how extensive the movement was, if it existed at all. Foner, *History of Cuba*, 1:122.

8. AGI, U 3548/49, "Carta de Manuel Ximenez Guarzo," 20 November 1825; cf. Hall, *Social Control*, 133.

9. Knight, *Slave Society*, 88–89; Foner, *History of Cuba*, 1:89; and see also Allahar, "Cuban Sugar Planters."

10. ANC, CM 11/1, "Testamento de Juan Prieto," 10 October 1834, fols. 331–32v. Although dated in 1834, the document states that it was a copy from the original will made in 1832.

11. In August 1832, the archbishop of the diocese of *San Cristóbal de la Habana*, Juan José Díaz de Espada y Fernánez de Landa, died from apoplexy at the age of seventy-six. He had held the most important religious position in Cuba since 1800. Following his death, there was an interregnum, a *sede vacante*, until Pope Gregory XVI appointed Francisco Ramón Valentín de Casaus y Torres as apostolic administrator in 1836. Figueroa y Miranda, *Religión y política*, 14.

12. Saco, "Dictamen que á la Junta," 158.

13. NA, FO 84/136, "Letter from Macleay to Palmerston," 16 April 1833, fol. 114.

14. Sagra counted 8,253 deaths by *castas* and by neighborhood. Saco totaled 8,315 based on cemetery records. Sagra, *Tablas necrologicas*, 9; and Saco, *Carta sobre*, 89–110.

Digitized records from Havana's church archives contain very few burial records between February and April 1833, except SSDA, NSR, vol. 2, "Defunciones," 1829–42.

15. The most cholera-related deaths occurred outside Havana's city walls in predominantly black and poor neighborhoods; thus, white people believed the initial outbreak arrived on board slave ships. In fact, the disease spread from India through Russia, Europe, and then to the Americas with European travelers and immigrants. It was not until the 1850s that scientists began to understand how *vibrio cholerae* thrived in water and food contaminated with the bacteria. People living in poorer conditions therefore had greater chances of contracting and dying from the disease. Kiple, *Caribbean Slave*, 135 and 146–48; see also Beldarraín Chaple and Espinosa Cortés, "El cólera"; Echenberg, *Time of Cholera*; King, *Another Dimension*, 147–57; Kiple, "Cholera and Race"; and López Denis, "Higiene pública."

16. Saco, "Examen de las tablas," 325–43.

17. ANC, CM 11/1, "Testamento de Juan Prieto," 10 October 1834, fol. 220.

18. D. Brown, *Santería Enthroned*, 305.

19. Santa Cruz y Mallen, *Historia de familias cubanas*, 5:265.

20. Iduate, "Noticias sobre sublevaciones," 124.

21. Seven documented slave ships arrived in Cuba from the Bight of Benin in 1832 and 1833. Voyages (database: 1832–33, Bight of Benin to Cuba).

22. ANC, EM 540B, "Relación de los negros no alzados, aprehendidos y presentados de la dotación de la finca San Salvador del dominio y propiedad de D. Francisco de Santiago Aguirre," 16–24 August 1833, fols. 173–76. Authorities determined that 219 enslaved Africans were directly involved, while eighty-eight people refused to participate. For a complete list, see Iduate, "Noticias sobre sublevaciones," 133–47.

23. Iduate, "Noticias sobre sublevaciones," 122.

24. Van Norman, *Shade-Grown Slavery*, 133 and 136.

25. Barcia, *West African Warfare*, 100.

26. ANC, EM 540B, "Deposición del negro Hermenegildo Lucumí ó Olló," 29 August 1833, fol. 167.

27. In this list, authorities documented African names of adult males but not women and children. There were also another twenty-four males who did not appear in the list because they had died, but witnesses identified their Christian and African names in testimonies. Interpretations of African names were obtained through independent interviews with Olatunji Ojo (Yorùbá), Abubakar Babajo Sani (Hausa), and Umar Hussein (Dagomba), April–September 2011. Philip Misevich contacted Mende speakers to interpret the Mandinga and Gangá names in an email 20 July 2011. ANC, EM 540B, "Relación de los negros no alzados, aprehendidos y presentados de la dotación de la finca San Salvador del dominio y propiedad de D. Francisco de Santiago Aguirre," 16–24 August 1833, fols. 173–76; and see also H. Lovejoy, "Old Oyo Influences," chap. 2.

28. ANC, EM 540B, "Declaración de Baltazara Piernas Aguirre," 19 August 1833, fols. 19–20.

29. ANC, EM 540B, "Declaración de Diego Barreiro, mayordomo," 19 August 1833, fols. 12–14.

30. Nicolas Mina was severely beaten for sounding a bell to signal for help. Tranquilino Mandinga described how they killed a man with a machete because he refused

to join. ANC, EM 540B, "Declaración del negro Nicolas Mina," 19 August 1833, fols. 20–21; ANC, EM 540B, "Declaración del moreno Tranquilino Mandinga, servicio del cafetal Catalina," 19 August 1833, fol. 100.

31. Iduate, "Noticias sobre sublevaciones," 124.

32. ANC, EM 540B, "Declaración de Blás Hernández, mayordomo," 19 August 1833, fols. 14–15.

33. Iduate, "Noticias sobre sublevaciones," 125.

34. ANC, EM 540B, "Declaracíon de Gonzalo Mandinga," 19 August 1833, fols. 125–27.

35. NA, T 70/1546, "Letter of Lionel Abson," 26 September 1783; cf. Law, *Contemporary Source Material*, 43; and Law, *Ouidah*, 75.

36. Iduate, "Noticias sobre sublevaciones," 127.

37. Fifteen women and one male child participated. ANC, EM 540B, "Relación de los negros no alzados, aprehendidos y presentados de la dotación de la finca San Salvador del dominio y propiedad de D. Francisco de Santiago Aguirre," 29 August 1833, fols. 173–76.

38. Iduate, "Noticias sobre sublevaciones," 133–47.

39. Iduate, 145.

40. ANC, EM 540B, "Declaración del negro Pascual Lucumí ó Ayaí," 19 August 1833, fol. 145.

41. ANC, EM 540B, "Declaración de Francisco Guiterrés," 19 August 1833, fol. 84.

42. Iduate, "Noticias sobre sublevaciones," 125.

43. Luis Gangá identified the drummers, who died in battle, as Antonio Lucumí, Elluvy, and Agustín Lucumí, Choból. ANC, EM 540B, "Declaración del negro Luis Gangá," 19 August 1833, fol. 137.

44. ANC, EM 540B, "Declaración del negro Matias Lucumí ó Egúyori," 19 August 1833 fol. 115.

45. Both quotations from ANC, EM 540B, "Declaración del negro José Mina," 19 August 1833, fols. 24–25. Interpretations of this documented Yorùbá phrase come from emails with Andrew Apter and Olatunji Ojo, February 2010.

46. Iduate, "Noticias sobre sublevaciones," 129.

47. Iduate, 129.

48. AHN, E 8034/21, "El Intendente de la Habana da cuenta de las medidas que se podían adoptar para preservar la Isla de riesgo que se teme de la población de color," 22 August 1833, doc. 2.

49. ANC, EM 540B, "Declaración de Diego Barreiro, mayordomo," 19 August 1833, fols. 12–14.

50. ANC, EM 540B, "Declaración de la negra Margarita Lucumí," 19 August 1833, fols. 24–24v.

51. ANC, EM 540B, "Declaración de la negra Guadalupe Lucumí," 19 August 1833, fols. 22–23.

52. ANC, EM 540B, "Decision de Tomas de Salazar," 4 September 1833, fol. 181v.

53. AGI, SD 1753/5118, *Diario de la Habana*, "Sentencia pronunciada por el Consejo de guerra de la comisión militar ejecutiva permanente de esta plaza," 18 September 1833, front page.

54. NA, FO84/91, "Sentence of the Firme," 12 December 1828, fol. 260.

Chapter Eight

1. W. Johnson, *History of Cuba*, 2:349.

2. *Correspondencia Reservada*, "Introducción," 16–17.

3. *Colección de documentos*, vol. 1, "Ley 150 Que los Negros no Trabajen los Dias de Fiesta y Guarden la Fiesta como los Cristianos," 1544, 231.

4. *Bando de buen gobierno*, 4 and 21–22.

5. Saco, "Memoria sobre," 31.

6. Deschamps Chapeaux, "Presencia religiosa," 102.

7. ANC, CM 11/1, "Declaración de Hermenegildo Lucumí," 12 July 1835, fol. 20.

8. ANC, CM 11/1, "Declaración de Narcisco Diaz," 12 July 1835, fol. 34.

9. ANC, CM 11/1, "D. Juan Bautista Velazques . . . presente sumaria," 15 July 1835, fols. 175–77v.

10. ANC, CM 11/1, "Certificación del cirujano," 12 July 1835, fol. 115.

11. ANC, CM 11/1, "En el pueblo de Calvario," 12 July 1835, fol. 102.

12. ANC, CM 11/1, "Lista de diez y nueve negros Emancipados," 12 July 1835, fol. 35.

13. NA, FO 313/58–59, "Cargamento del Bergatin Mercante Español Negrito," 5 January 1833. Refer to entry 29 (Blás), 44 (Leandro), 46 (Roman), 47 (Prudencio), 61 (Gabriel), 83 (Leon), 163 (Cirilo), and 167 (Anacleto).

14. ANC, CM 11/1, "Declaración" for Victor Lucumí, Florencio Congo, Miguel Lucumí, Agustin Lucumí, José Clemente de Dávila, Simon Lucumí, Juan de Mata Gonzales, Andrés Campos Lucumí, and Hermenegildo Jáuregui Lucumí, 13 July 1835, fols. 7–31.

15. ANC, CM 11/1, "Declaración del Negro José Clemente Dávila," 13 July 1835, fols. 11v–12.

16. ANC, CM 11/1, "Declaración de Narciso Serrano," 14 July 1835, fol. 43.

17. ANC, CM 11/1, "Declaración de José de los Santos Sotomayor," 14 July 1835, fol. 40; and ANC, CM 11/1, "Declaración de Bernardo Machado," 14 July 1835, fol. 41 (emphasis in original).

18. Fernando Lucumí insisted that "there were not any *negros* shouting Havana mine, kill white, white women mine!" Hermenegildo Jáuregui Lucumí claimed that "he did not have a white tail or a staff." ANC, CM 11/1, "Confesión de Fernando Lucumí," 14 July 1835, fol. 166; and ANC, CM 11/1, "Confesión de Hermenegildo Jáuregui Lucumí," 14 July 1835, fol. 167.

19. ANC, CM 11/1, "Declaración de D. Pedro Abreu," 14 July 1835, fol. 32.

20. ANC, CM 11/1, "Sumario de D. Antonio Lorenzo Baltanás," 13 July 1835, fol. 62.

21. D. Brown, *Santería Enthroned*, 182.

22. D. Brown, 191.

23. Deschamps Chapeaux, "Presencia religiosa," 102.

24. ANC, CM 11/1, "Capitania Pedaneo de Jesus Maria," 14 July 1835, fols. 211–211v.

25. ANC, CM 11/1, "D. Juan Bautista Velazques . . . presente sumaria," 15 Jul. 1835, fols. 175–77v.

26. "D. Juan Bautista Velazques," fols. 175–77v. Other participants arrested in the Lucumí disturbance included Juan de Mata Gonzales, Agustín Lucumí, Andres Campos, José Clemente Dávila and Fernando Lucumí.

27. AHN, E 8034/31, "El Capitan General de la Isla de Cuba participa el motin de un numero considerable des negros," 24 July 1835; and see also *Correspondencia reservada*, "Miguel Tacón al Ministro de Estado Habana," 24 July 1835, 175.

28. "Miguel Tacón al Ministro," 176n92.

29. *El noticioso y lucero: Diario mercantil, politico y literario*, "Sentencia de la Comisión Militar, Consulta del Auditor, Decreto de ejecución de la sentencia y certificación de su cumplimiento," 17 July 1835; and *Diario de la Habana*, "Sentencia de la Comisión Militar, Consulta del Auditor, Decreto de ejecución de la sentencia y certificación de su cumplimiento," 17 July 1835. Numerous copies of these newspapers scattered throughout AHN, E 8034/31.

30. AHN, E 8034/31, "Copia de una carta por Tacón al Ministro Plenipotenciario de S.M. en Londres," 17 July 1835, doc. 9; AHN, E 8034/31, "Copia de una carta por Tacón al Embajador en Paris," 17 July 1835, doc. 10; and AHN, E 8034/31, "Copia de una carta por Tacón al Consul General de S.M. en Genova," 17 July 1835, doc. 11.

31. AHN, E 8034/31, "Copia y traducción de una carta por Mollier al Consul General de Francia," 17 July 1835, doc. 3.

32. ANC, CM 11/1, "Declaración de D. Clemente Dávila," 17 July 1835, fols. 95–96.

33. SSDA, JMJ, Bautismos de Pardos y Morenos (BPM), vol. 7, "Pedro Lucumí adulto y esclavo de Don Clemente Davila," 26 October 1833, fol. 129v, entry 1480; SSDA, JMJ, BPM, "Felipe Lucumí adulto y esclavo de Don Clemente Davila," 26 October 1833, fol. 129v, entry 1481.

34. ANC, CM 11/1, "Declaración del Negro Manuel Lucumí," 17 July 1835, fols. 96–97v.

35. ANC, CM 11/1, "Diligencia de la libertad al Negro Manuel," 17 July 1835, fol. 199.

36. ANC, CM 11/1, "Declarción de D. Juan Fernandez," 18 July 1835, fols. 220–220v. For a photograph of the clothing style in modern-day practices see D. Brown, *Santería Enthroned*, 196 (fig. 4.26).

37. ANC, CM 11/1, "Declaración de D. Juan Fernandez," 18 July 1835, fols. 220–220v.

38. ANC, CM 11/1, "Declaración de D. José de Feria," 18 July 1835, fols. 220v–22.

39. ANC, CM 11/1, "Declaración de Juan Prieto," 18 July 1835, fols. 222v–25v. Fistulas are a narrow passage formed by a disease leading from an abscess to a free surface, or for one body cavity to another.

40. ANC, CM 11/1, "Declaración de Juan Prieto," 18 July 1835, fols. 222v–25v.

41. ANC, CM 11/1, "Declaración de Maria Guillerma Garcia," 18 July 1835, fols. 232–34.

42. The same *legajo* contains additional declarations for the *negro Lucumí* Anselmo Rodrigues and the *negro* Carabali Papá Antonio Diaz. See ANC, CM 11/1, fols. 234–37v.

43. ANC, CM 11/1, "Declaración de Juan Prieto," 18 July 1835, fols. 222v–25v.

44. ANC, CM 11/1, "Declaración de Juan Prieto," 18 July 1835, fols. 222v–25v. See also chap. 3.

45. ANC, CM 11/1, "Officio al Sub Inspector de morenos en relación à Juan Prieto," 18 July 1835, fol. 240v.

46. ANC, FL 21/83, "El Intendente da cuente de haber salido de la Habana al de Pensacola las tropas auxiliares," 28 June 1812.

47. AGI, PC 256B, "Primera Compañia de Morenos de la Habana," 1814; AGI, PC 250, "Hospital Militar Compañia de Morenos de la Habana," 31 May 1814; and AGI, PC 250, "Hospital Militar Compañia de Morenos de la Habana," 31 May 1814.

48. AGI, PC 256B, "Batallón de Morenos: Lista de los Individuos se embarcaron para la Habana en la Corbeta de la Real Armada la Diana," 8 September 1814.

49. See Childs, *1812 Aponte Rebellion*; and email with Matt D. Childs, June 2012.

50. ANC, CM 11/1, "Declaración de Juan Prieto," 18 July 1835, fols. 222v–25v.

51. AHN, E 8034/34, "Tacón al Secretario del Estado y del Despacho," 18 July 1835, doc. 6 (emphasis in original).

52. *Correspondencia reservada*, "Miguel Tacón al Ministro de Estado Habana," 24 July 1835, 174–75.

53. *Correspondencia reservada*, "Este oficina a lo Interior se transcribió en su fecha á Guerra y á Estado," 31 August 1835, 177–79.

54. A hard copy of this article could not been located, but it is referred to in NA, FO 84/172, "From Macleay to Palmerston," 6 November 1835, fols. 175–175v. This document states, "In the 'Times' newspaper of the 25th August last we have seen an Article, copied from the American Papers."

55. NA, FO 84/172, "From Macleay to Palmerston," 6 November 1835, fols. 175–175v.

56. Saco, "Memoria sobre," 35.

57. Prieto disappeared from historical record just as Ño Remegio Herrera, aka "Adechina" (Adéṣíná), emerged as the *capatáz* of another Lucumí *cabildo* devoted to La Virgen de Regla (Yẹmọja) in Regla. This mutual aid society formed from the mid-1830s and operated until the early 1890s. Prieto's disappearance also coincides with the oral traditions related to the consecration of *bàtá* drums in the mid-1830s. D. Brown, *Santería Enthroned*, 62–65; Ortiz, "Los 'bàtá,'" 221–22. For a discussion see also the conclusion.

Conclusion

1. Berlin, *Many Thousands Gone*, 94.

2. P. Lovejoy, "Identifying Enslaved Africans," 2.

3. Apter, "Blood of Mothers," 80.

4. Apter coined the term "lateral syncretism" in a lecture about lateral exchanges between African and even First Nation groups in the New World. Apter, "Steps toward an Ecology of Creolization," University of Chicago, 15 March 1995. Email with Apter, 25 November 2014.

5. Mintz and Price, *Anthropological Approach*, 43.

6. See Peel, *Religious Encounters*.

7. Landers, *Atlantic Creoles*, 3–5.

8. Bastide, *Les amériques noires*, 101.

9. D. Brown, *Santería Enthroned*, 70.

10. ANC, CM 11/1, "Declaración de Juan Prieto," 18 July 1835, fol. 225v.

11. Ortiz, *Los negros brujos*, 68–72.

12. Murphy, *Santería*, 33.

13. Brandon, *Santeria from Africa*, 74.

14. D. Brown, *Santería Enthroned*, 287.

15. Palmié, *Cooking of History*, 44 (emphasis in original).

16. Apter, *Oduduwa's Chain*, 13.

17. Carmen Barcia, *Los ilustres apellidos*, 414–17.

18. Mason, *Aráàràárá*, 154.

19. ANC, AH 99/1, "Cabildo Mandinga (Zape), 1568; cf. Carmen Barcia, *Los ilustres apellidos*, 425; and see also H. Lovejoy and Ojo, "'Lucumí' and 'Terranova.'"

20. López Valdés, *Africanos de Cuba*, 189.

21. The patron saints were Nuestra Señora del Rosario and Nuestra Señora de las Nieves. AGI, SD, 515/51, "Inventario de cabildos," 1755.

22. Mason, *Aráàràárá*, 154.

23. See Herskovits, "African Gods."

24. For Lucumí War see chap. 7; and for the Malê Uprising see Reis, *Rebelião escrava no Brasil*; and Da Costa e Silva, "Sobre a rebelião de 1835."

25. Ortiz, "Los batá,'" 221.

26. Ortiz, 221–22.

27. Ortiz, 221–22.

28. Interviews with Francisco Aguabella, May 2007; and Michael Marcuzzi, February 2005.

29. Mason, *Aráàràárá*, 151.

30. Mason, 161.

31. D. Brown, *Santería Enthroned*, 65.

32. Interview with Pedro Cosme Baños, 1 July 2004. Samuel Johnson shows similar scarification for people from Ọ̀yọ́ in *History of the Yorùbás*, 104.

33. Crowther, *Dictionary of the Yorùbá Language*, 33.

34. ANC, CM 11/1, "Declaración de Juan Prieto," 18 July 1835, fol. 225v.

35. Ortiz, "Los batá," 221–22.

36. Ortiz, 221–22.

37. ANC, CM 11/1, "Declaración de María Guillerma García," 18 July 1835, fol. 233v.

38. I have been unable to locate baptism records that would prove Isidrio, Paula, or Maria Guillerma García helped baptized an adult Lucumí slave named Filomeno.

39. ANC, GSC 1677/83995, "Lucumí Bragurá Santa Barbara," 1843.

40. Bremer, *Homes of the New World*, 3:181–85.

41. Ajisafe, *History of Abeokuta*, 11; and Law, *Ọyọ Empire*, 137.

42. D. Brown, *Santería Enthroned*, 52 and 316n67; and email from Olatunji Ojo, 26 May 2016.

43. ANC, GSC 1677/84010, "Cabildo Lucumí Ayones Santa Bárbara," 1868.

44. Cabrera, *El Monte*, 34 and 35n2.

45. See López Váldes, *Pardos y morenos*.

46. ANC, AH 228/1, "Sociedad de Socorros Mutuos de Nación Lucumí, sus hijos y descendientes, invocada a Santa Bárbara," 1891, fols. 403–9; cf. Carmen Barcia, *Los ilustres apellidos*, 417; and see also D. Brown, *Santería Enthroned*, 68–69.

47. The quotation refers to a Congo *cabildo* from 1881 that submitted similar regulations. R. Scott, *Slave Emancipation*, 265–66.

48. D. Brown, *Santería Enthroned*, 68–70; and see also Mason, *Aráàràarà*, 151.

49. ANC, Audiencia de la Habana, 228/1, fols. 403–9, "Articulo II: Reglamentos del Cabildo Africano Lucumi," 25 April 1910; cf. Carmen Barcia, *Los ilustres apellidos*, 417.

50. Carmen Barcia, 414.

Bibliography

Oral Data

Between 2001 and 2017, the author collected oral evidence in El Cerro, Guanabacoa, Regla, and Santiago de las Vegas in Havana, Cuba; and in Los Angeles and Toronto. Details of the informants whose evidence has been made in the present work are as follows:

Aguabella, Francisco. *Bátà* drummer and instructor at the University of California, Los Angeles, interviewed May 2007.

Cosme Baños, Pedro. Director of the Museo Municipal de Regla, interviewed 1 July 2004.

Hussein, Umar. Interpretation of African names with author, 10–20 September 2011.

Marcuzzi, Michael. *Bátà* drummer and instructor at York University, interviewed February 2005.

Mason, John. *Babaláwo*, interviewed 4 February 2017.

Miller, Ivor. Interviewed June–September 2016, May 2017.

Ojo, Olatunji. Interpretation of African names with author, 8 April–24 October 2011.

Ramirez, Alexander L. *Tata nganga briyumbia*, interviewed March 2012.

Sani, Abubakar Babajo. Interpretation of African names, 10 July–10 October 2011.

Segara Echevarría, Joaquín. *Oriaté pimienta rama*, interviewed 13 April 2012.

Tamayo, Ana Clara. *Madrina pimienta rama*, interviewed October 2011–May 2012.

Valdés Jané, Ernesto. Director of Proyecto Orunmila, *Efuche rama*, interviewed 2001–2012.

Villa, Ismael. *Oriaté pimienta rama*, interviewed 10 December 2011.

Villalba, Enrique. *Babaláwo* at the *casa-templo* Orichaoko in the neighborhood of Parraga, Havana, interviewed 30 March 2011.

Archival Sources

Archives Nationales, Paris (ANP)
Archivo General de Indias (AGI)
    Casa de la Contración (CC)
    Papeles de Cuba (PC)
    Santo Domingo (SD)
Archivo Histórico Nacional, Madrid (AHN)
    Estado (E)
    Ultramar (U)

Archivo Nacional de Cuba (ANC)
   Audencia de la Havana (AH)
   Comisión Militar (CM)
   Escribanía de Cabello (EC)
   Escribanía de Gobierno (EG)
   Escribanía de Guerra (EGu)
   Escribanía de Varios (EV)
   Escribanía de Vergel (EVer)
   Floridas (F)
   Gobierno General (GG)
   Gobierno Superior Civil (GSC)
   Intendencia General (IG)
   Miscelánea de Expedientes (ME)
Church Missionary Society (CMS)
   Original Papers (O)
Library of Congress (LOC)
   American State Papers (ASP)
The National Archives, England (NA)
   Colonial Office (CO)
   Foreign Office (FO)
   Treasury (T)
Merseyside Maritime Museum (MMM)
Slave Societies Digital Archive (SSDA)
   Espiritu Santo (ES)
   Jesus, María y José (JMJ)
   Nuestra Señora de la Asunción de Guanabacoa (NSAG)
   Nuestra Señora de Regla (NSR)
   San Carlos de Matanzas (SCM)
   Santo Angel Custodio (SAC)
   Santo Cristo del Buen Viaje (SCBV)
St. Kitts Archive (SKA)
University of Liverpool Library (ULL)
   Dumbell Papers (DP)

Newspapers

Diario de la Havana
Diario del gobierno de la Habana
El noticioso y lucero: Diario mercantil, politico y literario
Liverpool General Advertiser
Times

Published Primary Sources

Adams, John. *Remarks on the Country Extending from Cape Palmas to the River Congo, Including Observations on the Manners and Customs of the Inhabitants*. London: G. and W. B. Whittaker, 1823.

Ajayi, J. F. Ade. "Samuel Ajayi Crowther of Oyo." In *Africa Remembered: Narratives by West Africans from the Era of the Slave Trade*, edited by Philip D. Curtin, 289–316. Madison: University of Wisconsin Press, 1967.

Arango y Parreño, Francisco. *Obras del Excmo. Señor D. Francisco de Arango y Parreño*. Vol. 1. Havana: Impresa de Howson y Heinen, 1888.

Baba, Ahmad. "Belief, Unbelief, and Slavery in Hausaland." In *Nigerian Perspectives: An Historical Anthology*, translated by Thomas Hodgkin, 2nd ed., 155–56. Oxford: Oxford University Press, [1960] 1975.

———. *Mi'râj al-Su'ûd: Ahmad Bâbâ's Replies on Slavery*. Edited by John Hunwick and Fatima Harrak. Rabat: University Mohammed V, Souissi Institute of African Studies, 2000.

Bando de buen gobierno para la ciudad de la Havana. Havana: Reimpreso en la imprenta de la Capitanía General, 1792.

Bando de governación y policía de las isla de Cuba espedido por Excmo. Sr. D. Gerónimo Valdés, Gobernador y Capitán General. Havana: Imp. del Gobierno, 1842.

Barbot, Jean. *A Description of the Coasts of North and South Guinea; and of Ethiopia Inferior* . . . London: n.p., 1732.

Beatson, Robert. *Naval and Military Memoirs of Great Britain, from 1727 to 1783*. Vol. 5. Boston, MA: Gregg Press, 1972.

Bello, Muḥammad. *Infâq al-Maysûr fî Târîkh at-Takrûr*. Edited by Bahija Chadli. Rabat: Mohammed V University, Publications of the Institute of African Studies, 1996.

Bosman, William. *New and Accurate Description of the Gold Coast of Guinea*. London, 1705.

Boto Villa, Josef. *Plano del puerto de la Havana* . . . 1783. Map retrieved from the Library of Congress, https://www.loc.gov/item/74690699.

Bremer, Frederika. *The Homes of the New World: Impressions of America*. Translated by Mary Howitt. 3 vols. New York: Harper & Brothers, 1853.

Clapperton, Hugh. *Hugh Clapperton into the Interior of Africa: Records of the Second Expedition, 1825–1827*. Edited by Jamie Bruce Lockhart and Paul E. Lovejoy. Leiden: Koninklijke Brill N. V., 2005.

Colección de documentos para la historia de la formación social en hispanoamérica. Edited by Richard Konetzke. 3 vols. Madrid: Consejo Superior de Investigaciones Científicas, 1953–62.

Correspondencia reservada del capitan general Don Miguel Tacon con el gobierno de Madrid, 1834–1836. Edited by Juan Pérez de la Riva. Havana: Consejo Nacional de Cultura, 1963.

Crowther, Samuel Ajayi. *A Dictionary of the Yoruba Language*. London: Oxford University Press, [1843] 2007.

"Cuban Slaves in England." *Anti-Slavery Reporter* 2, no. 10. London: Peter Jones Bolton, 1854, 234–39.

Curtin, Philip. "Joseph Wright of the Egba." In *Africa Remembered: Narratives by West Africans from the Era of the Slave Trade*, edited by Philip Curtin, 313–33. Madison: University of Wisconsin Press, 1967.

Dalzel, Archibald. *The history of Dahomy, an inland Kingdom of Africa; compiled from authentic memoirs; with an introduction and notes.* London: T. Spilsbury & Son, 1793.

Dapper, Olfert. *Naukeurige beschryvinge der Africaenische gewesten Egypten, Barbaryen, and Naukeurige beschrijvinge der Africaenische eylanden* . . . Amsterdam, 1668.

Del Rio, D. Jose. *Plano del puerto y ciudad de la Havana* . . . 1793. Map retrieved from the Huntington Library, http://hdl.huntington.org/cdm/singleitem/collection /p15150coll4/id/10120/rec/13.

Des Marchais, Chevalier. *Voyage du chevalier des Marchais en Guinée, isles voisines, et à Cayenne, fait en 1725, 1726 & 1727* . . . Amsterdam: Aux dépens de la Compagnie, 1731.

Diario de las operaciones de la expedicion contra la plaza de Panzacola concluida por las armas de S. M. Católica, baxo las órdenes del mariscal de campo D. Bernardo de Galvez. Havana, 1781.

Diario de sesiones de las cortes generales y extraordinarias. Vol. 3. Madrid: Imprenta de J. A. García, 1870.

Duff, E. C. *Gazetteer of the Kontagora Province.* London: Waterlow, 1920.

Dumont, Henri. *Antropología y patología comparadas de los negros esclavos, 1876.* Translated by Israel Castellanos. Havana, 1922.

Eaton, John Henry. *The Life of Major General Andrew Jackson: Comparing a History of the War in the South* . . . Philadelphia: McCary & Davis, 1828.

Fadipe, N. A. *The Sociology of the Yoruba.* Edited by F. O. Okediji and O. O. Okediji. Ibadan: Ibadan University Press, 1970.

Gandarias, Alonso C. S., and Hernández E. Prieto. *Crónicas parlamentarias para la constitución de 1812: 24 de Septiembre de 1810–19 de Marzo de 1812.* Madrid: Congreso de Diputados, 2012.

Historia documentada de la conspiración de los soles y rayos de Bolívar. Edited by Roque E. Garrigó. 2 vols. Habana: La Imprenta El Siglo XX, 1929.

Humboldt, Alexander von. *Political Essay on the Island of Cuba.* Edited by Vera M. Kutzinski and Ottmar Ette. Translated by J. Bradford Anderson, Vera M. Kutzinski, and Anja Becker. Chicago: University of Chicago Press, [1826] 2011.

Irving, Edward. "Ijebu Country." *Church Missionary Intelligencer* 7 (1856): 65–72, 93–98, 118–20.

Isert, Paul Erdmann. *Letters on West Africa and the Slave Trade: Paul Erdmann Isert's Journey to Guinea and the Caribbean Islands in Columbia (1788).* Translated by Selena A. Winsnes. Accra: Sub-Saharan Publishers, [1992] 2007.

Johnson, Rev. Samuel. *The History of the Yorùbás from the Earliest Times to the Beginning of the British Protectorate.* London: Routledge & Sons Limited, 1921.

Journal of the Commissioners for Trade and Plantations, 1704–1782. Vol. 14. London: H. M. S. O., 1920.

Lambert, Sheila, ed. *House of Commons Sessional Papers of the Eighteenth Century.* Wilmington, DE: Scholarly Resources, 1975.

———. *Slave Trade 1788–1790*. Vol. 67 of Lambert, *House of Commons Sessional Papers of the Eighteenth Century*.

———. *Minutes of Evidence on the Slave Trade 1788 and 1789*. Vol. 68 of Lambert, *House of Commons Sessional Papers of the Eighteenth Century*.

———. *Report of the Lords of Trade on the Slave Trade 1789, Part I*. Vol. 69 of Lambert, *House of Commons Sessional Papers of the Eighteenth Century*.

———. *Minutes of Evidence on the Slave Trade 1790, Part I*. Vol. 71 of Lambert, *House of Commons Sessional Papers of the Eighteenth Century*.

———. *Minutes of Evidence on the Slave Trade 1790, Part II*. Vol. 72 of Lambert, *House of Commons Sessional Papers of the Eighteenth Century*.

———. *Minutes of Evidence on the Slave Trade 1790, Part III*. Vol. 73 of Lambert, *House of Commons Sessional Papers of the Eighteenth Century*.

———. *Slave Trade 1791 and 1792*. Vol. 82 of Lambert, *House of Commons Sessional Papers of the Eighteenth Century*.

Lander, Richard. *Records of Captain Clapperton's Last Expedition to Africa*. 2 vols. London: Colburn and Bentley, 1830.

Lander, Richard, and John Lander. *Journal of an Expedition to Explore the Course and Termination of the Niger*. 2 vols. London: John Murray, 1832.

Las siete partidas del sabio rey Don Alonso el Nono. Madrid: Oficina de B. Cano, 1789.

Le Herissé, A. *L'ancien royaume de Dahomey*. Paris: E. Larose, 1911.

Liverpool Plantation Registers, 1744–1773 and 1779–1784 in the Custom House. East Ardsley: Microform Academic Publishers, [1978] 2005.

Lloyd, Peter C. "Osifekunde of Ijebu." In *African Remembered: Narratives by West Africans from the Era of the Slave Trade*, edited by Philip Curtin, 217–88. Prospect Heights: Waveland Press, 1967.

Lloyd's Register 1783. London: Wyman & Sons, 1783.

Lloyd's Register 1784. London: Wyman & Sons, 1784.

Marshall, John. *Royal Naval Biography, or, Memoirs of the Services of All the Flag Officers, Superannuated Rear-Admirals, Retired-Captains, Post-Captains and Commanders . . .* London: Printed for Longman, Rees, Orme, Brown and Green, [1823] 1983.

Minutes of the Evidence Taken at the Bar of the House of Lords, upon the Order Made for Taking into Consideration the Present State of the Trade to Africa, and Particularly the Trade in Slaves . . . London, 1792.

The Nautical Magazine: A Journal of Papers on Subjects Connected with Maritime Affairs. London: Simpkin, Marshall, and Co., 1837.

Norris, Robert. *A Short Account of the African Slave Trade: Collected from Local Knowledge, from the Evidence Given at the Bar of Both Houses of Parliament, and, from Tracts Written upon That Subject*. Liverpool: Printed at Ann Smith's Navigation Shop, 1788.

———. *Memoirs of the Reign of Bossa Ahádee*. London: Printed for W. Lowndes, 1789.

Ogilby, John. *Africa: Being an Accurate Description of the Regions of Ægypt, Barbary, Lybia, and Billedulgerid, the Land of Negroes . . .* London: Printed by Tho. Johnson for the author . . . , 1670.

Parliamentary Debates from the Year 1803 to the Present Time: Forming a Continuation of the Work Entitled "The Parliamentary History of England from the Earliest Period to the Year 1803." Vol. 37. London: T. C. Hansard, 1818.

Pérez, Louis A., Jr. ed. *Slaves, Sugar, and Colonial Society: Travel Accounts of Cuba, 1801–1899*. Willington, DE: Scholarly Resources, 1992.

Pichardo, Esteban. *Diccionario provincial casi-razonado de vozes y frases cubanas*. 3rd ed. Havana: Imprenta la Antilla, [1836] 1862.

Real cédula por la que Su Majestad concede libertad para el comercio de negros con las islas de Cuba, Sto. Domingo, Puerto Rico, y provincial de Caracas a los españoles y extranjeros. Madrid: Impresa Nacional, 1789.

Reglamento de Esclavos de 1826. Transcribed by Zavala Trías Sylvia. http://freepages .genealogy.rootsweb.ancestry.com/~poncepr/reglamento.html.

Reglamento para las milicias de infantería y caballería de la Isla de Cuba. Havana: D. Guillermo del Rio, [1769] 1795.

Ritter, Carl. "Mittheilungen über einige westafricanische Stämme in Cuba, gesamelt von Hesse." In *Monatsberichte über die Verhandlungen der Gesellschaft für Erdkunde zu Berlin*, edited by T. E. Gumprecht, 12–16. Berlin: Bei Simo Schropp und Comp., 1853.

Romans, B., and R. Sayer. *Plan of the Harbour of Pensacola*. London: Printed for R. Sayer, 1788. Map retrieved from the Library of Congress, https://www.loc.gov /item/73694474.

Saco, José Antonio. *Carta sobre el cólera morbo-asiático*. Habana: Impresa del Gobierno, 1833.

———. "Dictamen que á la Junta de gobierno del Real Consulado de la Habana presentó una comision de su propio seno sobra la reforma de los ramos de la administraction pública." *Revista Bimestre Cubana* 3, no. 7 (1832): 145–72.

———. "Examen de las tablas necrológicas del cólera-morbus en la ciudad de la Habana y sus arrabales, formadas á escitacion del exmo. señor intendente de ejército conde de Villanueva, por Don Ramon de la Sagra." *Revista Bimestre Cubana* 9, no. 1 (1834): 325–43.

———. "Memoria sobre la vagancia en la isla de Cuba." *Revista Bimestre Cubana* 3, no. 6 (1832): 19–64.

Sagra, Ramon de la. *Plano de la ciudad y del puerto de la Habana* . . . Paris: Imprimerie Lemercier et Cie., 1842. Map retrieved from the Biblioteca Digital Hispánica, http://bdh.bne.es/bnesearch/detalle/bdh0000020336.

———. *Tablas necrologicas del cholera-morbus en la ciudad de la Havana y sus arrabalaes*. Havana: n.p., 1833.

Smith, Adam. *An Inquiry into the Nature and Causes of the Wealth of Nations*. 2 vols. London: W. Strahan, 1776.

Stanfield, James Field. *The Guinea Voyage: A Poem, in Three Books*. London: James Phillips, 1789.

———. *Observations on a Guinea Voyage. In a Series of Letters Addressed to the Rev. Thomas Clarkson*. London: James Phillips, George-Yard, Lombard-Street, 1788.

Taylor, John Glanville. *The United States and Cuba: Eight Years of Change and Travel*. London: Bentley, 1851.

Treaty between His Britannic Majesty and His Catholic Majesty, for Preventing Their Subjects from Engaging in Any Illicit Traffic in Slaves, Sept. 23, 1817, http://www .pdavis.nl/Treaty_1817.html.

Turnbull, David. *Travels in the West: Cuba, with Notices of Porto Rico and the Slave Trade*. London: Longman, Orme, Brown, Greens and Longman, 1840.

Digital Resources

Cuban Genealogy Center: Resources for those Searching for their Cuban Roots. http://www.cubagenweb.org/index.htm. [Accessed 2018].

Dictionary of Caribbean and Afro-Latin American Biography. http://hutchinscenter.fas.harvard.edu/DCALAB. Directed by Henry Louis Gates Jr., Franklin Knight, and Steven J. Niven. [Accessed 2018].

The Kings Candle Sticks. http://www.thekingscandlesticks.com/index.htm. [Accessed 2018].

Legacies of British Slave-ownership. https://www.ucl.ac.uk/lbs/. Directed by Keith McClelland. [Accessed 2018].

Liberated Africans. http://liberatedafricans.org/. Directed by Henry B. Lovejoy. [Accessed 2018].

"Our Lady." *Montserrat*. http://www.montserratvisita.com/en/spirituality/our-lady.

"Patronazgo del Cuerpo de Infantería de Marina." *Armada Española*. http://www.armada.mde.es/ArmadaPortal/page/Portal/Armadaespannola/conocenos_organizacion/prefLang_es/03_Flota—04_Flota-Fuerza-Infanteria-Marina—03_patronazgo-cuerpo-infanteria-marina_es. [Accessed 2018].

SHADD: Studies in the History of the African Diaspora – Documents. http://tubman.info.yorku.ca/publications/shadd/. Directed by Paul E. Lovejoy. [Accessed 2018].

Slave Societies Digital Archive. https://slavesocieties.org/. Directed by Jane Landers. [Accessed 2018].

Voyages: The Trans-Atlantic Slave Trade Database. http://www.slavevoyages.org/. Directed by David Eltis. [Accessed 2018].

Secondary Sources

Abrams, Susan M. "Cherokees in the Creek War: A Band of Brothers." In *Tohopeka: Rethinking the Creek War & War of 1812*, edited by Kathryn E. Holland Braund, 122–45. Tuscaloosa: University of Alabama Press, 2012.

Adams, Henry. *History of the United States of America during the Second Administration of James Madison*. Vol. 1. New York: Charles Scribner's Sons, 1891.

Adderley, Rosanne Marion. *"New Negroes from Africa": Slave Trade Abolition and Free African Settlement in the Nineteenth-Century Caribbean*. Bloomington: Indiana University Press, 2006.

———. "Yoruba Ethnic Groups or Yoruba Ethnic Group? A Review of the Problem of Ethnic Identification." *África: Revista do Centro de Estudos Africanos da Universidade de São Paulo, Brasil* 7 (1984): 57–70.

Aimes, Hubert H. S. "African Institutions in America." *Journal of American Folklore* 18, no. 68 (1905): 15–32.

———. *History of Slavery in Cuba, 1511–1868*. New York: G. P. Putnam's Sons, 1907.

Ajayi, J. F. Ade, and Robert Sydney Smith. *Yoruba Warfare in the 19th Century*. Cambridge: Cambridge University Press, 1964.

Ajisafe, Ajayi Kolawole. *The History of Abeokuta*. Abeokuta, Nigeria: Fola Bookshops, 1964.

Akinjogbin, Isaac Adeagbo. *The Cradle of a Race (Ife from the Beginning to 1980)*. Port Harcourt, Nigeria: Sunray Publications, 1992.

———. *Dahomey and Its Neighbours*. Cambridge: Cambridge University Press, 1967.

———. "The Expansion of Oyo and the Rise of Dahomey, 1600–1800." In *The History of West Africa*, vol. 1, edited by J. F. Ade Ajayi and Michael Crowther, 305–46. New York: Columbia University Press, 1972.

———. "The Prelude to the Yoruba Civil Wars of the Nineteenth Century." *Odu* 24, no. 46 (1965): 81–86.

Akinnaso, F. Niyi. "The Sociolinguistic Basis of Yoruba Personal Names." *Anthropological Linguistics* 22, no. 7 (1980): 275–304.

———. "Traditional Yoruba Names and the Transmission of Cultural Knowledge." *Names* 31 (1983): 139–58.

Allahar, Antón L. "The Cuban Sugar Planters (1790–1820): The Most Solid and Brilliant Bourgeois Class in All of Latin America." *Americas* 41, no. 1 (1984): 37–57.

Amores, Juan B. *Cuba en la época de Ezpeleta (1785–1790)*. Pamplona, Spain: Ediciones Universidad de Navarra, S. A., 2000.

Angarica, Nicolás Valentín. *Manual de Orihaté: Religión Lucumi*. Havana: n.p., 1955.

Apter, Andrew. *Black Critics and Kings: The Hermeneutics of Power in Yorùbá Society*. Chicago: University of Chicago Press, 1992.

———. "The Blood of Mothers: Women, Money, and Markets in Yoruba-Atlantic Perspective." *Journal of African American History* 98, no. 1 (2013): 72–98.

———. "The Embodiment of Paradox: Yoruba Kingship and Female Power." *Cultural Anthropology* 6 (1991): 212–29.

———. "Herskovits's Heritage: Rethinking Syncretism in the African Diaspora." *Diaspora: A Journal of Transnational Studies* 1, no. 3 (1991): 235–60.

———. "The Historiography of Yoruba Myth and Ritual." *History in Africa* 14 (1987): 1–25.

———. "Notes on Orisha Cults in the Ekiti Yoruba Highlands: A Tribute to Pierre Verger." *Cahiers d'Etudes Africaines* 39, no. 2 (1995): 369–401.

———. *Oduduwa's Chain: Locations of Culture in the Yoruba Diaspora*. Chicago: Chicago University Press, 2017.

———. "On African Origins: Creolization and Connaissance in Haitian Vodou." *American Ethnologist* 29, no. 2 (2002): 233–60.

Arrom, José Juan. "La Virgen del Cobre: Historía, leyenda y símbolo sincrético." In *Estudios Afro-Cubanos*, edited by Lázara Menédez, 269–310. Habana, Cuba: Facultad de Artes y Letras Universidad de la Habana, [1959] 1990.

Arthur, Stanley, George C. H. Kernion, and Charles P. Dimitry. *Old Families of Louisiana*. New Orleans: Harmanson, 1931.

Artola, Miguel. *La España de Fernando VII*. Madrid: Espasa-Calpe, 1999.

Artola, Miguel, and Orti M. Morán. *Las cortes de Cádiz*. Madrid: Marcial Pons, 1991.

Atienza y Navajas, Julio de. *Nobiliario español: Diccionario heráldico de apellidos españoles y de títulos nobiliarios*. Madrid: M. Aguilar, [1948] 1954.

Avoseh, Theophilus Ọláb̀ọ́dé. *A Short History of Badagry*. Lagos: Ife-Olu Print, 1938.

Ayisi, Eric O. *Saint Eustatius: The Treasure Island of the Caribbean*. Trenton, NJ: Africa World Press, 1992.

Ayorinde, Christine. *Afro-Cuban Religiosity, Revolution, and National Identity*. Gainesville: Florida University Press, 2004.

Babayemi, S. O. "Bere Festival in Oyo." *Journal of the Historical Society of Nigeria* 7, no. 1 (1973): 121–24.

———. "Sango Traditions and Cult Organisation in Oyo." *West Africa Journal of Archaeology* 18 (1988): 95–110.

Balogun, Kolawole. *Government in Old Oyo Empire*. Lagos: Africanus Publishers, 1985.

Barber, Karin. *I Could Speak until Tomorrow: Oriki, Women, and the Past in a Yoruba Town*. Edinburgh: Edinburgh University Press for the International African Institute, 1991.

Barcia, Manuel. *The Great African Slave Revolt of 1825*. Baton Rouge: Louisiana State University Press, 2012.

———. *Seeds of Insurrection: Domination and Resistance on Western Cuban Plantations, 1808-1848*. Baton Rouge: Louisiana University Press, 2008.

———. "West African Islam in Colonial Cuba." *Slavery and Abolition* 35, no. 2 (2013): 292–305.

———. *West African Warfare in Bahia and Cuba: Soldier Slaves in the Atlantic World, 1807-1844*. Oxford: Oxford University Press, 2014.

Barka, Norman F. "Citizens of St. Eustatius, 1781: A Historical and Archaeological Study." In *The Lesser Antilles in the Age of European Expansion*, edited by Robert L. Paquette and Stanley L. Engerman, 223–40. Gainesville: University Press of Florida, 1996.

Barnes, Sandra T. *Africa's Ogun: Old World and New*. Bloomington: Indiana University Press, [1989] 1997.

Bascom, William. *Drums of the Yoruba of Nigeria*. CD liner notes. Washington: Smithsonian Folkways Records, [1953] 1992.

———. "The *Esusu*: A Credit Institution of the Yoruba." *Journal of the Royal Anthropological Institute* 82 (1952): 63–69.

———. "The Focus of Cuban Santería." *Southwestern Journal of Anthropology* 6, no. 1 (1950): 64–68.

———. *Ifá Divination: Communication between Gods and Men in West Africa*. Bloomington: Indiana University Press, 1991.

———. *Sixteen Cowries: Yoruba Divination from Africa to the New World*. Bloomington: Indiana University Press, 1980.

———. "The Sociological Role of the Yoruba Cult Group." *American Anthropologist* 46, no. 1 (1944): 1–75.

———. "Yoruba Acculturation in Cuba." *Mémoires de l'Institut Français d'Afrique Noire* 27 (1953): 163–67.

Bastide, Roger. *Les amériques noires: Les civilisations africaines dans le nouveau monde*. Paris: Payot, 1967.

Bay, Edna G. "Belief, Legitimacy, and the 'Kpojito': An Institutional History of the 'Queen Mother' in Precolonial Dahomey." *Journal of African History* 36, no. 1 (1995): 1–27.

———. *Wives of the Leopard: Gender, Politics, and Culture in the Kingdom of Dahomey.* Charlottesville: University of Virginia Press, 1998.

Behrendt, Stephen D. "The Captains in the British Slave Trade from 1785 to 1807." *Transactions of the Historic Society of Lancashire and Cheshire*, 140 (1991): 79–140.

———. "Crew Mortality in the Transatlantic Slave Trade in the Eighteenth Century." *Slavery and Abolition* 18, no. 1 (1997): 49–71.

Beier, Ulli. "The Historical and Psychological Significance of Yoruba Myths." *Odu* 1 (1955): 17–25.

———. "Yoruba Enclave." *Nigeria* 58 (1953): 238–40.

———. *Yoruba Myths.* Cambridge: Cambridge University Press, 1980.

Beldarraín Chaple, Enrique, and Luz María Espinosa Cortés. "El cólera en la Habana en 1833: Su impacto demográfico." *Diálogos* 15, no. 1 (2013): 155–73.

Bencomo, Juan. "Crafting These Sacred Bata Drums." In *Afro-Cuban Voices: On Race and Identity in Contemporary Cuba*, edited by Pedro Pérez Sarduy and Jean Stubbs, 140–46. Gainesville: University Press of Florida, 2000.

Bennett, Robert J. *The Voice of Liverpool Business: The First Chamber of Commerce and the Atlantic Economy, 1774–c. 1796.* Liverpool: Liverpool Chamber of Commerce, 2010.

Bergad, Laird W. *The Comparative Histories of Slavery in Brazil, Cuba, and the United States.* Cambridge: Cambridge University Press, 2007.

Bergad, Laird W., Fe Iglesias Garcia, and María del Carmen Barcia. *The Cuban Slave Market, 1790–1880.* Cambridge: Cambridge University Press, 1995.

Berlin, Ira. *Many Thousands Gone: The First Two Centuries of Slavery in North America.* Cambridge, MA: Harvard University Press, 2000.

Bettelheim, Judith., ed. *Cuban Festivals: A Century of Afro-Cuban Culture.* Princeton, NJ: Markus Wiener, 2001.

Bilby, Kenneth. "Swearing by the Past, Swearing to the Future: Sacred Oaths, Alliances, and Treaties among the Guianese and Jamaican Maroons." *Ethnohistory* 44, no. 4 (1997): 655–89.

Biobaku, Saburi, ed. *The Egba and Their Neighbours, 1842–1872.* Oxford: Clarendon Press, 1965.

———. "An Historical Sketch of the Egba Traditional Authorities." *Africa* 22, no. 1 (1952): 35–49.

———. *Sources of Yorùbá History.* Oxford: Clarendon Press, 1973.

Bivar, A. D. H., and M. Hiskett. "The Arabic Literature of Nigeria to 1804: A Provisional Account." *Bulletin of the School of Oriental and African Studies* 25, no. 1 (1962): 104–48.

Blackburn, Robin. *The Overthrow of Colonial Slavery, 1776–1848.* London: Verso, 1988.

Bly, Antonio T. "'Pretends He Can Read:' Runaways and Literacy in Colonial America, 1730–1776." *Early American Studies* 6, no. 2 (2008): 261–94.

Bolanle, Awe. "Militarism and Economic Developments in Nineteenth Century Yoruba Country: The Ibadan Example." *Journal of African History* 14, no. 1 (1973): 65–77.

Bolívar Aróstegui, Natalia. *Los orishas en Cuba*. Havana: Ediciones Unión, Unión de Escritores y Artistas de Cuba, 1990.

Bolívar Aróstegui, Natalia, and Mario López Cepero. *¿Sincretismo Religioso? Santa Barbara Chango*. Havana: Pablo de la Torriente Editorial, 1995.

Borucki, Alex, David Eltis, and David Wheat. "Atlantic History and the Slave Trade to Spanish America." *American Historical Review* 120, no. 2 (2015): 433–61.

Brandon, George. *Santería from Africa to the New World: The Dead Sell Memories*. Bloomington: Indiana University Press, 1993.

Braund, Kathryn E. Holland. *Deerskins and Duffels: The Creek Indian Trade with Anglo-Americans, 1683-1815*. Lincoln: University of Nebraska Press, 1993.

———. "Red Skins." In *Tohopeka: Rethinking the Creek War and War of 1812*, edited by Kathryn E. Holland Braund, 84–104. Tuscaloosa: University of Alabama Press, 2012.

Brown, David H. "The Afro-Cuban Festival 'Day of the Kings': An Annotated Bibliography." In *Cuban Festivals: A Century of Afro-Cuban Culture*, edited by Judith Bettelheim, 49–98. Princeton, NJ: Markus Weiner, 2001.

———. "Garden in the Machine: Afro-Cuban Sacred Art and Performance in Urban New Jersey and New York." PhD diss., Yale University, 1989.

———. *Santería Enthroned: Art, Ritual, and Innovation in an Afro-Cuban Religion*. Chicago: University of Chicago Press, 2003.

Brown, Vincent. *Reaper's Garden: Death and Power in the World of Atlantic Slavery*. Cambridge: Cambridge University Press, 2010.

Brubaker, Rogers, and Frederick Cooper. "Beyond 'Identity.'" *Theory and Society* 29, no. 1 (2000): 1–47.

Buckner, Timothy R. "The Slave Trade's Apex in the Eighteenth Century." In *The Atlantic World, 1450-2000*, edited by Toyin Falola and Kevin D. Roberts, 96–113. Bloomington: Indiana World Press, 2008.

Bunn, Mike, and Clay Williams. *Battle for the Southern Frontier: The Creek War and the War of 1812*. Charleston, SC: History Press, 2008.

Cabrera, Lydia. *El Monte*. Havana: Ediciones SI-MAR, [1954] 1996.

———. "El sincretismo religioso en Cuba." *Orígenes* 11, no. 36 (1954): 8–20.

———. *La lengua sagrada de los ñáñigos*. Miami, FL: Ediciones CR, 1988.

———. *La regla Kimbisa del Santo Cristo del Buen Viaje*. Miami: Peninsular Printing, 1977.

———. *Vocabulario Lucumí (El Yoruba que se habla en Cuba)*. Havana: Colleción del Chiherekú, 1957.

———. *Yemayá y Ochún. Kariochas, Iyalochas y Olorichas*. Madrid: Edición C. R., 1974.

Candido, Mariana P. *An African Slaving Port and the Atlantic World: Benguela and Its Hinterland*. Cambridge: Cambridge University Press, 2013.

Capone, Stefania. *La quête de l'Afrique dans le candomblé: Pouvoir et tradition au Brésil*. Paris: Karthala, 1999.

Cardoso Morais, Christianni. "Ler e escrever: Habilidades de escravos e forros? Comarca do Rio das Mortes, Minas Gerais, 1731-1850." *Revista Brasileira de Educação* 12, no. 36 (2007): 493–504.

Carmen Barcia, María del. *La otra familia: Parientes, redes y descendencia de los esclavos en Cuba.* Santiago de Cuba: Editorial Oriente, 2009.

———. *Los ilustres apellidos: Negros en la Habana colonial.* Havana: Editorial de Ciencias Social, 2009.

Carvalho Soares, Mariza de. *Devotos da cor: Identidade étnica, religiosidade e escravidão, século XVIII.* Rio de Janeiro: Civilização Brasileira, 2000.

Castellanos, Israel. *La brujería y el ñañiguismo en Cuba desde el punto de vista médico-legal.* Havana: Lloredo y Compañia, 1916.

Caughey, John Walton. *Bernardo de Gálvez in Louisiana, 1776-1783.* Berkeley: University of California Press, 1934.

Chance, John K., and William B. Taylor. "Estate and Class in a Colonial City: Oaxaca in 1792." *Comparative Studies in Society and History* 19, no. 4 (1977): 454-87.

———. "Estate and Class: A Reply." *Comparative Studies in Society and History* 21, no. 3 (1979): 434-42.

Chandler, David G. *The Campaigns of Napoleon.* New York: Macmillan, 1966.

Chávez, Thomas E. *Spain and the Independence of the United States: An Intrinsic Gift.* Albuquerque: University of New Mexico Press, 2002.

Chenoweth, Michael. *The 18th Century Climate of Jamaica: Derived from the Journals of Thomas Thistlewood, 1750-1786.* Philadelphia, PA: American Philosophical Society, 2003.

Childs, Matt D. *The 1812 Aponte Rebellion in Cuba and the Struggle against Atlantic Slavery.* Chapel Hill: University of North Carolina Press, 2006.

———. "'The Defects of Being a Black Creole': The Degrees of African Identity in the Cuban Cabildos de Nación." In *Slaves, Subjects, and Subversives: Blacks in Colonial Latin America,* edited by Barry Robinson and Jane Landers, 209-46. Albuquerque: University of New Mexico Press, 2006.

———. "Gendering the African Diaspora in the Iberian Atlantic: Religious Brotherhoods and the *Cabildos de Nación.*" In *Women in the Iberian Atlantic,* edited by Sarah E. Owens and Jane Mangan, 230-62. Baton Rouge: Louisiana State University Press, 2012.

———. "Re-creating African Ethnic Identities in Cuba." In *The Black Urban Atlantic in the Age of the Slave Trade,* edited by Jorge Cañizares-Esguerra, Matt D. Childs, and James Sidbury, 85-100. Philadelphia: University of Pennsylvania Press, 2013.

Childs, Matt D., and Toyin Falola. "The Yoruba Diaspora in the Atlantic World: Methodology and Research." In *The Yoruba Diaspora in the Atlantic World,* edited by Toyin Falola and Matt D. Childs, 1-14. Bloomington: Indiana University Press, 2004.

Christopher, Emma. *Slave Ship Sailors and their Captive Cargoes, 1750-1807.* Cambridge: Cambridge University Press, 2006.

———. *They Are We.* Brooklyn, NY: Icarus Films, 2015.

Coker, William. *Indian Traders of the Southeastern Spanish Borderlands: Panton, Leslie &Company and John Forbes &Company, 1783-1847.* Pensacola: University of West Florida Press, 1986.

Coker, William, and Douglas Inglis. *The Spanish Censuses of Pensacola, 1784-1820: A Genealogical Guide to Spanish Pensacola.* Pensacola, FL: Perdido Bay Press, 1980.

Coker, William, and Susan Parker. "The Second Spanish Period in the Two Floridas." In *The New History of Florida*, edited by Michael Gannon, 150–66. Gainesville: University Press of Florida, 2012.

Comaroff, Jean, and John L. Comaroff. *Of Revelation and Revolution*. Chicago: University of Chicago Press, [1991] 1997.

Cornelius, Janet Duitsman. "'We Slipped and Learned to Read': Slave Accounts of the Literacy Process, 1830–1865." *Phylon* 44, no. 3 (1983): 171–86.

———. *"When I Can Read My Title Clear": Literacy, Slavery, and Religion in the Antebellum South*. Columbia: University of South Carolina Press, 1991.

Covington, James W. "The Negro Fort." *Gulf Coast Historical Review* 5 (1990): 72–91.

Curtin, Philip D. *The Atlantic Slave Trade: A Census*. Madison: University of Wisconsin Press, 1969.

Cusick, James G. *The Other War of 1812: The Patriot War and the American Invasion of Spanish Florida*. Gainesville: University Press of Florida, 2003.

Da Costa e Silva, Alberto. "Sobre a rebelião de 1835 na Bahia." *Revista Brasileira* 8, fase 7, no. 31 (2003): 1–33.

Davis, Natalie Zemon. *Trickster Travels: A Sixteenth-Century Muslim between Worlds*. New York: Hill & Wang, 2006.

Debien, Gabriel. "Les origines des esclaves des Antilles." *Bulletin de l'Institut Français d'Afrique Noire* 25, no. 3 (1963): 215–65.

De la Fuente, Alejandro. *Havana and the Atlantic in the Sixteenth Century*. Chapel Hill: University of North Carolina Press, 2011.

———. "Slaves and the Creation of Legal Rights in Cuba: *Coartación* and *Papel*." *Hispanic American Historical Review* 87, no. 4 (2007): 659–92.

Deschamps Chapeaux, Pedro. "Cabildos: solo para esclavos." *Cuba* 7, no. 69 (1968): 50–51.

———. *El negro en la economía habanera del siglo XIX*. Havana: Ediciones Unión, 1970.

———. "La Habana de intra y extramuros y los cabildos de nación." In *Comisión de Activistas de Historia del Regional 10 de Octubre*. Havana: Conferencia el 23 de Octubre, 1972, 19–25.

———. *Los batallones de pardos y morenos libres*. Havana: Editorial Arte y Literatura, 1976.

———. "Marcas tribales de los esclavos en Cuba." *Etnología y folklore* 8 (1969): 65–78.

———. "Presencia religiosa en las sublevaciones de esclavos." *Del Caribe* 6, no. 16 (1990): 101–5.

———. "Rebeliones, cimarronje y libertad en el Caribe." *Del Caribe* 4, no. 8 (1987): 72–79.

Díaz, María Elena. "Rethinking Tradition and Identity: The Virgin of the Charity of El Cobre." In *Cuba, the Elusive Nation: Interpretations of National Identity*, edited by Damián J. Fernández and Madeline Cámara Betancourt, 43–59. Gainesville: University of Florida Press, 2000.

———. *The Virgin King, and the Royal Slaves of El Cobre: Negotiating Cuba in Colonial Cuba, 1670–1780*. Stanford, CA: Stanford University Press, 2000.

Dodson, Julynne E. *Sacred Spaces and Religious Traditions in Oriente Cuba*. Albuquerque: University of Mexico Press, 2008.

Doortmont, Michel R. "The Invention of the Yorubas: Regional Pan-African Nationalism versus Ethnic Provincialism." In *Self-Assertion and Brokerage: Early Cultural Nationalism in West Africa*, edited by Paulo Fernando de Moraes Farias and Karin Barber, 101–8. Birmingham: Centre of West African Studies, University of Birmingham, 1990.

Dorsey, Joseph C. *Slave Traffic in the Age of Abolition: Puerto Rico, West Africa, and the Non-Hispanic Caribbean, 1815–1859*. Gainesville: University Press of Florida, 2003.

Dowd, Gregory Evans. *A Spirited Resistance: The North American Indian Struggle for Unity, 1745–1815*. Baltimore, MD: Johns Hopkins University Press, 1993.

Draper, Nicholas. *The Price of Emancipation: Slave-Ownership and British Society at the End of Slavery*. Cambridge: Cambridge University Press, 2010.

Drewal, Henry John, and Margaret Thompson Drewal. *Gẹlẹdẹ: Art and Female Power among the Yoruba*. Bloomington: Indiana University Press, 1990.

DuBois, Laurent, and John Garrigus. *Slave Revolution in the Caribbean, 1789–1804: A Brief History with Documents*. New York: Palgrave Macmillan, 2006.

Du Bois, W. E. B. *The Souls of Black Folk*. New York: Dover Publications, 1903.

Duharte, Rafael. *El negro en la sociedad colonial*. Santiago de Cuba: Editorial Oriente, 1988.

DuVal, Kathleen. *Independence Lost: Lives on the Edge of the American Revolution*. New York: Random House, 2015.

Echenberg, Myron. *Africa in the Time of Cholera: A History of Pandemics from 1817 to the Present*. New York: Cambridge University Press, 2010.

Egharevba, Jacob U. *A Short History of Benin*. Ibadan, Nigeria: Ibadan University Press, [1936] 1968.

Elder, Melinda. "The Liverpool Slave Trade, Lancaster, and Its Environs." In *Liverpool and Transatlantic Slavery*, edited by David Richardson, Suzanne Schwarz, and Anthony Tibbles, 119–37. Liverpool: Liverpool University Press, 2007.

Eltis, David. "The Diaspora of Yoruba Speakers, 1650–1865: Dimensions and Implications." In *The Yoruba Diaspora in the Atlantic World*, edited by Toyin Falola and Matt Childs, 19–39. Bloomington: Indiana University Press, 2004.

———. *Economic Growth and the Ending of the Transatlantic Slave Trade*. New York: Oxford University Press, 1987.

———. "Fluctuations in Sex and Age Ratios in the Transatlantic Slave Trade, 1663–1864." *Economic History Review* 46 (1993): 308–23.

———. "interAmertoSpanAmer database." Unpublished dataset.

———. "The Middle Passage." In *Voyages: The Trans-Atlantic Slave Trade Database*. 2007. http://www.slavevoyages.org/assessment/essays#.

———. "Nutritional Trends in Africa and the Americas: Heights of Africans, 1819–1839." *Journal of Interdisciplinary History* 22 (1982): 453–75.

———. "The Volume, Age/Sex Ratios, and African Impact of the Slave Trade: Some Refinements of Paul Lovejoy's Review of the Literature." *Journal of African History* 31, no. 3 (1990): 485–92.

Ely, Roland. *La economía cubana entre las dos Isabeles, 1492–1830*. Havana: Librería Martí, 1960.

Enthoven, Victor. "'That Abominable Nest of Pirates': St. Eustatius and the North Americans, 1680-1780." *Early American Studies: An Interdisciplinary Journal* 10, no. 2 (2012): 239-301.

Esdaile, Charles J. *The Peninsular War: A New History*. New York: Palgrave Macmillan, 2003.

Ethridge, Robbie. *Creek Country: The Creek Indians and Their World*. Chapel Hill: University of North Carolina Press, 2003.

Fabre, Geneviève. "The Slave Ship Dance." In *Black Imagination and the Middle Passage*, edited by Maria Diedrich, Henry Louis Gates Jr., and Carl Pedersen, 33-46. Oxford: Oxford University Press, 1999.

Falola, Toyin. *Ìbàdàn: Foundation Growth and Change*. Ibadan: Bookcraft, 2012.

———. *The Political Economy of a Pre-Colonial African State: Ibadan, 1830-1900*. Ife, Nigeria: University of Ife Press, 1984.

———. *The Power of African Cultures*. Rochester, NY: University of Rochester Press, 2003.

———. "Warfare and Trade Relations between Ibadan and the Ijebu in the Nineteenth Century." In *Warfare and Diplomacy in Precolonial Nigeria*, edited by Toyin Falola and Robin Law, 26-30. Madison: African Studies Program University of Wisconsin-Madison, 1992.

———, ed. *Yoruba Historiography*. Madison: African Studies Program of Wisconsin-Madison, 1991.

Falola, Toyin, and Akanmu G. Adebayo. *Culture, Politics, and Money among the Yoruba*. New Brunswick, NJ: Transaction Publishers, 2000.

Falola, Toyin, and Akintunde Akinyemi, eds. *Encyclopedia of the Yorùbá*. Bloomington: Indiana University Press, 2016.

Falola, Toyin, and Theophilus Olabode Avoseh. "The Minor Works of T. O. Avoseh." *History in Africa* 19 (1992): 237-62.

Falola, Toyin, and Ann Genova, ed. *Òrìsà: Yorùbá Gods and Spiritual Identity in Africa and the Diaspora*. Trenton, NJ: Africa World Press, 2005.

Ferreira, Roquinaldo Amaral. *Cross-Cultural Exchange in the Atlantic World: Angola and Brazil during the Era of the Slave Trade*. New York: Cambridge University Press, 2012.

Ferrer, Ada. *Freedom's Mirror: Cuba and Haiti in the Age of Revolution*. New York: Cambridge University Press, 2014.

———. "Noticias de Haití en Cuba." *Revista de Indias* 63, no. 229 (2003): 675-94.

Fett, Sharla M. *Recaptured Africans: Surviving Slave Ships, Detention, and Dislocation in the Final Years of the Slave Trade*. Chapel Hill: University of North Carolina Press, 2017.

Figarola, Joel James. *La brujería cubana: El Palo Monte*. Santiago de Cuba: Editorial Oriente, 2009.

Figueroa y Miranda, Miguel. *Religión y política en la Cuba del siglo XIX: El obispo Espada visto a la luz de los archivos romanos, 1802-1832*. Miami, FL: Ediciones Universal, 1975.

Finch, Aisha K. *Rethinking Slave Rebellion in Cuba: La Escalera and the Insurgencies of 1841-1844*. Chapel Hill: University of North Carolina Press, 2015.

Fisher, Ruth Anna. "The Surrender of Pensacola as Told by the British Source."
American Historical Review 54, no. 2 (1949): 326–29.

Folayan, Kola. "Egbado to 1832: The Birth of a Dilemma." *Journal of the Historical Society of Nigeria* 4, no. 1 (1967): 15–33.

Foner, Philip. *A History of Cuba and Its Relations with the United States.* 2 vols. New York: International Publishers, 1962.

Font, Mauricio A., and Alfonso W. Quiroz, ed. *Cuban Counterpoint: The Legacy of Fernando Ortiz.* Lanham, MD: Lexington Books, 2005.

Fraginals, Manuel Moreno. "Aportes Culturales y Deculturación." In *África en América Latina*, edited by Manuel Moreno Fraginals, 13–33. México: Siglo XXI Editores, [1977] 1996.

———. *El ingenio: el complejo ecónomico cubano del azucar.* Havana: Comisión Nacional Cubana de la UNESCO, 1964.

Franco, José Luciano. *Comercio clandestino de esclavos.* Havana: Ciencias Sociales, [1980] 1996.

———. *Historia de la revolución de Haití.* Havana: Instituto de Historia, Academia de Ciencias, 1966.

———. *La conspiración de Aponte, 1812.* Havana: Editorial Ciencias Sociales, [1963] 2006.

———. *Las conspiraciones de 1810 y 1812.* Havana: Editorial de Ciencias Sociales, 1977.

———. *Los palenques de los negros cimarrones.* Havana: Colección Historia, 1973.

Franklin, Sarah L. *Women and Slavery in Nineteenth-Century Colonial Cuba.* Rochester, NY: University of Rochester Press, 2012.

Froelich, Jean-Claude, and Pierre Alexandre. "Histoire traditionnelle des Kotokoli et des Bi-Tchambi du Nord-Togo." *Bulletin de l' L'Institut Français d'Afrique Noire* 22, no. 1 (1960): 211–75.

Froelich, Jean-Claude, Pierre Alexandre, and Robert Cornevin. *Les populations du nord-Togo.* Paris: Presses Universitaires de France, 1963.

Fuentes, Marisa J. *Dispossessed Lives: Enslaved Women, Violence, and the Archive.* Philadelphia: University of Pennsylvania Press, 2016.

Gárate, Ojanguren M. *Comercio ultramarino e ilustración: La real compañia de la Habana.* Donostia: Departamento de Cultura del Gobierno Vasco, 1994.

García, León J. M. *Liberty under Siege: The Cadiz Parliament of 1812 and Spain's First Constitution.* Cádiz: Quorum, Editores, 2012.

García, Mouton Pilar. *El Español de América, 1992.* Madrid: Consejo Superior de Investigaciones Científicas, 2003.

García Grasa, Rafael. "Apuntes sobre los cabildo africanos en Camagüey." *Simposio nacional sobre la cultura popular tradicional cubana.* Camagüey: Dirección de Orientación y Extensión Cultural, Department de Estudios Culturales, 1981.

García Rodríguez, Gloria. "A propósito de La Escalera: El esclavo como sujeto político." *Boletín del Archivo Nacional* 12 (2000): 1–13.

———. *Conspiraciones y revueltas: La actividad política de los negros en Cuba (1790-1845).* Santiago de Cuba: Oriente, 2003.

———. "El mercado de fuerza de trabajo en Cuba: El comercio esclavista (1760-1790)." *La esclavitud en Cuba*, 124–48. Havana: Editorial Academia, 1986.

————. *La esclavitud desde la esclavitud*. Havana: Ciencias Sociales, 2003.

————. *Voices of the Enslaved in Nineteenth-Century Cuba: A Documentary History*. Translated by Nancy Westrate. Chapel Hill: University of North Carolina Press, 2011.

Gates, Henry Louis Jr. *The Signifying Monkey: A Theory of African-American Literary Criticism*. Oxford: Oxford University Press, 1988.

Geggus, David Patrick. *The Impact of the Haitian Revolution in the Atlantic World*. Columbia: University of South Carolina Press, 2001.

————. "Slave Resistance in the Spanish Caribbean in the mid-1790s." In *A Turbulent Time: French Revolution and the Greater Caribbean*, edited by David Barry Gaspar and David Patrick Geggus, 131–55. Bloomington: Indiana University Press, 1997.

————. "Slavery, War, and Revolution in the Greater Caribbean, 1789–1815." In *A Turbulent Time: French Revolution and the Greater Caribbean*, edited by David Barry Gaspar and David Patrick Geggus, 1–50. Bloomington: Indiana University Press, 1997.

Genovese, Eugene D. *From Rebellion to Revolution: Afro-American Slave Revolts in the Making of the Modern World*. Baton Rouge: Louisiana State University Press, 1979.

Gilroy, Paul. *The Black Atlantic: Modernity and Double Consciousness*. Cambridge, MA: Harvard University Press, 1993.

Gleason, Judith. *Orisha: The Gods of Yorubaland*. New York: Atheneum, 1971.

Glélé, Maurice Ahanhanzo. *Le Danxome: Du pouvoir Aja à la nation Fon*. Paris: Nubia, 1974.

Gomez, Michael A. *Black Crescent: The Experience and Legacy of African Muslims in the Americas*. New York: Cambridge University Press, 2005.

González Quintana, Marta. "María Teresa de Ambulodi, una noble cubana de finales del siglo XVIII." *Coloquio de historia canario—americano* 13 (1988): 1205–12.

González-Ripoll, María Dolores, Consuelo Naranjo, Ada Ferrer, Gloría García, and Josef Opatrny. *El rumor de Haití en Cuba: Temor, raza y rebeldía, 1789–1844*. Madrid: Consejo Superior de Investigaciones Científicas, 2005.

Goveia, Elsa V. "The West Indian Slave Laws of the 18th Century." In *Chapters in Caribbean History*, 7–54. Barbados: Caribbean University Press, 1970.

Grandío Moráguez, Oscar. "The African Origins of Slaves Arriving in Cuba, 1789–1865." In *Extending the Frontiers: Essays on the New Transatlantic Slave Trade Database*, edited by David Eltis and David Richardson, 176–202. New Haven, CT: Yale University Press, 2008.

Green, Michael D. *The Politics of Indian Removal: Creek Government and Society in Crisis*. Lincoln: University of Nebraska Press, 1985.

Greene, Sandra. "Cultural Zones in the Era of the Slave Trade: Exploring the Yoruba Connection with the Anlo-Ewe." In *Identity in the Shadow of Slavery*, edited by Paul E. Lovejoy, 86–101. New York: Continuum, [2000] 2009.

Guanche, Jesús. *Africanía y etnicidad en Cuba*. Havana: Editorial de Ciencias Sociales, 2009.

Guran, Milton. *Agudás: Os 'brasileieros' do Benin*. Rio de Janeiro: Editora Nova Fronteira S.A., 1999.

Hagedorn, Katherine J. *Divine Utterances: The Performance of Afro-Cuban Santería.* Washington, DC: Smithsonian Institution Press, 2001.

Haggerty, Sheryllynne. *'Merely for Money'? Business Culture in the British Atlantic, 1750–1815.* Liverpool: Liverpool University Press, 1988.

Haggerty, Sheryllynne, and John Haggerty. "Visual Analytics of an Eighteenth-Century Business Network." *Enterprise and Society* 11, no. 1 (2010): 1–25.

Hall, Gwendolyn Midlo. "African Ethnicities and the Meaning of 'Mina.'" In *Trans-Atlantic Dimensions of Ethnicity in the African Diaspora*, edited by Paul E. Lovejoy and David V. Trotman, 65–81. New York: Continuum, 2003.

———. *Slavery and African Ethnicities in the Americas: Restoring the Links.* Chapel Hill: University of North Carolina Press, 2005.

———. *Social Control in Slave Plantation Societies: A Comparison of St. Domingue and Cuba.* Baltimore, MD: Johns Hopkins Press, 1971.

Hall, Neville, and Barry W. Higman. *Slave Society in the Danish West Indies: St. Thomas, St. John, and St. Croix.* Baltimore, MD: Johns Hopkins University Press, 1992.

Handler, Jerome S. "The Middle Passage and the Material Culture of Captive Africans." *Slavery and Abolition* 30, no. 1 (2009): 1–26.

Hanger, Kimberly S. *Bounded Lives, Bounded Places: Free Black Society in Colonial New Orleans.* Durham, NC: Duke University Press, 1997.

Harbron, John D. *Trafalgar and the Spanish Navy.* London: Naval Institute Press, 1988.

Helg, Aline. *Our Rightful Share: The Afro-Cuban Struggle for Equality, 1886–1912.* Chapel Hill: University of North Carolina Press, 2000.

Herskovits, Melville J. *Acculturation: The Study of Culture Contact.* New York: J. J. Augustin, 1938.

———. "African Gods and Catholic Saints in New World Negro Belief." *American Anthropologist* 39 (1937): 635–43.

———. *Dahomey, an Ancient West African Kingdom.* New York: J. J. Augustin, 1938.

———. *Myth of the Negro Past.* New York: Harper & Brothers, 1941.

———. "The New World Negro as an Anthropological Problem." *Man* 31 (1931): 68–69.

Heywood, Linda M. *Central Africans and Cultural Transformations in the American Diaspora.* Cambridge: Cambridge University Press, 2002.

Hilgers, Joseph. "Sabbatine Privilege." In *The Catholic Encyclopedia*, vol. 13. New York: Robert Appleton Company, 1912.

Hogendorn, Jan S., and Marion M. Johnson. *The Shell Money of the Slave Trade.* Cambridge: Cambridge University Press, 1986.

Holes, Jack. "West Florida, 1779–1821." In *A Guide to the History of Florida*, edited by Paul George, 3–76. New York: Greenwood, 1989.

Horton, Robin. "Ancient Ife: A Reassessment." *Journal of the Historical Society of Nigeria* 9, no. 4 (1979): 69–149.

Howard, Philip A. *Changing History: Afro-Cuban Cabildos and Societies of Color in the Nineteenth Century.* Baton Rouge: Louisiana State University Press, 1998.

Hunt, Lynn. *Inventing Human Rights: A History.* New York: W. W. Norton, 2008.

Hunwick, John. "Ahmad Baba on Slavery." *Sudanic Africa* 11 (2000): 131–39.

————. "A New Source for the Biography of Aḥmad Bābā al-Tinbuktī (1556–1627)." *Bulletin of the School of Oriental and African Studies* 27, no. 3 (1964): 568–93.

Hunwick, John, and Fatima Harrak. *Mi'raj al-Su'ud: Ahmad Baba's Replies on Slavery.* Rabat: Institute of African Studies, 2000.

Idowu, E. Bolaji. *Olódùmarè: God in Yoruba Belief.* London: Longmans, 1962.

Iduate, Juan. "Noticias sobre sublevaciones y conspiraciones de esclavos: Cafetal Salvador, 1833." *Revista de la Biblioteca Nacional José Martí* 73, no. 24 (1982): 117–52.

Iznaga, Diana. *Transculturación en Fernando Ortiz.* Havana: Editorial de Ciencias Sociales, 1989.

Jameson, J. Franklin. "St. Eustatius in the American Revolution." *American Historical Review* 8, no. 4 (1903): 683–708.

Jennings, Evelyn P. "Paths to Freedom: Imperial Defense and Manumission in Havana, 1762–1800." In *Paths to Freedom: Manumission in the Atlantic World*, edited by Rosemary Brana-Shute and Randy Sparks, 121–41. Columbia: University of South Carolina Press, 2009.

————. "State Enslavement in Colonial Havana." In *Slavery without Sugar: Diversity in Caribbean Economy and Society since the 17th Century*, edited by Verene Shepherd, 152–82. Gainesville: University Press of Florida, 2002.

————. "War as the 'Forcing House of Change': State Slavery in Late-Eighteenth-Century Cuba." *William and Mary Quarterly* 62, no. 3 (2005): 411–40.

Jensen, Ove. "Horseshoe Bend: A Living Memorial." In *Tohopeka: Rethinking the Creek War and War of 1812*, edited by Kathryn E. Holland Braund, 146–57. Tuscaloosa: University of Alabama Press, 2012.

Johnson, Marion. "The Ounce in Eighteenth-Century West African Trade." *Journal of African History* 7, no. 2 (1966): 197–214.

Johnson, Sherry. *Climate and Catastrophe in Cuba and the Atlantic World in the Age of Revolution.* Chapel Hill: University of North Carolina Press, 2011.

————. "Maintaining the Home Front: Widows, Wives, and War." In *Gender, War, and Politics: Transatlantic Perspectives, 1775–1830*, edited by Karen Hagemann, Gisela Mettele, and Jane Rendall, 206–24. New York: Palgrave Macmillan, 2010.

————. *The Social Transformation of Eighteenth-Century Cuba.* Gainesville: University of Florida Press, 2001.

Johnson, Willis Fletcher. *The History of Cuba.* 2 vols. New York: B. F. Buck, 1920.

Jutta, Paul. "La santería como resultado del proceso de transculturación en Cuba." *Revista de la Biblioteca Nacional de José Martí* 3 (1981): 123–36.

Keefer, Katrina. "Scarification and Identity in the Liberated Africans Department Register, 1814–1815." *Canadian Journal of African Studies* 47, no. 3 (2014): 537–53.

Kelley, Sean M., and Henry B. Lovejoy. "The Origins of the African-Born Population in Antebellum Texas: A Research Note." *Southwestern Historical Quarterly* 120, no. 2 (2016): 216–32.

King, Virginia Himmelsteib. *Another Dimension to the African Diaspora: Diet, Disease, and Racism.* Cambridge: Cambridge University Press, 1981.

Kiple, Kenneth F. *Blacks in Colonial Cuba, 1774–1899.* Gainesville: University Presses of Florida, 1976.

———. *The Caribbean Slave: A Biological History*. Cambridge: Cambridge University Press, 1984.

———. "Cholera and Race in the Caribbean." *Journal of Latin American Studies* 17, no. 1 (1985): 157–77.

Kirsch, Johann Peter. "St. John Nepomucene." In *The Catholic Encyclopedia*, vol. 8. New York: Robert Appleton, 1910.

Klein, Debra L. *Yorùbá Bàtá Goes Global: Artists, Culture Brokers, and Fans*. Chicago: University of Chicago Press, 2007.

Klein, Herbert S. "The Colored Militia of Cuba." *Caribbean Studies* 6, no. 2 (1966): 17–27.

Knight, Franklin W. "Origins of Wealth and the Sugar Revolution in Cuba, 1750–1850." *Hispanic American Historical Review* 57, no. 2 (1977): 231–53.

———. *Slave Society in Cuba during the Nineteenth Century*. Madison: University of Wisconsin Press, 1970.

Krapf-Askari, Eva. *The Social Organization of the Owe*. 2 vols. Ibadan: African Notes, Institute of African Studies, 1965.

Kuethe, Allan J. *Cuba, 1753–1815: Crown, Military, and Society*. Knoxville: University of Tennessee Press, 1986.

———. "Havana in the Eighteenth Century." In *Atlantic Port Cities: Economy, Culture, and Society in the Atlantic World, 1650–1850*, edited by Franklin K. Knight and Peggy K. Liss, 13–39. Knoxville: University of Tennessee Press, 1991.

———. *Military Reform and Society in New Granada, 1773–1808*. Gainesville: University Presses of Florida, 1978.

Kuethe, Allan J., and Kenneth J. Andrien. *The Spanish Atlantic World in the Eighteenth Century: War and the Bourbon Reforms, 1713–1796*. New York: Cambridge University Press, 2014.

Kuznesof, Elizabeth A. "Ethnic and Gender Influences on 'Spanish' Creole Society in Colonial Spanish America." *Colonial Latin American Review* 4, no. 1 (1995): 153–76.

———. "More Conversation on Race, Class, and Gender." *Colonial Latin American Review* 5, no. 1 (1996): 129–33.

Lacerda, Marcos Branda. *Yoruba Drums from Benin, West Africa*. CD liner notes. Washington, DC: Smithsonian Folkways Recordings, 1996.

Lachatañeré, Rómulo. *Manual de santería: El sistema de cultos "lucumís."* Havana: Editorial Caribe, 1942.

———. "La religión santera y el milagro de la Caridad del Cobre." *Del Caribe* 21 ([1936] 1991): 79–81.

———. "Tipos étnicos africanos que concurrieron en la amalgama cubana." *Actas de folklore* 1, no. 3 (1961): 5–12.

Landers, Jane. *Atlantic Creoles in the Age of Revolution*. London: Harvard University Press, 2010.

———. *Black Society in Spanish Florida*. Urbana: University of Illinois Press, 1999.

———. "Catholic Conspirators? Religious Rebels in Nineteenth-Century Cuba." *Slavery and Abolition* 36, no. 3 (2015): 495–520.

———. "Transforming Bondsmen into Vassals: Arming Slaves in Colonial Spanish America." In *Arming Slaves: From Classical Times to the Modern Age*, edited by

Christopher Leslie Brown, and Philip D. Morgan, 120–45. New Haven, CT: Yale University Press, 2006.

Langley, Lester D. *The Americas in the Age of Revolution, 1750–1850*. New Haven, CT: Yale University Press, 1996.

Lavrin, Asunción. "In Search of the Colonial Woman in Mexico: The Seventeenth and Eighteenth Centuries." In *Latin American Women: Historical Perspectives*, edited by Asunción Lavrin, 23–59. Westport, CT: Greenwood Press, 1978.

Law, Robin. "The Career of Adele at Lagos and Badagry, c. 1807–c. 1837." *Journal of the Historical Society of Nigeria* 9, no. 2 (1978): 35–60.

———. *Contemporary Source Material for the History of the Old Oyo Empire, 1627–1824*. Toronto: York University and UNESCO Nigerian Hinterland Project, [1992] 2001.

———. "Dahomey and the North-West." *Cahiers du Centre de Recherches Africaines* 8 (1994): 149–67.

———. "Dahomey and the Slave Trade: Reflections on the Historiography of the Rise of Dahomey." *Journal of African History* 27, no. 2 (1986): 237–67.

———. "The Dynastic Chronology of Lagos." *Lagos Notes and Records* 2, no. 2 (1968): 46–54.

———. "Ethnicities of Enslaved Africans in the Diaspora: On the Meanings of 'Mina' (Again)." *History in Africa* 32 (2005): 247–67.

———. "Ethnicity and the Slave Trade: 'Lucumí' and 'Nagô' as Ethnonyms in West Africa." *History in Africa* 24 (1997): 205–19.

———. *The Horse in West African History*. Oxford: Oxford University Press, 1980.

———. "Ideologies of Royal Power: The Dissolution and Reconstruction of Political Authority on the Slave Coast." *Africa* 57 (1987): 321–44.

———. "Jean Barbot as a Source for the Slave Coast of West Africa." *History of Africa* 9 (1982): 155–73.

———. *The Kingdom of Allada*. Leiden: Research School CNWS, 1997.

———. "A Lagoonside Port on the Eighteenth Century Slave Coast: The Early History of Badagri." *Canadian Journal of African Studies* 28 (1994): 35–50.

———. "'My Head Belongs to the King': On the Political and Ritual Significance of Decapitation in Pre-Colonial Dahomey." *Journal of African History* 30, no. 3 (1989): 399–415.

———. *Ouidah: The Social History of a West African Slaving 'Port,' 1727–1892*. Athens: Ohio University Press, 2004.

———. "Ouidah as a Multiethnic Community." In *The Black Urban Atlantic in the Age of the Slave Trade*, edited by Jorge Cañizares-Esguerra, Matt D. Childs, James Sidbury, 42–62. Philadelphia: University of Pennsylvania Press, 2013.

———. "The Oyo-Dahomey Wars, 1726–1823: A Military Analysis." In *Warfare and Diplomacy in Precolonial Nigeria*, edited by Toyin Falola and Robin Law, 9–25. Madison: African Studies Program University of Wisconsin-Madison, 1992.

———. *The Oyo Empire, c. 1600–c. 1836: A West African Imperialism in the Era of the Atlantic Slave Trade*. Oxford: Clarendon Press, [1977] 1991.

———. *The Slave Coast of West Africa, 1550–1750: The Impact of the Atlantic Slave Trade on an African Society*. Oxford: Clarendon Press, 1991.

———. "Slave-Raiders and Middlemen, Monopolists and Free-Traders: The Supply of Slaves for the Atlantic Trade in Dahomey, c. 1715–1850." *Journal of African History* 30 (1988): 45–68.

———. "Trade and Politics behind the Slave Coast: The Lagoon Traffic and the Rise of Lagos, 1500–1800." *Journal of African History* 24 (1983): 321–48.

———. "A West African Cavalry State: The Kingdom of Oyo." *Journal of African History* 16, 1 (1975): 1–15.

Law, Robin, and Paul E. Lovejoy. *The Biography of Mahommah Gardo Baquaqua: His Passage from Slavery to Freedom in Africa and America*. Princeton, NJ: Markus Wiener, 2001.

———. "Borgu in the Atlantic Slave Trade." *African Economic History* 27 (1999): 69–92.

Law, Robin, and Silke Strickrodt. *Ports of the Slave Trade (Bights of Benin and Biafra)*. Stirling: Center of Commonwealth Studies, University of Stirling, 1999.

Lewis, James A. "Anglo-American Entrepreneurs in Havana: The Background and Expulsion of 1784–1785." In *American Role in the Spanish Imperial Economy, 1760-1819*, edited by Jacques Barbier and Allan J. Kuethe, 112–26. Manchester: Manchester University Press, 1984.

Llaverías, Joaquín. *La comisión militar ejecutiva y permanente de la isla de Cuba*. Habana: El Siglo XX, A. Muñez y Hno., 1929.

Lloyd, Peter C. "The Political Development of Yoruba Kingdoms in the Eighteenth and Nineteenth Centuries." *Royal Anthropological Institute Occasional Paper* 31 (1971): 1-55.

———. *Power and Independence*. London: Routledge & Kegan Paul, 1974.

———. "The Status of the Yoruba Wife." *Sudan Society* 2 (1963): 35–42.

———. "Yoruba Myths—A Sociologist's Interpretation." *Odu* 2 (1955): 20–28.

López Denis, Adrián. "Higiene pública contra higiene privada: Cólera, limpieza y poder en La Havana colonial." *Estudios Interdisciplinarios de América Latina y el Caribe* 14, no. 1 (2003): 11–34.

López Valdés, Rafael. *Africanos de Cuba*. San Juan, P.R.: Centro de Estudios Avanzados de Puerto Rico y el Caribe y el Instituto de Cultura Puertorriqueña, 2002.

———. *Componentes africanos en el etnos cubano*. Havana: Editorial de Ciencias Sociales, 1985.

———. "Notas para el estudio etnohistórico de los esclavos lucumí de Cuba." *Anales del Caribe* 6 (1986): 54–74.

———. *Pardos y morenos: Esclavos y libres en Cuba y sus instituciones en el Caribe Hispano*. San Juan, P.R.: Centro de Estudios Avanzados de Puerto Rico y el Caribe, 2007.

Lovejoy, Henry B. "The Arrest Report and Declaration of Juan Nepomuceno Prieto, c. 1818–1835." *Studies in the History of the African Diaspora—Documents* 20 (2012): 1–18.

———. "Drums of Ṣàngó: Bàtá Drum and the Symbolic Reestablishment of the Oyo Empire in Colonial Cuba, c. 1817–1836." In *Ṣàngó in Africa and the African Diaspora*, edited by Joel Tishken, Toyin Falola, and Akintunde Akinyemi, 284–308. Bloomington: Indiana University Press, 2009.

―――. "Mapping the Collapse of Oyo and the trans-Atlantic Slave Trade from the Bight of Benin on an Annual Basis, 1816–1836." *Journal of Global Slavery* (forthcoming, 2019).

―――. "Old Oyo Influences on the Transformation of Lucumí Identity in Colonial Cuba." PhD diss., University of California, Los Angeles, 2012.

―――. "Ọ̀ṣun Becomes Cuban: The Nationalist Discourse over the *Mulata* in Lucumí and Cuban Popular Culture." *Atlantic Studies* (forthcoming, 2019).

―――. "The Proyecto Orunmila Texts of Osha-Ifá in Regla, Cuba." *Studies in the History of the African Diaspora—Documents* 3 (2002): 1–3.

―――. "Redrawing Historical Maps of the Bight of Benin Hinterland, c. 1780." *Canadian Journal of African Studies* 47, no. 3 (2013): 443–63.

―――. "The Registers of Liberated Africans of the Havana Slave Trade Commission: Implementation and Policy, 1824–1841." *Slavery and Abolition* 37, no. 1 (2016): 23–44.

―――. "The Registers of Liberated Africans of the Havana Slave Trade Commission: Transcription Methodology and Statistical Analysis." *African Economic History* 38 (2010): 107–36.

―――. "Santería: An Afro-Cuban Religion." *Queen's Journal*, February 2002.

―――. "The Transculturation of Yoruba Annual Festivals: The *Día de Reyes* in Colonial Cuba in the Nineteenth Century." In *Carnival—Theory and Practice*, edited by Christopher Innes, Annabel Rutherford, and Brigitte Bogar, 33–50. Trenton, NJ: Africa World Press, 2011.

Lovejoy, Henry B., and Olatunji Ojo. "'Lucumí' and 'Terranova,' and the Origins of the Yoruba Nation." *Journal of African History* 56, no. 3 (2015): 353–72.

Lovejoy, Paul E. "The African Diaspora: Revisionist Interpretations of Ethnicity, Culture, and Religion under Slavery." *Studies in the World History of Slavery, Abolition, and Emancipation* 2, no. 1 (1997): no page numbers. http://www.2.h-net.msu.edu/~slavery/essays/esy9701love.html.

―――. *Caravans of Kola: The Hausa Kola Trade, 1700–1900*. Zaria, Nigeria: Ahmadu Bello University Press, 1980.

―――. "The Context of Enslavement in West Africa: Aḥmad Bābā and the Ethics of Slavery." In *Slaves, Subjects, and Subversives: Blacks in Colonial Latin America*, edited by Barry Robinson and Jane Landers, 9–38. Albuquerque: University of New Mexico Press, 2006.

―――. "Departure from Calabar during the Slave Trade." In *Calabar on the Cross River*, edited by David Imbua, Paul E. Lovejoy, and Ivor L. Miller, 23–50. Trenton, NJ: African World Press, 2017.

―――. "Identifying Enslaved Africans in the African Diaspora." In *Identity in the Shadow of Slavery*, edited by Paul E. Lovejoy, 1–29. London: Continuum, 2000.

―――. *Jihād in West Africa during the Age of Revolutions*. Athens: Ohio University Press, 2016.

―――. "The 'Middle Passage': The Enforced Migration of Africans across the Atlantic." Ann Arbor, MI: ProQuest Information and Learning, 2006.

————. "The Role of the Wangara in the Economic Transformation of the Central Sudan in the Fifteenth and Sixteenth Centuries." *Journal of African History* 19, no. 2 (1978): 173–93.

————. "Scarification and the Loss of History in the African Diaspora." In *Activating the Past: History and Memory in the Black Atlantic World*, edited by Andrew Apter and Robin Derby, 99–138. Newcastle Upon Tyne: Cambridge Scholars Publishing, 2010.

————. *Transformations in Slavery: A History of Slavery in Africa*. 3rd ed. Cambridge: Cambridge University Press, [1983] 2012.

————. "The Yoruba Factor in the Trans-Atlantic Slave Trade." In *The Yoruba Diaspora in the Atlantic World*, edited by Toyin Falola and Matt Childs, 40–55. Bloomington: Indiana University Press, 2004.

Lovejoy Paul E., and David Richardson. "British Abolition and Its Impact on Slave Prices along the Atlantic Coast of Africa, 1783–1850." *Journal of Economic History* 55, no. 1 (1995): 98–119.

————. "Competing Markets for Male and Female Slaves: Prices in the Interior of West Africa, 1780–1850." *International Journal of African Historical Studies* 28, no. 2 (1995): 261–93.

Lovett, Gabriel. *Napoleon and the Birth of Modern Spain*. New York: New York University Press, 1965.

Lucena Salmoral, Manuel. "El derecho de la coartación del esclavo en la América Española." *Revista de Indias* 59, no. 216 (1999): 357–73.

Lufríu, René. *El impulso inicial: Estudio histórico de los tiempos modernos de Cuba*. Havana: Imprenta El Siglo XX, 1930.

Mabogunje, M. A., and J. Omer-Cooper. *Owu in Yoruba History*. Ibadan: Ibadan University Press, 1971.

MacGaffey, Wyatt. *Kongo Political Culture: The Conceptual Challenge of the Particular*. Bloomington: Indiana University Press, 2000.

Mann, Kristin. *Slavery and the Birth of an African City: Lagos, 1760–1900*. Bloomington: Indiana University Press, 2007.

Marcuzzi, Michael D. "A Historical Study of the Ascendant Role of Bàtá Drumming in Cuban Òrìsà Worship." PhD diss., York University, 2005.

Martin, Joel. *Sacred Revolt: The Muskogees' Struggle for a New World*. Boston, MA: Beacon Press, 1991.

Martín, Juan Luís, *De dónde vinieron los negros de Cuba. Los mandingos, gangás, carabalíes, arará: Su historia antes de la esclavitud*. Havana: Editorial Atalaya S.A., 1939.

Masó y Velázquez, Calixto. *Historia de Cuba*. Miami, FL: Ediciones Universal, 1976.

Mason, John. *Aráàràárá: Wondrous Inhabitor of Thunder*. Brooklyn, NY: Yoruba Theological Archministry, 2012.

————. *Orin Òrìsà: Songs for Selected Heads*. Brooklyn, NY: Yoruba Theological Archministry, 1992.

Matory, J. Lorland. *Black Atlantic Religion: Tradition, Transnationalism, and Matriarchy in the Afro-Brazilian Candomblé*. Princeton, NJ: Princeton University Press, 2005.

———. "The English Professors of Brazil: On the Diasporic Roots of a Yoruba Nation." *Comparative Studies in Society and History* 41, no. 1 (1999): 72–103.

———. *Sex and the Empire That Is No More: Gender and Politics of Metaphor in Oyo Yoruba Religion*. Minneapolis: University of Minnesota Press, 1994.

McAlister, Lyle N. *The "Fuero Militar" in New Spain, 1764–1800*. Gainesville: University of Florida Press, 1957.

———. "Pensacola during the Second Spanish Period." *Florida Historical Quarterly* 37, no. 3 (1959): 281–327.

McCaa, Robert, Stuart B. Schwartz, and Arturo Grubessich. "Race and Class in Colonial Latin America: A Critique." *Comparative Studies in Society and History* 21, no. 3 (1979): 421–33.

McIntosh, Marjorie Keniston. *Yoruba Women, Work, and Social Change*. Bloomington: Indiana University Press, 2009.

McKenzie, Peter Rutherford. *Hail Orisha: A Phenomenology of a West African Religion in the Mid-Nineteenth Century*. Leiden: Brill, 1997.

Miller, Ivor L. "Calabar on the Cross." In *Calabar on the Cross River*, edited by David Imbua, Paul E. Lovejoy, and Ivor L. Miller, 1–10. Trenton, NJ: African World Press, 2017.

———. "The Relationship between Early Forms of Literacy in Old Calabar and the Inherited Manuscripts of the Cuban Abakuá Society." In *Calabar on the Cross River*, edited by David Imbua, Paul E. Lovejoy, and Ivor L. Miller, 177–216. Trenton, NJ: African World Press, 2017.

———. *Voice of the Leopard: African Secret Societies and Cuba*. Jackson: Mississippi University Press, 2009.

Miller, Joseph C. *Way of Death: Merchant Capitalism and the Angolan Slave Trade, 1730–1830*. Madison: University of Wisconsin Press, 1988.

Millett, Nathaniel. "Britain's 1814 Occupation of Pensacola and America's Response: An Episode of the War of 1812 in the Southeastern Borderlands." *Florida Historical Quarterly* 84, no. 2 (2005): 229–55.

———. "Defining Freedom in the Atlantic Borderlands of the Revolutionary Southeast." *Early American Studies: An Interdisciplinary Journal* 5, no. 2 (2007): 367–94.

Milligan, John D. "Slave Rebelliousness and the Florida Maroon." *Journal of the National Archives* 6 (1974): 5–18.

Mintz, Sidney. "History and Anthropology: A Brief Reprise." In *Race and Slavery in the Western Hemisphere: Quantitative Studies*, edited by Stanley Engerman and Eugene D. Genovese, 477–94. Princeton, NJ: Princeton University Press, 1975.

———. *Sweetness and Power: The Place of Sugar in Modern History*. New York: Viking, 1985.

Mintz, Sidney, and Richard Price. *An Anthropological Approach to the Afro-American Past: A Caribbean Perspective*. Philadelphia, PA: Institute for the Study of Human Issues, 1976.

———. *The Birth of African-American Culture: An Anthropological Perspective*. Boston, MA: Beacon Press, [1976] 1992.

Moliner Castañeda, Israel. *Los cabildos afrocubanos en Matanzas*. Matanzas: Ediciones Matanzas, 2002.

Moreno, Isidoro. *La antigua hermandad de los negros de Sevilla: Etnicidad, poder y sociedad en 600 años de historia*. Sevilla: Universidad de Sevilla y Junta de Andalucía-Consejería de Cultura, 1997.

Morgan, Gwenda, and Peter Rushton. *Banishment in the Early Atlantic World*. London: Bloomsbury, 2013.

Morgan, Kenneth. "Liverpool's Dominance in the British Slave Trade, 1740–1807." In *Liverpool and Transatlantic Slavery*, edited by David Richardson, Suzanne Schwarz, and Anthony Tibbles, 14–42. Liverpool: Liverpool University Press, 2007.

Morrison, Karen Y. *Cuba's Racial Crucible: The Sexual Economy of Social Identities, 1750–2000*. Bloomington: Indiana University Press, 2015.

———. "Slave Mothers and White Fathers: Defining Family and Status in Late Colonial Cuba." *Slavery and Abolition* 31, no. 1 (2010): 29–55.

Morton-Williams, Peter. "The Oyo Yoruba and the Atlantic Trade, 1670–1830." *Journal of the Historical Society of Nigeria* 3, no. 1 (1964): 25–45.

Mouléro, Thomas. "Guézo ou Guédizo Massigbé." *Etudes dahoméennes* 4, no. 5 (1965): 52–53.

Murphy, Joseph M. *Santería: An African Religion in America*. Boston: Beacon Press, 1988.

Murphy, Joseph M., and Mei-Mei Sanford, eds. *Òṣun across the Waters: A Yoruba Goddess in Africa and the Americas*. Bloomington: Indiana University Press, 2001.

Murray, David J. *Odious Commerce: Britain, Spain, and the Abolition of the Cuban Slave Trade*. Cambridge: Cambridge University Press, 2002.

Nwokeji, G. Ugo, and David Eltis. "The Roots of the African Diaspora: Methodological Considerations in the Analysis of Names in the Liberated African Registers of Sierra Leone and Havana." *History in Africa* 29 (2002): 365–79.

Obayemi, Ade. "The Sokoto Jihad and the 'O-Kun' Yoruba: A Review." *Journal of the Historical Society of Nigeria* 9, no. 2 (1978): 61–87.

Obrando Andrade, Rafael Ángel. "Manumisión, coartación y carta de venta: Tres de los mecanismos legales de obtención de la libertad para los esclavos negros en la América Española." *Revista de historia de América* 145 (2011): 103–25.

Ochoa, Todd Ramón. *Society of the Dead: Quita Manaquita and Palo Praise in Cuba*. Berkeley: University of California Press, 2010.

Oduyoye, Modupe. *Yoruba Names: Their Structure and Meaning*. London: Karnak House, 1987.

Ogundiran, Akinwumi. "Living in the Shadow of the Atlantic World: History and Material Life in a Yoruba-Edo Hinterland, ca. 1600–1750." In *Archaeology of Atlantic Africa and the African Diaspora*, edited by Akinwumi Ogundiran and Toyin Falola, 77–99. Bloomington: Indiana University Press.

O'Hear, Ann. *Power Relations in Nigeria: Ilorin Slaves and Their Successors*. Rochester, NY: University of Rochester Press, 1997.

Ojo, G. J. Afolabi. *Yoruba Culture*. Ife, Nigeria: University of Ife Press, 1966.

Ojo, Olatunji. "'Heepa' (Hail) Òrìsà: The Òrìsà Factor in the Birth of Yoruba Identity." *Journal of Religion in Africa* 39 (2009): 30–59.

———. "The Organization of the Atlantic Slave Trade in Yorubaland, ca. 1777 to ca. 1856." *International Journal of African Historical Studies* 41, no. 1 (2008): 77–100.

———. "The Slave Ship Manuelita and the Story of a Yoruba Community, 1833–1834." *Tempo* 23, no. 2 (2017): 360–82.

Olupona, Jacob K., and Terry Rey, ed. *Òrìṣà Devotion as World Religion: The Globalization of Yorùbá Religious Culture*. Madison: University of Wisconsin Press, 2008.

O'Malley, Gregory E. *Final Passages: The Inter-Colonial Slave Trade of British America, 1619–1807*. Chapel Hill: University of North Carolina Press, 2014.

———. "inter-Caribbean database." Unpublished dataset.

Ortiz, Fernando. *Contrapunteo cubano del tabaco y el azúcar*. Havana: J. Montero, 1940.

———. *Hampa afro-cubana: los negros esclavos*. Havana: Revista Bimestre Cubana, 1916.

———. "La semi luna de la Virgen de la Caridad del Cobre." *Archivos del folklore cubano* 4, no. 2 (1929): 161–63.

———. "La 'tragedia' de los ñáñigos." *Cuadernos Americanos* 52, no. 4 (1950).

———. "Los 'batá.'" In *Los instrumentos de la música afrocubana*, vol. 4, 205–342. Habana: Dirección de Cultura del Ministerio de Educación, 1954.

———. *Los cabildos y la fiesta afrocubanos del Día de Reyes*. Havana: Editorial de Ciencias Sociales, [1921] 1992.

———. *Los negros brujos: Apuntes para un estudio de etnología criminal*. Miami, FL: Ediciones Universal, [1906] 1973.

Ortiz, Fernando, and Matos Arévalo. *La Virgen de la Caridad del Cobre: Historia y etnografía*. Havana: Fundación Fernando Ortiz, 2012.

Otero, Solimar. *Afro-Cuban Diasporas in the Atlantic World*. Rochester, NY: University of Rochester Press, 2010.

Palmié, Stephen. *The Cooking of History: How Not to Study Afro-Cuban Religion*. Chicago: University of Chicago Press, 2013.

———. "Ethnogenic Processes and Cultural Transformations in Afro-American Slave Populations." In *Slavery in the Americas*, edited by Wolfgang Binder, 337–63. Würzburg, Germany: Könighausen and Neumann, 1993.

———. *Wizards and Scientists: Explorations in Afro-Cuban Modernity and Tradition*. Durham, NC: Duke University Press, 2002.

Paquette, Robert L. *Sugar Is Made with Blood: The Conspiracy of La Escalera and the Conflict between Empires over Slavery in Cuba*. Middletown, CT: Wesleyan University Press, 1988.

Parrinder, E. G. *The Story of Ketu: An Ancient Yoruba Kingdom*. Edited by I. A. Akinjogbin. Ibadan: Ibadan University Press, [1956] 1967.

Parry, J. H. "Eliphalet Fitch: A Yankee Trader in Jamaica during the War of Independence." *History* 40, no. 138 (1955): 84–98.

———. *The Spanish Seaborne Empire*. Berkeley: University of California Press, [1966] 1990.

Patrick, Rembert W. *Florida Fiasco: Rampant Rebels on the Georgia-Florida Frontier*. Athens: University of Georgia Press, 1954.

Peel, John David Yeadon. *Religious Encounter and the Making of the Yorùbá*. Bloomington: Indiana University Press, 2000.

Pemberton, John III. "A Cluster of Sacred Symbols: Orisa Worship among the Igbomina Yoruba of Ila-Ọrangun." *History of Religions* 17, no. 1 (1977): 1–28.

Perera Díaz, Aisnara, and María de los Angeles Meriño Fuentes. *Esclavitud, familia y parroquia en Cuba: Otra mirada desde la microhistoria*. Santiago de Cuba: Editorial Oriente, 2008.

Perez, Elizabeth. "The Virgin in the Mirror: Reading Images of a Black Madonna through the Lens of Afro-Cuban Women's Experiences." *Journal of African American History* 95, no. 2 (2010): 202–28.

Pérez, Louis A., Jr. *Cuba: Between Reform and Revolution*. New York: Oxford University Press, 1988.

———. *Winds of Change: Hurricanes and the Transformation of Nineteenth-Century Cuba*. Chapel Hill: University of North Carolina Press, 2001.

Peukert, Werner. *Der Atlantische sklavenhandel von Dahomey, 1740–1797*. Wiesbaden: Steiner, 1978.

Pike, Ruth. *Aristocrats and Traders: Sevillian Society in the Sixteenth Century*. Ithaca, NY: Cornell University Press, 1972.

Pino-Santos, Oscar. *Historia de Cuba: Aspectos fundamentals*. Havana: Editorial Nacional, 1964.

Platero Fernández, Carlos. "Los apellidos en las islas Canarias (españoles y castellanizados)." *Caja Insular de Ahorros de Gran Canaria*, 179 (1988): 12–15.

Polanyi, Karl. *Dahomey and the Slave Trade: An Analysis of an Archaic Economy*. Seattle: University of Washington Press, 1966.

Pollis, Edna. "An Analysis of the Pre-Colonial Polity of Dahomey, West Africa." *Papers in Anthropology* 15, no. 1 (1974): 1–22.

Poot-Herrera, Sara. "Los criollos: Nota sobre su identidad y cultura." *Colonial Latin American Review* 4, no. 1 (1995): 177–83.

Porter, Kenneth Wiggins. "Negroes and the Seminole War, 1817–1818." *Journal of Negro History* 36, no. 3 (1951): 249–80.

Portuondo Zúñiga, Olga. *Entre esclavos y libres de Cuba colonial*. Santiago de Cuba: Editorial Oriente, 2003.

———. *La Virgen de la Caridad del Cobre: Símbolo de cubanía*. Santiago de Cuba: Editorial Oriente, 2001.

Quadri, Y. A. "An Appraisal of Muhammad Bello's Infâq al-Maysûr fî Târîkh at-Takrûr." *Journal of Arabic and Religious Studies* 3 (1986): 53–62.

Radburn, Nicholas. "Guinea Factors, Slave Sales, and the Profits of the Transatlantic Slave Trade in Late Eighteenth-Century Jamaica: The Case of John Tailyour." *William and Mary Quarterly* 72, no. 2 (2015): 243–86.

Ramos, Arthur. *As culturas negras no novo mundo*. Rio de Janeiro: Civilizãa Brasileira S. A. Editora, 1937.

Ramos, Miguel. "The Empire Beats On: Oyo, Bata Drums and Hegemony in Nineteenth-Century Cuba." MA thesis, Florida International University, 2000.

———. "Lucumí (Yoruba) Culture in Cuba: A Reevaluation (1830s–1940s)." PhD diss., Florida International University, 2013.

Ranston, Jackie. *The Lindo Legacy*. London: Toucan Books, 2000.

Redfield, Robert, Ralph Linton, and Melville J. Herskovits. "Memorandum for the Study of Acculturation." *American Anthropologist* 38, no. 1 (1936): 149–52.

Rediker, Marcus. *The Slave Ship: A Human History*. New York: Viking, 2007.

Reid-Vasquez, Michele. *The Year of the Lash: Free People of Color in Cuba and the Nineteenth-Century Atlantic World*. Athens: University of Georgia Press, 2011.

———. "The Yoruba in Cuba: Origins, Identities, and Transformations." In *The Yoruba Diaspora in the Atlantic World*, edited by Toyin Falola and Matt D. Childs, 111–29. Bloomington: Indiana University Press, 2004.

Reis, João José. 2003. *Death is a Festival: Funeral Rites and Rebellion in Nineteenth Century Brazil*. Chapel Hill: University of North Carolina Press, 2003.

———. *Domingos Sodré, um sacerdote africano: Escravidão, liberdade e candomblé na Bahia do século XIX*. São Paulo: Companhia das Letras, 2008.

———. *Rebelião escrava no Brasil: A história do levante dos Malês em 1835*. São Paulo: Companhia das Letras, [1987] 2004.

Reis, João José, and Beatriz Gallotti Mamigonian. "Nagô and Mina: The Yoruba Diaspora in Brazil." In *The Yoruba Diaspora in the Atlantic World*, edited by Toyin Falola and Matt D. Childs, 77–110. Bloomington: Indiana University Press, 2004.

Richard, Robert, and Gabriel Debien. "Les origines des esclaves des Antilles." *Bulletin de l'IFAN* 24, no. 1 (1963): 1–39.

Richards, Jeffrey H. "Samuel Davies and the Transatlantic Campaign for Slave Literacy in Virginia." *Virginia Magazine of History and Biography* 111, no. 4 (2003): 333–78.

Richardson, David. "Shipboard Revolts, African Authority, and the Atlantic Slave Trade." *William and Mary Quarterly* 58, no. 1 (2001): 69–92.

Roche y Monteagudo, Rafael. *Los policías y sus misterios*. Havana: Imprenta "La Prueba," [1908] 1952.

Rodgers, Nini. *Ireland, Slavery, and Anti-Slavery: 1645–1865*. New York: Palgrave, 2007.

Rodrigues, Raymundo Nina. *L'animisme fétichiste de nègres de Bahia*. Bahia, Brazil: Reis & Comp., 1900.

Rodríguez, Jaime E. O. *The Independence of Spanish America*. Cambridge: Cambridge University Press, 1998.

Roldán de Montaud, Inés. "En los borrosos confines de la libertad: El caso de los negros emancipados en Cuba, 1817–1870." *Revista de Indias* 71 (2011): 159–92.

———. "La diplomacia británica y la abolición del tráfico de esclavos cubanos: Una nueva aportación." *Revista complutense de historia de América* 2 (1981): 219–50.

Ronen, Dov. "On the African Role in the Trans-Atlantic Slave Trade in Dahomey." *Cahiers d'études Africaines* 11 (1971): 5–13.

Rosa, Gabino la. *Los palenque del oriente de Cuba: Resistencia y acoso*. Havana: Editorial Academia, 1991.

Rosa, Gabino la, and Mirtha T. González. *Cazadores de esclavos: Diarios*. Havana: Fundación Fernando Ortiz, 2004.

Ross, David. "The Dahomean Middleman System, 1727–c. 1818." *Journal of African History* 28, no. 3 (1987): 357–75.

Rudé, George F. E. *Hanoverian London, 1714–1808*. Berkeley: University of California Press, 1971.

Rushing, Fannie Theresa. "Afro-Cuban Social Organization and Identity in a Colonial Slave Society, 1800–1888." *Colonial Latin American Historical Review* 11, no. 2 (2002): 177–201.

Sàlàkọ́, Ruhollah Ajíbọ́lá. *Ọ̀tà: Biography of the Foremost Àwórì Town*. Ota: Penink Publicity, 1998.

Sánchez, Joseph P. "African Freedmen and the Fuero Militar: A Historical Overview of Pardo and Moreno Militiamen in the Late Spanish Empire." *Colonial Latin American Historical Review* 3 (1994): 165–84.

Santa Cruz y Mallen, Francisco Xavier de. *Historia de familias cubanas*. 9 vols. Miami, FL: Editorial Hércules, 1940.

Sarracino, Rodolfo. *Los que volvieron a África*. Havana: Editorial de Ciencias Sociales, 1988.

Sartorius, David. *Ever Faithful: Race, Loyalty, and the Ends of Empire in Spanish Cuba*. Durham, NC: Duke University Press, 2014.

———. "Free-Colored Militias in Cuba and the Ends of Spanish Empire." *Journal of Colonialism and Colonial History* 5, no. 2 (2004): 1–25.

Saunt, Claudio. *A New Order of Things: Property, Power, and the Transformation of the Creek Indians, 1733–1816*. Cambridge: Cambridge University Press, 2004.

Schneider, Elena. "African Slavery and Spanish Empire: Imperial Imaginings and Bourbon Reform in Eighteenth-Century Cuba and Beyond." *Journal of Early American History* 5, no. 1 (2015): 3–29.

Schwartz, Stuart B. "Colonial Identities and the Sociedad de Castas." *Colonial Latin American Review* 4, no. 1 (1995): 185–201.

Schwarz, L. D. *London in the Age of Industrialisation: Entrepreneurs, Labour Force, and Living Conditions, 1700–1850*. Cambridge: Cambridge University Press, 1992.

Scott, Julius S. *The Common Wind: Currents of Afro-American Communication in the Era of the Haitian Revolution*. n.p., 1986.

Scott, Rebecca J. *Slave Emancipation in Cuba: The Transition to Free Labor, 1860–1899*. Pittsburgh, PA: University of Pittsburgh Press, 2007.

Scott, Rebecca J., and Jean M. Hébrard. *Freedom Papers: An Atlantic Odyssey in the Age of Emancipation*. Cambridge, MA: Harvard University Press, 2012.

Smallwood, Stephanie E. *Saltwater Slavery: A Middle Passage Africa to American Diaspora*. Cambridge, MA: Harvard University Press, 2007.

Smith, Robert Sydney. *Kingdoms of the Yoruba*. London: Methuen, 1969.

Sorensen-Gilmour, Caroline. "Badagry 1784–1863: The Political and Commercial History of a Pre-Colonial Lagoonside Community in South West Nigeria." PhD diss., University of Stirling, 1995.

Sparks, Randy J. *The Two Princes of Calabar: An Eighteenth-Century Atlantic Odyssey*. Cambridge, MA: Harvard University Press, 2008.

Spitta, Silvia. *Between Two Waters: Narratives of Transculturation in Latin America*. College Station: Texas A&M University Press, 2006.

Stilwell, Sean. *Slavery and Slaving in African History*. New York: Cambridge University Press, 2014.

Stolke, Verena. *Marriage, Class, and Colour in Nineteenth-Century Cuba: A Study of Racial Attitudes and Sexual Values in a Slave Society*. 2nd ed. Ann Arbor: University of Michigan Press, [1974] 1989.

Suárez, Federico. *Las cortes de Cádiz*. Madrid: Rialp, 2002.

Sublette, Ned. *Cuba and Its Music from the First Drums to the Mambo*. Chicago: Chicago Review Press, 2004.

Sweet, James H. *Domingos Álvares, African Healing, and the Intellectual History of the Atlantic World*. Chapel Hill: University of North Carolina Press, 2013.

Sweet, John W., and Lisa A. Lindsay. *Biography and the Black Atlantic*. Philadelphia: University of Pennsylvania Press, 2014.

Taylor, William B. *Magistrates of the Sacred: Priests and Parishioners in Eighteenth Century Mexico*. Stanford, CA: Stanford University Press, 1996.

Thieme, Darius L. "A Descriptive Catalogue of Yoruba Musical Instruments." PhD diss., Catholic University of America, 1969.

Thompson, Robert Farris. "An Aesthetic of the Cool." *African Arts* 7 (1973): 40–43, 64–67, 89–91.

———. "The Sign of the Divine King." In *African Art and Leadership*, edited by Douglas Turner and Herbert M. Cole, 227–60. Madison: University of Wisconsin Press, 1972.

Thornton, John K. *Africa and the Africans in the Making of the Atlantic World, 1400–1800*. Cambridge: Cambridge University Press, [1992] 1998.

Thrower, Robert G. "Casualties and Consequences of the Creek War: A Modern Creek Perspective." In *Tohopeka: Rethinking the Creek War and War of 1812*, edited by Kathryn E. Holland Braund, 10–29. Tuscaloosa: University of Alabama Press, 2012.

Timi de Ede, Laoye I. "Los tambores Yoruba." *Actas del folklore bolétin mensual del centro de estudios del folklore* 1 (1961): 17–31.

Tomich, Dale W. *Through the Prism of Slavery: Labor, Capital, and World Economy*. Lanham, MD: Rowman & Littlefield, 2004.

Tomich, Dale W., and Michael Zeuske. "Introduction, the Second Slavery: Mass Slavery, World-Economy, and Comparative Microhistories." *Review* 31, no. 2 (2008): 91–100.

Torres Ramirez, Bibano. *La compañía Gaditana de negros*. Sevilla: Escuela de Estudios Hispano-Americanos, 1973.

Trotman, David. "Reflections on the Children of Shango: An Essay on a History of Orisa Worship in Trinidad." *Slavery and Abolition* 28, no. 2 (2007): 211–34.

Trujillo y Monagas, D. José. *Los criminales en Cuba y el inspector Trujillo: Narración de los servicios, prestados en cuerpo de policía de La Havana*. Barcelona: F. Giró, 1882.

Usman, Aribidesi. "Empires and Their Peripheries: A Case of Oyo and the Northern Yoruba." In *The Changing Worlds of Atlantic Africa: Essays in Honor of Robin Law*, edited by Toyin Falola and Matt D. Childs, 31–50. Durham, NC: Carolina Academic Press, 2009.

Van Norman, William. *Shade-Grown Slavery: The Lives of Slaves on Coffee Plantations in Cuba*. Nashville, TN: Vanderbilt University Press, 2013.

Vansina, Jan. *How Societies Are Born: Governance in West Central African before 1600*. Charlottesville: University of Virginia Press, 2004.

————. *La tradition orale et la methode historique* . Tervuren: Musee Royal de l'Afrique Centrale, 1961.

————. *Paths in the Rainforests: Toward a History of Political Tradition in Equatorial Africa*. Madison: University of Wisconsin Press, 1990.

Varella, Claudia. "The Price of 'Coartación' in the Hispanic Caribbean: How Much Freedom Does the Master Owe to the Slave?" *International Journal of Cuban Studies* 4, no. 2 (2012): 200–10.

Verger, Pierre Fatoumbi. "America Latina en África." In *África en América Latina*, edited by Moreno Fraginals, 363–77. Madrid: UNESCO, 1977.

————. "Les côtes d'Afrique occidentale entre 'rio Volta' et 'rio Lagos' (1535–1773)." *Journal de la société des africanistes* 38, no. 1 (1968): 35–58.

————. *Orisha: Les dieux Yorouba en Afrique et au nouveau monde*. Paris: Editions A.M. Metailie, [1957] 1982.

————. *Trade Relations between the Bight of Benin and Bahia from the 17th to the 19th Century*. Translated by Evelyn Crawford. Ibadan, Nigeria: Ibadan University Press, [1968] 1976.

Warner-Lewis, Maureen. *Archibald Monteath: Igbo, Jamaican, Moravian*. Kingston: University of West Indies Press, 2007.

Watson, Alan. *Slave Law in the Americas*. Athens: University of Georgia Press, 1989.

Wescott, Joan, and Peter Morton-Williams. "The Symbolism and Ritual Context of the Yoruba Laba Shango." *Journal of the Anthropological Institute of Great Britain and Ireland* 92, no. 1 (1962): 23–37.

Wetohossou, Blandine. "Las migraciones africanas y afro-cubanos entre la llamada costa de los esclavos y Cuba, 1850–1886." PhD diss., Universidad de Costa Rica, 2007.

Wheat, David. *Atlantic Africa and the Spanish Caribbean, 1570–1640*. Chapel Hill: University of North Carolina Press, 2016.

Williams, Harry F. "Old French Lives of Saint Barbara." *Proceedings of the American Philosophical Society* 119, no. 2 (1975): 156–85.

Wright, J. Leitch, Jr. "A Note on the First Seminole War as Seen by the Indians, Negroes, and Their British Advisors." *Journal of Southern History* 34 (1968): 565–75.

Yoder, John C. "Fly and Elephant Parties: Political Polarization in Dahomey, 1840–1870." *Journal of African History* 15, no. 3 (1974): 417–32.

Zúñiga, Olga Portuondo. *Entre esclavos y libres de Cuba colonial*. Santiago de Cuba: Editorial Oriente, 2003.

Index

Envisioning Cuba

HENRY B. LOVEJOY, *Prieto: Yorùbá Kingship in Colonial Cuba during the Age of Revolutions* (2018).

A. JAVIER TREVIÑO, *C. Wright Mills and the Cuban Revolution: An Exercise in the Art of Sociological Imagination* (2017).

ANTONIA DALIA MULLER, *Cuban Émigrés and Independence in the Nineteenth-Century Gulf World* (2017).

JENNIFER L. LAMBE, *Madhouse: Psychiatry and Politics in Cuban History* (2017).

DEVYN SPENCE BENSON, *Antiracism in Cuba: The Unfinished Revolution* (2016).

MICHELLE CHASE, *Revolution within the Revolution: Women and Gender Politics in Cuba, 1952–1962* (2015).

AISHA K. FINCH, *Rethinking Slave Rebellion in Cuba: La Escalera and the Insurgencies of 1841–1844* (2015).

CHRISTINA D. ABREU, *Rhythms of Race: Cuban Musicians and the Making of Latino New York City and Miami, 1940–1960* (2015).

ANITA CASAVANTES BRADFORD, *The Revolution Is for the Children: The Politics of Childhood in Havana and Miami, 1959–1962* (2014).

TIFFANY A. SIPPIAL, *Prostitution, Modernity, and the Making of the Cuban Republic, 1840–1920* (2013).

KATHLEEN LÓPEZ, *Chinese Cubans: A Transnational History* (2013).

LILLIAN GUERRA, *Visions of Power in Cuba: Revolution, Redemption, and Resistance, 1959–1971* (2012).

CARRIE HAMILTON, *Sexual Revolutions in Cuba: Passion, Politics, and Memory* (2012).

SHERRY JOHNSON, *Climate and Catastrophe in Cuba and the Atlantic World during the Age of Revolution* (2011).

MELINA PAPPADEMOS, *Black Political Activism and the Cuban Republic* (2011).

FRANK ANDRE GURIDY, *Forging Diaspora: Afro-Cubans and African Americans in a World of Empire and Jim Crow* (2010).

ANN MARIE STOCK, *On Location in Cuba: Street Filmmaking during Times of Transition* (2009).

ALEJANDRO DE LA FUENTE, *Havana and the Atlantic in the Sixteenth Century* (2008).

REINALDO FUNES MONZOTE, *From Rainforest to Cane Field in Cuba: An Environmental History since 1492* (2008).

MATT D. CHILDS, *The 1812 Aponte Rebellion in Cuba and the Struggle against Atlantic Slavery* (2006).

EDUARDO GONZÁLEZ, *Cuba and the Tempest: Literature and Cinema in the Time of Diaspora* (2006).

JOHN LAWRENCE TONE, *War and Genocide in Cuba, 1895–1898* (2006).

SAMUEL FARBER, *The Origins of the Cuban Revolution Reconsidered* (2006).

LILLIAN GUERRA, *The Myth of José Martí: Conflicting Nationalisms in Early Twentieth-Century Cuba* (2005).

RODRIGO LAZO, *Writing to Cuba: Filibustering and Cuban Exiles in the United States* (2005).

ALEJANDRA BRONFMAN, *Measures of Equality: Social Science, Citizenship, and Race in Cuba, 1902–1940* (2004).

EDNA M. RODRÍGUEZ-MANGUAL, *Lydia Cabrera and the Construction of an Afro-Cuban Cultural Identity* (2004).

GABINO LA ROSA CORZO, *Runaway Slave Settlements in Cuba: Resistance and Repression* (2003).

PIERO GLEIJESES, *Conflicting Missions: Havana, Washington, and Africa, 1959–1976* (2002).

ROBERT WHITNEY, *State and Revolution in Cuba: Mass Mobilization and Political Change, 1920–1940* (2001).

ALEJANDRO DE LA FUENTE, *A Nation for All: Race, Inequality, and Politics in Twentieth-Century Cuba* (2001).